CW00750336

The decline and fall of

THE WESTERHAM RAILWAY

A Prelude to Beeching

Ron Strutt

ISBN 9781909328471

First published 2018 by Crécy Publishing Ltd

A CIP record for this book is available from the British Library

Publisher's Note: Every effort has been made to identify and correctly attribute photographic credits. Any error that may have occurred is entirely unintentional.

Printed in Malta by Gutenberg Press

Crécy Publishing Limited
1a Ringway Trading Estate
Shadowmoss Road
Manchester M22 5LH

www. crecy.co.uk

Front cover: The typical Westerham branch train from the final years. 'H' class 0-4-4T No 31522 at the branch terminus with a two coach pull-push set converted from steam-railmotor vehicles and ready for the shuttle back to Dunton Green. As with the railway and the rolling stock seen, so No 31522 would be subsequently condemned being taken out of use at the end of 1963.

Rear cover: 'O1' No 31065, one of the hoped for engines to be used on a resurrected Westerham service to be operated under private enterprise. (Full caption details will be found on page 146.)' © *Dave Cobbe Collection/Rail Photoprints*

Frontsipiece: The archetypical Westerham branch train of latter years: an 'H' class tank engine with pull-push set seen here at the main line junction of Dunton Green. By rights a similar scene should be possible today, albeit with 21st century stock but still serving the community and terminus at Westerham. The fact this has not been possible for what is fast approaching sixty years is a shameful example of railway and government policy of the period.

Contents

Detailed appendices including a production list are available to download. Please contact enquiries@crecy.co.uk
The appendices include the following:

Appendix 1: Westerham branch operating instructions 1955
Appendix 2: BR estimates of savings from Westerham branch closure
Appendix 3: 'Proposed Closing of Westerham Branch': paper to Southern Area Board February 1960
Appendix 4: Closure proposal submitted to the TUCC March 1960
Appendix 5: Internal BR Report on the Westerham branch May 1960
Appendix 6: Costs of using two-car demus June 1960 34
Appendix 7: Comparative costs of Westerham branch traction July 1960
Type 3 diesel, electric mu, and diesel-electric mu
Appendix 7A: Detailed comparative costs of Westerham branch traction July 1960
Type 3 diesel, electric mu, and diesel-electric mu
Appendix 7B: Comparative costs of Westerham branch traction July 1960
Diesel railbus and battery-electric railcar
Appendix 8: BR internal review of objections June 1960
Including passenger loadings in relation to alternative buses
Appendix 9: BR response to TUCC July 1960
Appendix 10: 'Alternative Means of Traction to replace Steam Working': Memo dated 24 November 1960 from P.A. White, Assistant General Manager (Traffic) to General Manager, Southern Region
Appendix 11: TUCC Questionnaire and BR Answers January 1961
Including season ticket costs (January 1961)
Appendix 12: Scottish Region report on railbus operation December 1960
Appendix 13: Extract from the minutes of the London TUCC meeting on 8 February 1961 and notes of deputations' comments
Appendix 14: Adjournment debate in the House of Commons 19 October 1961
Appendix 15: How much did BR really save by closing the Westerham branch?
Steam service costs and possible savings
Comparison of costs between steam and electric working
Appendix 16: Proposed WVRA commuter timetable 148
Appendix 17: MOT (HMRI) questionnaire: WVRA answers
Appendix 18: Ministry of Transport report on the South Orbital Road c1961

Publisher's note: It is with regret that as with not being able to travel on the line itself, Ron Strutt sadly passed away before his book was published. As publisher's we hope we have done justice to his memory and not too many 'tweaks' have been omitted! Ron's work is believed to be without equal when it comes to recording the fate of any short branch line. Some might even say a book of this length just on the closure and subsequent ill-fated attempts to reopen the railway might be excessive, when read however it clearly becomes apparent why so little in the way of editing was required or indeed necessary. Instead this book will stand testament to a man who was simply not prepared to see the Westerham closure story brushed under the carpet and forgotten. Railway management and and politicians of the period might well hang their heads in shame at their action/inaction. To Ron Strutt though must go all credit for his fortitude, perseverance and downright determination that the story of the demise of Westerham should not go unnoticed and similarly never be forgotten. The events reported may indeed belong to a past generation but it remains a lesson to be learnt and remembered both from the past and for the future, one that must never be forgotten and equally never be repeated.

Introduction

The railway to Westerham may only have been a small branch line but it has an outstandingly rich story that has waited years to be revealed. Local people had a hard fight to get their railway in the first place and only 70 years after it opened they found themselves fighting even harder to keep it. In the end their campaign turned out to be in vain when, for the first-ever time, Ernest Marples ordered the line to be closed against the recommendation of the transport consultative committees. However, the passengers' determined struggle was to change the way the subsequent Beeching closures were carried out.

Closure was not the end of the story, though. Railway enthusiasts joined with local people to try to reopen the line for weekday commuters and weekend tourists. This book reveals, for the first time, how Whitehall and British Railways decided that they should not succeed. Their hostility towards the very idea of preserved railways and the patronising attitude they displayed towards enthusiasts will shock many. There has long been a belief that the line was sacrificed so that the M25 could be built on its course but the real reasons for the collapse of the preservation scheme are far more intriguing.

* * *

We are fortunate that, unlike many railway closures, the official Westerham files have survived largely intact. They give us a unique, detailed insight into the way such things

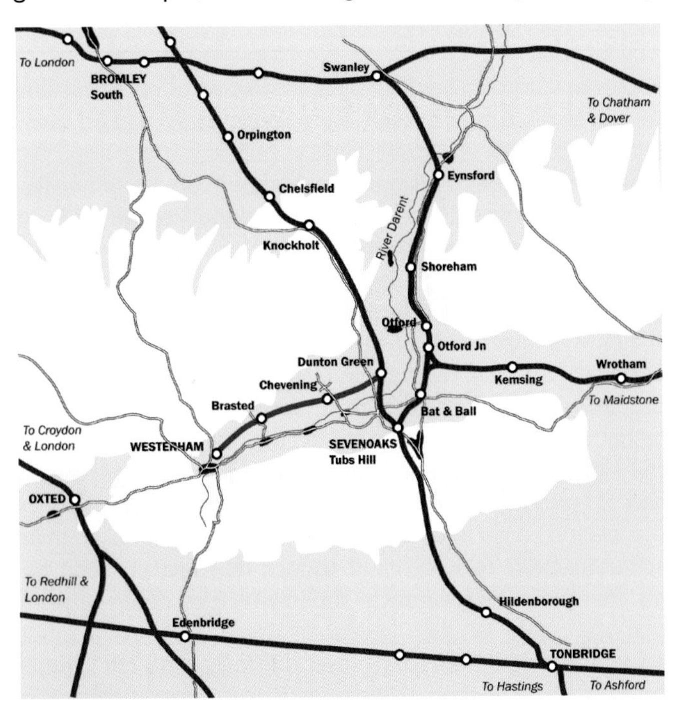

The Westerham branch in relation to other railways and pre-motorway roads in West Kent. High ground is shown by lighter shading. ***Author***

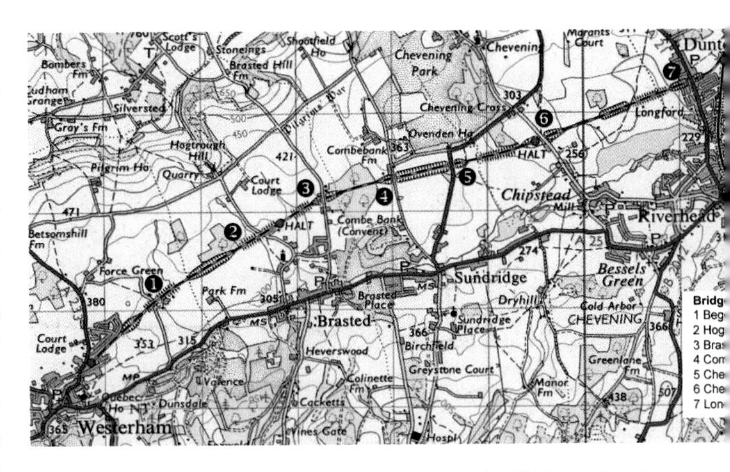

Ordnance Survey One-Inch Map sheet No 171, revised 1961, showing railway bridges. ***Crown Copyright***

were dealt with in the early 1960s and reveal what really went on behind closed doors in both BR and Whitehall.

* * *

I was aware of the Westerham branch before it closed but, sadly, I never managed to travel on it. I remember looking at the map in the back of my father's Southern Region timetable. The Westerham branch was shown by a thin line signifying it as steam-worked, standing out amidst those 'to be electrified'. It was my childhood's closest steam branch but it was just a little too far away for me to reach in its working days. By the time I had reached an age at which I could travel independently, it had closed. The best I could manage was to walk the length of the track with my school friend, Iain Whitlam, not long before the track was torn up, in preparation for a talk we gave to our school's Railway Society.

A few years after the line closed, I met David Kitton, the active Publicity Officer of the Westerham Valley Railway Association, which had fought to re-open the line. The fight to save it was over by then but he encouraged my interest in the branch. Indeed, he urged me to seek out the hidden truths and write this book – I am only sorry that he did not live long enough to read my revelations.

The loss of the line is sad but it has not gone entirely. The locomotives and rolling stock bought for it are now to be found on other heritage railways – some on the Bluebell in the south and the rest on the Worth Valley in the north. Many of the Westerham enthusiasts moved to the struggling Kent & East Sussex preservation scheme and maybe the hard lessons they had learned helped to bring about eventual success there. Even one of the GWR diesel railcars that had been considered for the Westerham commuter service is now at Tenterden.

And when, as an idealistic but inexperienced 15-year-old, I

wanted to save something of the railways of the Isle of Wight, among the people I turned to were some who had battled at Westerham. They helped to bring realism to my youthful ambitions and ensured that we eventually succeeded.

So, the spirit of the Westerham branch lives on, and not just beneath the tarmac of the M25.

When writing this book I set out to contact those who were involved in its final years. I managed to find a few of the younger ones but, sadly, age has caught up with most and they are no longer with us. I hope that my efforts will do them proud and that they will be pleased by the story I have uncovered.

Ron Strutt

Diss, Norfolk

2016

Acknowledgements

I could not have completed this book without the help of a great many people over a long period of time. My interest in the Westerham branch was shared by my school friend Iain Whitlam and together we walked along the line in 1964 and 1965 in preparation for a talk we gave to our school's railway society. Some of the photographs he took on those occasions can be found in these pages. They brought back many happy memories for me.

Over the years I have talked to a great many people about the Westerham branch and many of their ideas, thoughts and memories have found their way into this book. They include Roy Edwards, the late David Kitton, and the late Richard Ferris, all of whom were members of the Westerham Valley Railway Association, Nick Pallant of the Kent & East Sussex Railway, John Warde, whose ancestors played a key part in building the line in the first place, Nick Catford of the Disused Stations website, Richard Greenwood, and all the members of the Southern Email Group (SEmG). Richard Shawyer, curator of the Kent & East Sussex Railway archives at Tenterden, willingly assisted by tracking down the few remaining papers and ephemera of the Westerham Valley Railway Association. Chris Marshall of the CBRD website helped me enormously in my attempt to unravel the tangled story of the South Orbital Road, known today as the M25.

Thank you, too, for all the people who have helped by providing photographs of the line, without which this would be a far duller work.

Thanks are also due to the staff of the National Archives at Kew, who do such a marvellous job and who provide such an efficient service for researchers. Similarly, the Parliamentary Archives are always a delight to visit, not least because the staff are so helpful and friendly.

Above all, my partner Jane has given me massive encouragement and support as I have struggled to complete what has been a task of a lifetime. I cannot thank her enough for all she has done.

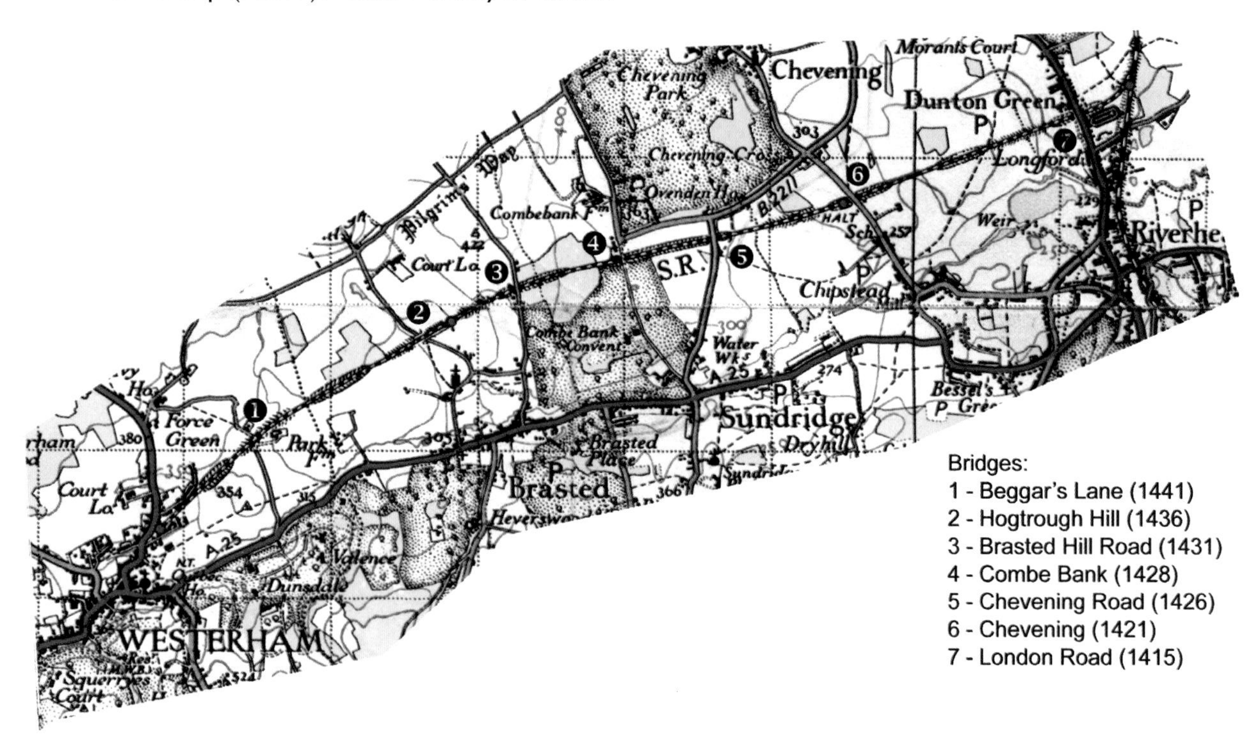

Ordnance Survey New Popular Edition One-Inch Map sheet No 171, revised 1946. ***Crown Copyright***

Sources and Further Reading

The Westerham branch

For detailed information about the branch itself, the main work is David Gould's *The Westerham Valley Railway*, published by Oakwood Press. The second edition, published in 1999, is an extended version of the first but there are illustrations in the 1974 first edition that didn't make it into the second. Gould covers matters such as the locomotive and carriage history of the line in detail and his second edition also includes excellent drawings of Westerham's station building, signal box, water tower, and goods shed, essential material for anyone wanting to model the station.

Another drawing of Westerham station building appears in *Southern Country Stations: 2 South Eastern & Chatham Railway* by John Minnis, published by Ian Allan in 1985. There are track and signalling plans in Pryor and Bowring's *An Historical Survey of Selected Southern Stations*, published by OPC in 1980.

Archives

I cannot list every document that I consulted at the National Archives at Kew; there were hundreds, totalling thousands of pages, ranging from once-secret Cabinet Minutes, with their records of discussions about the future of the railways, to detailed BR documents. The main series that I consulted are listed below. AN files are created by BR, MT the Ministry of Transport. Within each of these series are the individual files. These vary enormously: some are amazingly comprehensive, others bare, while some have gems amidst much else.

AN 177/245 Westerham–Dunton Green: correspondence, reports and cuttings 1 Nov 1951–30 Jun 1960AN 177/246 Westerham–Dunton Green: correspondence and reports 1 Jan 1960–28 Feb 1961
AN 177/247 Westerham–Dunton Green: correspondence, report and closure arrangements 1 Jul 1961–31 Jan 1963
AN 177/248 Westerham–Dunton Green: 1 Jul 1963–30 Apr 1965
AN 177/249 Westerham–Dunton Green: objections 1 Apr 1960–31 Jul 1960
AN 177/250 Westerham–Dunton Green: replies to questionnaire (date estimated) 1 Jan 1960–31 Dec 1960
AN 177/251 Westerham–Dunton Green: maps (date estimated) 1 Jan 1960–31 Dec 1960
AN 177/252 Westerham-Dunton Green: staff matters 1 Mar 1960–30 Sep 1961
MT 124/658 Southern Region: Westerham branch line 1962–70
MT 114/634 Westerham/Dunton Green branch, Kent: purchase of Westerham branch by Westerham Valley Association (Railway Inspectorate)MT 57 various: includes South Orbital Road and Sevenoaks Bypass documents
MT 95 various: includes South Orbital Road documents
MT 106 various: includes South Orbital Road documents
MT 110/12 Long term projects: South Orbital Road; Dartford Tunnel implications 1958–1961
MT 110/62 Development plans: long term projects; South Orbital Road, Dartford Tunnel implications 1961–1963

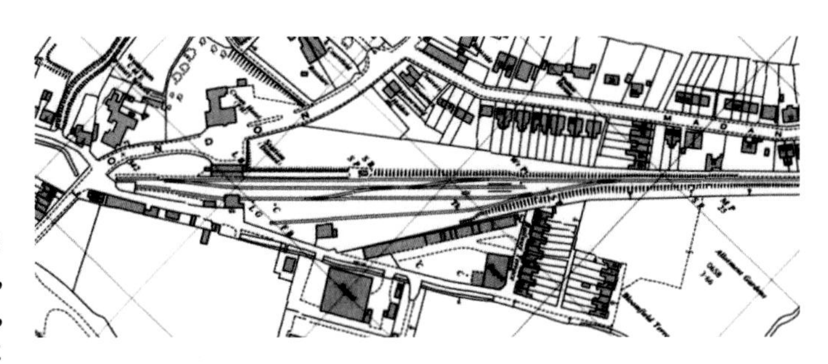

Westerham track layout 1963 (after closure) from OS 1:2500 map. ***Crown copyright***

Newspapers

Newspapers covering the Westerham area included the *Sevenoaks Chronicle*, the *Sevenoaks News*, the Westerham Herald and the *Kent & Sussex Courier*, of which only the first and last survive.

In Passing

Almost every railway album on branch lines in the south of England includes at least a photo or two of the Westerham branch; there are too many to list here. The line features in railway periodicals from time to time, ranging from single pictures through photo features and reminiscences to the occasional detailed article. Rather than list them all here, there is a superb index on the internet at www.steamindex.com. However, this does not include the magazine *British Railways Illustrated*, often known as *BRILL*, which had a good feature on Westerham in its January 1995 issue.

The Closure Era

The Westerham closure was part of the wider railway story of the 1950s and 60s, a period that is still poorly understood and about which myth still tends to overwhelm the truth. It was tempting to extend this book into a detailed commentary on the whole era but I have done my best to stay focussed and direct readers elsewhere instead. There is a good selection.

Clough, David N., *Dr Beeching's Remedy*, Ian Allan, 2013
Faulkner, Richard, and Austin, Chris, *Holding the Line – How Britain's Railways Were Saved*, OPC/Ian Allan, 2012
Gibbins, E. A., *The Railway Closure Controversy*, Leisure

Products, 2000
Gourvish, T. R., *British Railways 1948–73: A Business History*, Cambridge University Press, 1986
Hardy, R. H. N., *Beeching – Champion of the Railway?*, Ian Allan, 1989
Henshaw, David, *The Great Railway Conspiracy*, Leading Edge, 1991
Loft, Charles, *Last Trains: Dr Beeching and the Death of Rural England*, Biteback Publishing, 2013

Gourvish's *British Railways 1948–73* is the official history of BR and provides a detailed account of a complex period of BR's life. Needless to say, it is a source to which all other volumes refer. It is a heavyweight volume (literally), scholarly, but nevertheless readable.

Loft's *Last Trains* was published to mark the 50th anniversary of the Beeching Report. It was based on his earlier *Government, the Railways and the Modernization of Britain*, which started out as a PhD thesis. Despite its academic origins, *Last Trains* reads well and includes a chapter specifically on Westerham. Loft looks at the era in the context of Whitehall's attempt to modernise the management of Britain's economy, coupled with the desire to reduce public spending, though he understates the roles played by government in creating the railway problem in the first place and by railway management in failing to adapt to a changing world. It is also heavy in its academic reliance on the opinions, views and epithets of sundry other writers, but I can recommend it to those who want a deeper understanding of what the Beeching era was about.

Clough and Faulkner/Austin adopt a more illustrated approach to the subject, Clough's weakness being the lack of an index.

Hardy offers a view from within the railway ranks, claiming that Beeching was the saviour of Britain's railways. He combines a biography of the man with a history of the period but, while he details the events that led to Beeching's appointment, he offers little analysis of the problems that brought it about and too readily assumes that Beeching's prescription was the only answer.

The title of Henshaw's *The Great Railway Conspiracy* gives a clue to his approach. As the cover blurb says, he shows how 'Britain's railways were "stitched up" by powerful political interests in the roads lobby during the 1950s and 1960s'. It is worth reading but needs to be treated with caution.

Of Gibbins' *The Railway Closure Controversy*, the least said the better. A former railway manager, his thrust is that those who objected to railway closures were ignorant of the principles of economics, finance, politics and railway operations, their sole purpose in life being to frustrate the work of railway managers. His efforts to decry every objection become tedious. As this book shows, railway managers could and did get it wrong.

Dunton Green in 1961 from OS 1:2500 map. *Crown copyright*

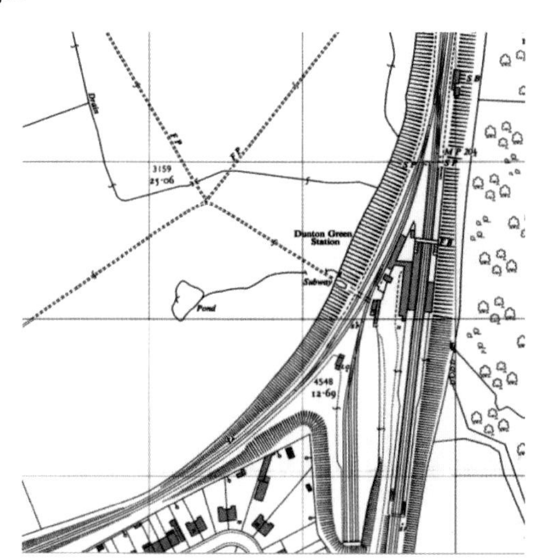

Acknowledgements
This book contains public sector information licensed under the Open Government Licence v3.0

A Few Notes

Abbreviations

Referred to as

AGM	Assistant General Manager
BR	British Railways
BR(SR)	British Railways (Southern Region) Southern Region
BRB	British Railways Board 'the Board'
BTC	British Transport Commission
CCE	Chief Civil Engineer
CRO	Chief Regional Officer
CTCC	Central Transport Consultative Committee
Demu	Diesel-electricmultiple unit
Emu	Electric multiple-unit
GM	General Manager
HMRI	Her Majesty's Railway Inspectorate

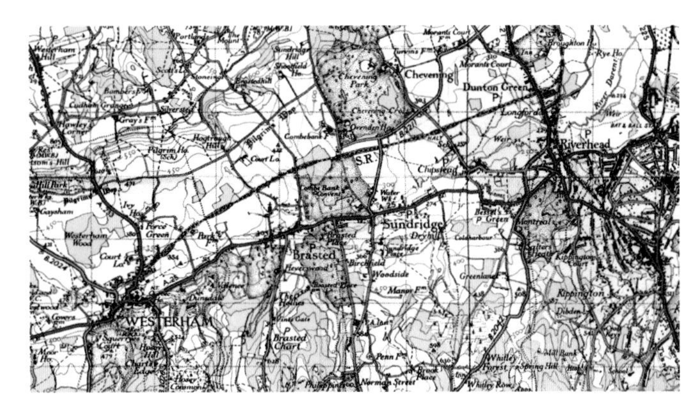

Ordnance Survey New Popular Edition One-Inch Map sheet No 171, revised 1946. *Crown Copyright*

K&ESR	Kent & East Sussex Railway
KCC	Kent County Council the county council
LNER	London & North Eastern Railway
LT	London Transport Executive (later Board) London Transport
MOT	Ministry of Transport 'the Ministry'
RI	See HMRI
TUCC	Transport Users' Consultative Committee (regional)
WBRPA	Westerham Branch Railway Passengers' Association
WVRA	Westerham Valley Railway Association

Money

Until 1971 the UK monetary system was based on pounds, shillings and pence. There were 12 pence to the shilling and 20 shillings to the pound. The decimal equivalent of one shilling is 5p. The abbreviation '£ s d' was widely used – thus £2 3s 6d represents two pounds, three shillings and sixpence. An amount of shillings and pence can also be shown as, say, 3/6. It was quite common for amounts in excess of £1 to be shown as shillings, especially the price of railway tickets (eg 35/6).

Inflation has eroded the value of money substantially, even since the 1960s. There is no single 'correct' way of comparing values then and now and simply increasing prices in line with inflation does not always give a sensible answer. I have mostly based comparisons of costs and values on the measure referred to as economic status, using the superb www.measuringworth.com/ukcompare/.

Measurements

Britain's railways were built using the imperial system and, to a great extent, are still measured by it.
1 mile = 1.61km
1 mile = 80 chains = 1760 yards1 chain = 22 yards = distance between wickets on a cricket pitch
On railways, distances are given in miles and chains, for example 12m 20ch, which is 12¼ miles. Land area was measured in acres:
1 acre = 0.4 hectares = 4840 square yards

Cast of Characters

Bolland, T. R. V. (Tim) (1922–?)

After war service in the Royal Navy, Bolland joined the Southern Railway as a Cadet in 1946. In 1960 he was appointed to the new position of Line Traffic Manager of the Southern Region's South Eastern Division2, having previously been the division's Traffic Superintendent.

In 1963 he left the Southern and became Line Manager of the Eastern Region's Great Northern Line before moving to the Freightliner Division of BR as Traffic Manager. In 1969 he became assistant managing director of Freightliners Ltd and in the following year joined the board of British Road Services. This subsequently became part of the National Freight Corporation, where he was director of technical services and market development from 1974 until his retirement in 1978, having switched his allegiance from rail to road. He subsequently became Chairman of the Kent Area Health Authority and a member of the Health Service Supply Council and was appointed a CBE in 1982.

Cobb, R. L. P. (Robert) (1917–1998)

After wartime service in the Royal Engineers in France and India, in which he reached the rank of Lt-Colonel, Cobb joined the Southern Railway as assistant to the Stores Superintendent, transferring to the Eastern Region in 1951 as Senior Assistant to the Stores Superintendent. In 1952 he moved to London Transport, becoming Assistant to the Chief Supplies Officer. In 1954 he became Senior Assistant to the Purchasing Officer and the following year he was promoted to Purchasing Officer. In 1957 he returned to the Southern Region as Stores Superintendent and, when the department was reorganised the following year, he became Supplies and Contracts manager, a position that he held until 1962 when he became one of the region's AGMs. When BR set up a new shipping and international services division in 1968 he became Irish and Channel Islands Traffic Manager and Chief Commercial Manager, Irish & Estuarial, the following year.

Ellison, Douglas V. (1923–2012)

At the time of the Westerham closure Ellison was

Assistant (Finance and General) in the General Manager's office of the Southern Region and shortly afterwards became Works & Planning Manager. In the early 1970s he became Chief Passenger Marketing Manager at BRB headquarters.

Hopkins, Charles P. (1901–?)
Hopkins won a Traffic Apprenticeship with the North Eastern Railway in 1921, having been placed first in the company's examination. Developing a flair for traffic problems, he made a speciality of wagon movement and control, but broadened his experience through a spell with the Continental Traffic Manager at Liverpool Street and later as assistant to the superintendent (Eastern Section). He returned to York in 1941 and joined the chief general manager's staff a year later. He later took charge of the Central Traffic Office at Marylebone, represented the LNER on the Operating Committee of the wartime Railway Executive Committee and finally reached the position of AGM (Traffic and Statistics) on the LNER. In 1948 he was a surprise appointment as CRO of BR's North Eastern Region when the railways were nationalised. (He was the youngest of all the CROs.) He moved to the Southern Region as CRO in 1950, becoming Chief Regional Manager in 1953, and General Manager from 1955 until 1962.

Langley, Brigadier Charles Ardagh, CB CBE (1897–1987)
One of HM Inspecting Officers of Railways from 1946 and HM Chief Inspecting Officer from 1958 to 1963, when he was succeeded by Col McMullen. He ended a distinguished military career in the Royal Engineers as Commandant of the Transportation Training Centre at Longmoor in 1946.

Marples, (Alfred) Ernest, PC (1907–1978)
Marples was Minister of Transport 1959-1964. Born in Manchester, he worked as a miner, postman and chef before qualifying as an accountant. After wartime service in the Royal Artillery in 1941, he joined the Conservative Party and was elected MP for Wallasey in 1945. After serving as a junior minister from 1951–55, he was appointed Postmaster-General in 1955 and Minister of Transport in 1959. He is most noted for bringing in the Beeching era on the railways. He retired from Parliament in 1974 and was created a peer.

In 1948 he co-founded a civil engineering company, Marples Ridgway and Partners. When he became a junior minister in 1951, he stepped down as Managing Director of Marples Ridgway but continued to hold some 80 per cent of the firm's shares. When he became Transport Minister in 1959 he undertook to sell his shareholding in the company but had not done so by January 1960 when Marples Ridgeway won the tender

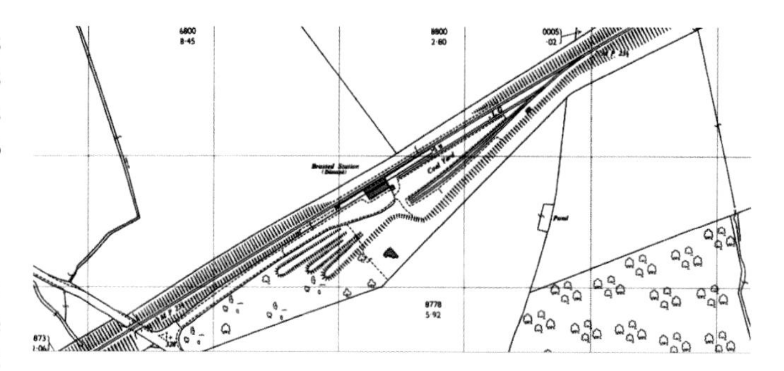

Brasted's final track layout from OS 1:2500 map. ***Crown copyright***

to build the Hammersmith Flyover. Under pressure, he finally transferred his shares – some say to his wife, some to a blind trust.

Early in 1975 Marples suddenly fled to Monaco after learning that he was suspected of tax fraud. The Treasury froze most of his assets in Britain but he had already transferred most of his wealth to bank accounts in Lichtenstein. He never returned to Britain.

McKenna, David, CBE (1911–2003) Came from LT to become AGM of the Southern Region in 1955. In 1962 he became Chief Commercial Officer at BTC HQ, working with Beeching on the reshaping of the network which culminated in the Beeching report, before becoming GM of the Southern Region and Chairman of its Board in 1963. He was appointed a member of the BRB from 1968 until his retirement in 1976, and was Chairman of British Transport Advertising from 1968 to 1981.

In the 1960s McKenna fought BR headquarters over the closure of the Ashford–Hastings and Alton–Winchester lines. Like the better-known Gerard Fiennes, McKenna saw no reason to close lines where the savings would be small, especially when a substantial loss of revenue was likely. He saved Ashford–Hastings but could only delay the closure of Alton–Winchester.

McMullen, Col Denis (1902–1973)
After service in the Royal Engineers, became one of HM Inspecting Officers of Railways from 1948 and HM Chief Inspecting Officer from 1963 to 1968 when he was succeeded by Col Robertson. He conducted the Inquiry into the 1967 Hither Green crash.

Robertson, Col John Richard Hugh, CBE (1912–1977)
Another former Royal Engineers officer, became one of HM Inspecting Officers of Railways in 1959 and was HM Chief Inspecting Officer from 1969 to 1973.

Scott-Malden, C. Peter (1918–2001)
An Under-Secretary at the MOT during the Westerham

era. He joined the Ministry of Transport in 1939 and retired as a Deputy Secretary at the Department of the Environment, where he was involved in both road and rail matters. In 1978 he was appointed a member of the Transport Tribunal.

Serpell, Sir David Radford (1911–2008)

After 15 years at the Treasury, became Deputy Secretary at the MOT in 1959 with responsibility for railways and was a member of the Stedeford Advisory Group which made recommendations on the future of BR in the run-up to the Beeching era. Beeching was a fellow member of the Group and Serpell claimed that it was he who persuaded Beeching to accept the Chairmanship of BR. He became Permanent Secretary at the MOT in 1968 and the Department of the Environment in 1970.

On his retirement in 1972 Serpell became chairman of the Nature Conservancy Council and was also a member of the National Environment Research Council and of the council of the National Trust. He served as a member of the BRB from 1974 to 1982.

In 1982–3 he produced a report on the future of the railways, setting out a number of options, of which the most notorious involved a huge cut to the network. After the report was leaked, public outcry ensured that the report was shunted into the sidings. Serpell felt the criticism and even abuse heaped on him was unfair. A minister had asked a question and he had answered it; it was not his fault if the question was not a sensible one. Many saw this as inadequate and indicative, stemming from what his obituary in *The Guardian* described as 'his traditional civil service approach – the neutral presentation of options, however outlandish' regardless of his real views. He was regarded as a stickler for the rules, one of his senior colleagues recalling him as a martinet. BR chairman Sir Peter Parker found him 'as cosy as a razor blade'.

Tunbridge, Graham (1899–1981)

Joined the railways in 1945 in the north-east and ended his career as Estates & Rating Surveyor of the Southern Region, retiring in December 1963. One of his final tasks was to ensure that the Kent County Council succeeded in its bid to buy the Westerham line.

Nine years later, Tunbridge was disgraced when his links with the corrupt architect John Poulson – a friend since his early days on the railways – were revealed. Poulson had earned fees totalling £409,330 in relation to railway property developments which Tunbridge had steered in his direction, including the development of

Ordnance Survey New Popular Edition One-Inch Map sheet No 171, revised 1946. ***Crown Copyright***

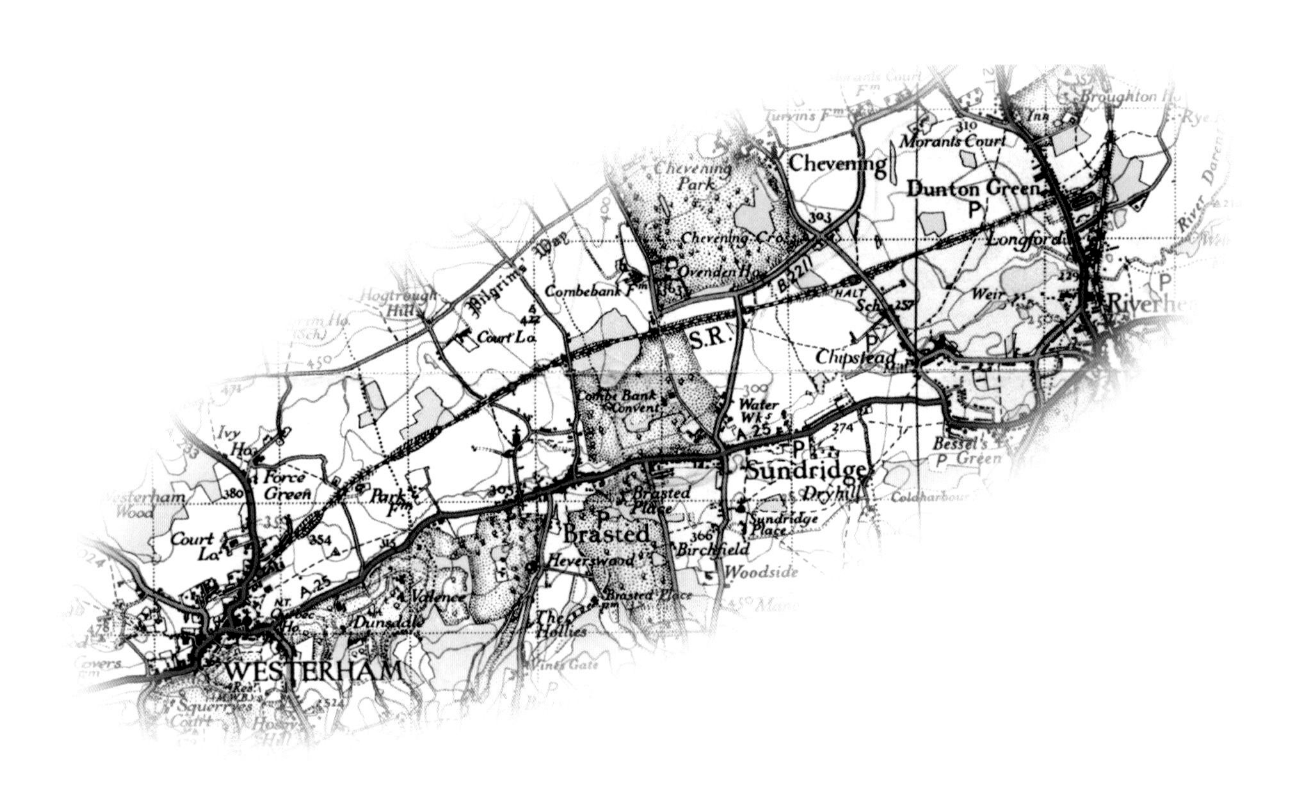

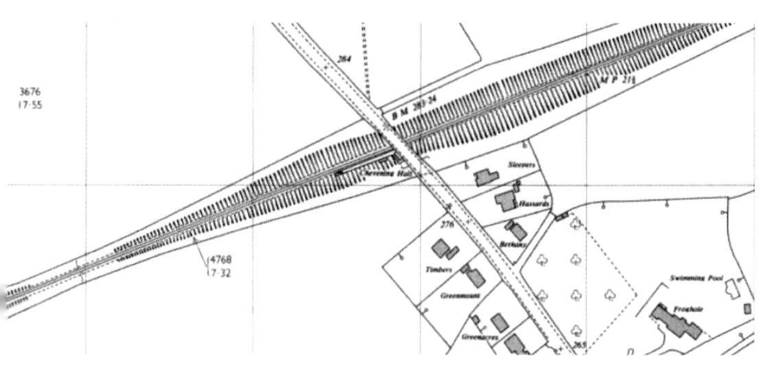

Chevening in 1964 (after closure) from OS 1:2500 map. *Crown copyright*

Cannon Street station, the building of Southern House (next to East Croydon station), and the York Road redevelopment at Waterloo.

Between 1949 and 1964, Tunbridge received at least £8,547 in cash and kind from Poulson, including a weekly income of £25 (£1,300 a year). Shortly before receiving the Cannon Street contract, Poulson gave him a cheque for £200 and a suit worth £80. He also gave him the use of a car worth £2,000. These were very substantial sums – in 1962 the average annual salary was about £800 and the average house price £2,700 – to the point at which it is hard to understand how friends and colleagues were not suspicious that he was living beyond his BR salary. When he pleaded guilty to corruption charges, Tunbridge received a 15-month suspended sentence, a fine of £4,000, and was ordered to pay £1,000 towards the prosecution costs – again, huge sums.

Poulson has been described as an 'avid Freemason' and is said to have used use Masonry as a back door to obtaining business[4]. It seems unlikely that Tunbridge was not also part of that network.

Wansbrough-Jones, Major-General Llewellyn, CB CBE (1900–1974)

Secretary-General of the BTC from 1955 to 1961 and Secretary to the BRB until his retirement in about 1965. He had previously been Principal Staff Officer to Field-Marshal Montgomery at Supreme Headquarter Allied Powers Europe (SHAPE) and as a Royal Engineers officer had some railway training. Gourvish, in his *British Railways 1948-1973*, describes him as 'industrious' while recording that he came into conflict with Beeching because of his 'by the book' way of working.

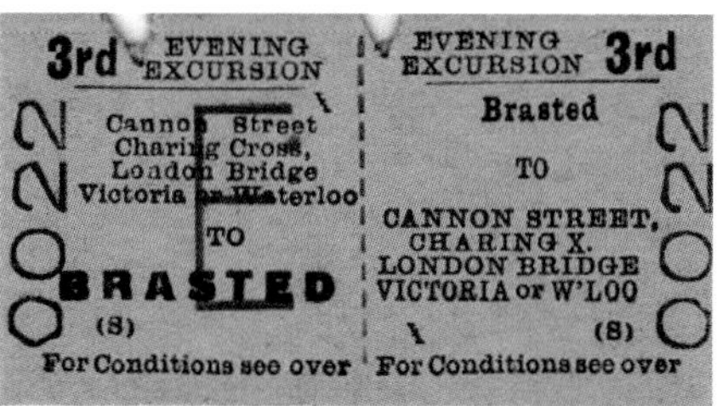

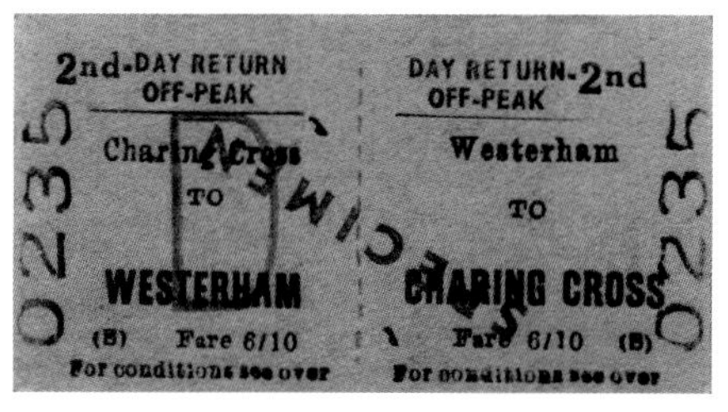

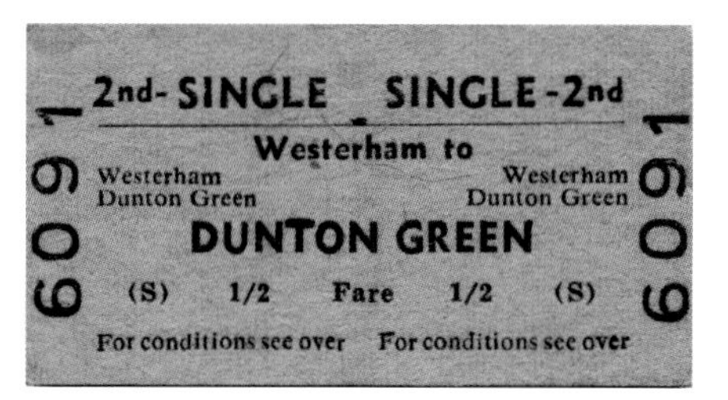

1

CLOSURE LOOMS

By the 1950s Britain's railways were heading into financial meltdown, no longer earning enough to cover their direct operating costs, let alone the interest on their capital and other central charges[5]. Inevitably, the question of closures arose and in 1949 the newly-formed British Transport Commission (BTC)[6] set up a Branch Lines Committee to review the least-used lines.

Rumours soon began to spread that the Westerham branch was one that might be condemned. In November 1951 Brasted resident Lord Kilmaine wrote to the BTC asking if the line was to close. The reply admitted that the branch was being considered but it was too early to say what the outcome might be; if it was decided that closure was justified, affected users would be able to appeal to the local Transport Users Consultative Committee (TUCC).

The role of the consultative committees

The consultative committees play a key role in our story and the Westerham closure was to change the way they worked. Set up by the 1947 Transport Act[7] to represent users' views about BTC services, the regional TUCCs[8] reported to the CTCC which, in turn, made

Westerham on Saturday 19 April 1952 with the 12.11 arrival from Dunton Green. Passengers can be seen giving up their tickets as they leave the platform. The train is formed of the unique pull-push set No 659, a rare visitor to the line. It was converted from SECR non-corridor stock; an accident-damaged composite vehicle was fitted with a driving compartment and a small brake van. Its partner brake third was unaltered, even retaining its distinctive 'birdcage' lookout, which can just be seen at the far end of the second carriage. Between the carriages and the engine ('H' class No 31523) is a four-wheel van, fitted for working in pull-push trains. There must have been a lot of parcels to be cleared from Westerham that day. *J. H. Aston*

On 1 August 1953 Westerham's porter-signalman talks to the fireman of 'H' class 0-4-4T No 31548 after handing over the token for the next trip to Dunton Green. Judging by the very full state of the bunker, the engine has not long started its duty, so the midday locomotive changeover may only just have taken place. The effectiveness of Wainwright's 'pagoda' roof design is obvious here – the fireman is leaning well outside the cab but is still protected by the roof. *Photo by Maurice Jarnoux/ Paris Match via Getty Images*

recommendations to the Minister of Transport. The Minister could direct the BTC to take action as a result of these recommendations but he was not compelled to do so.

The TUCCs started with no specifically defined role as far as railway closures were concerned but in 1951 the Minister of Transport suggested that all closure proposals should be referred to them and gradually a process evolved. BR would announce that it wanted to close a line and the TUCC would seek the views of the line's users before considering the proposal at one of its meetings, at which a BR representative would make the case for the closure. Users and local authorities could then voice their objections.

As time went on, the TUCCs expected BR to provide detailed financial information although, to begin with, the figures were not given to objectors. The hearings also began to take on a quasi-judicial air although there was never any legal basis for this. At the same time, the committees began to see it as their job to decide whether a closure was justified in the national interest. In its report on the 1958 case of the Lewes–East Grinstead 'Bluebell' line in East Sussex, it was decided that a railway that lost £33,000 a year could not be kept open unless there was:

'some major overriding consideration of national policy which can be satisfied only by keeping the railway running . . . regardless of disturbance, inconvenience, and sometimes even hardship which might be caused in a rural community by such a decision.'[9] If they refused closure the TUCCs saw it as their job to say how the service could be operated more economically, a curious state of affairs which seemed to absolve railway managers of any need to consider economies themselves. Conversely, if the TUCCs could not show how loss-making lines could be operated more cheaply, they felt obliged to agree to closure.

Nobody was happy. Users felt that the TUCCs sided with BR, partly because BR was represented on the committees and partly because most closures were approved. Their role to champion the cause of the user seemed to have been forgotten. At the same time, BR complained that the investigations had become too detailed, delaying its ability to make savings.

An unusual view of Westerham's station building and an unknown member of staff on 1 August 1953. Note the poster for the Shepherd Neame brewery. Unlike Westerham's own Black Eagle brewery, which closed in 1965, Shepherd Neame is still going strong. This was taken by a ***Paris Match*** **photographer who was on his way to Chartwell to photograph Winston Churchill but on the way he took a number of pictures of Westerham itself.** *Photo by Maurice Jarnoux/Paris Match via Getty Images*

Off-peak cutbacks

In February 1954 the Branch Lines Committee gave its verdict on the Westerham branch. The service was to be retained but was to be cut back to peak hours only on weekdays, saving £8,000 a year. The figures behind the decision have not survived but, in effect, the committee thought that, by cutting one-third of the trains, it would save one-third of the costs – a deeply flawed conclusion. When BR finally calculated the line's costs properly, it became embarrassingly clear that off-peak trains on the branch had not only covered their costs but even made a small profit[10]. Far from helping to save the line, the cuts had weakened it. This was just one of a number of dubious decisions in the Westerham case – decisions that trapped BR in corners from which it could not escape without raising doubts about its competence.

There was uproar locally when it was announced that the branch service was to be reduced from the start of the 1955 winter timetable on 19 September. On Mondays to Fridays there were to be no trains between the 9.54am from Westerham and the 4.25pm from Dunton Green and tThe timetable was adjusted so that it could be worked by a single locomotive and crew, wrongly referred to as 'one-engine-in-steam' working[11]. On Saturdays, the service restarted with a 12 noon departure – in those days, many people worked a 5½-day week so lunchtime commuter trains were needed; the service then ran throughout the afternoon but not in the evening. The hourly Sunday service continued, with trains leaving Dunton Green from 7.55am to 10.0pm but only from late March to the end of October.

'H' class No 31548 waits to depart from Westerham on 1 August 1953. Judging by other photographs taken at the same time, it looks as though this was a middle of the day scene – the lack of any members of the public seems to support that. The man in the foreground is presumably the porter-signalman as he is carrying the pouch with the single line token in it. He has just removed the red lamp from what was the rear of the train. The man further down the train may be the 'junior' porter who sold tickets on the train – staff past retiring age often performed this role. *Photo by Maurice Jarnoux/ Paris Match via Getty Images*

Brasted became an unstaffed halt, which led to some minor changes to the branch operating procedures as shown in Appendix 1.

Some passengers complained that they would be unable to leave London after 7pm if they wanted to catch a branch connection but BR countered with the results of a 1952 census of the evening departures from Dunton Green.

	Mon	Tue	Wed	Thu	Fri	Sat	Average
9.0pm	2	3	1	1	2	2	2
10.0pm	3	5	3	4	8	6	5
11.0pm	2	1	2	4	6	2	3

One BR manager claimed that these evening services were, in effect, special trains being paid for by the wider public, but this raises the question: why did BR wait three years before taking off such poorly used trains? People complained that they were being deprived of an evening out in London (although the figures suggest that few took advantage of the opportunity) and the remaining service must have been made less attractive if potential passengers thought there was a risk of being delayed leaving London and having no way of getting home.

There were complaints about the lack of notice, which BR had to admit were justified. Even though the changes had been decided the previous March, passengers were only told about them when chalked notices appeared days before they were introduced. Even BR's Southern Area Board complained that it had not been asked to approve the cuts and it was angry about the inadequate publicity for the changes.

Replying to the wider complaints about the reductions, BR insisted that it hoped to keep the branch's loss small enough to make it worthwhile, taking into account the traffic it contributed to the main line. David McKenna, assistant general manager of the Southern Region, noted that:

'We hope ... to keep the line in being until such time as we can operate it by more modern and efficient methods of transport such as electrification or diesel-electrification but I am bound to say that on account of its geographical position in relation to the main line railway routes

For a change, pull-push set No 481 is in use on the branch, seen here being propelled away from Brasted (station, as it then was) towards Dunton Green by an unrecorded 'H' class locomotive on Sunday 17 April 1955. Note the considerable depth of ballast required on this notoriously waterlogged stretch of the line. *Bluebell Railway Museum – Colin Hogg*

Chevening Halt on a Saturday in May 1960 with the 3.50pm train from Dunton Green. The road bridge was less than 10 years old but is already smoke-stained. The extensive drainage needed in this difficult cutting is obvious. Officially, the locomotive's single headcode disc should have been above the other buffer to indicate a Westerham branch train but this was rarely adhered to. *J. H. Aston*

'H' class 0-4-4T No 31164 has just arrived at Westerham on 20 October 1956 with a train of one of the two pull-push sets formed out of the ex-SECR railmotors. A curious feature of these sets was that their doors opened inwards, often confusing anyone who wasn't a regular user. In the mid-1950s it seems to have been the norm to run the service with the locomotive at the London end of the train. Note the horse box in the goods shed siding. *Author's collection*

Westerham will never be a very attractive passenger train service proposition except in the business periods when most of the present traffic is in fact carried. Ultimately electrification of the main line to the coast may stimulate a modest traffic also in that direction.'

* * *

The protests faded away in time but rumours continued that the line might close. Less than a year after the Westerham cutbacks were implemented, the BTC decided that there should be a mass programme of rail closures – in effect, an early version of the later Reshaping report. Regions were asked to nominate candidates and Westerham was on the Southern's list.

Track renewals deferred

In 1951, when it had first been considered for closure, the chief civil engineer (CCE) had been asked to defer spending on the line[12] and after five years the backlog was becoming a problem. Much of the track needed replacing and there were two serious earth slips, one at Chevening, the other near Brasted, which required urgent attention[13]. By August 1956 renewal of track with new sleepers and second-hand rails was needed on three sections of the line, totalling one mile 49 chains, at a cost of £16,000 (around £350,000 today). The work needed to be carried out within three or four months, the alternative being heavy patchwork repairs at considerable expense. A further £4,500 was needed to renew half a mile of track at Chevening in 1957. McKenna wanted to postpone this spending for six months to give the Branch Lines Committee time to decide the future of the line. He suggested imposing speed restrictions and decelerating the service but this would have required a second locomotive, train and crew to maintain the frequency. The idea was dropped when the costs were worked out.

By November 1956, with the repairs still not authorised, the CCE reported that he would do his best but he could no longer guarantee to keep the line running.

'. . . Apart from the steady deterioration in the condition of the Permanent Way materials, due to continued postponement of normal relaying and resleepering, there are two slips which should have been dealt with a long time ago. The slips tend to become worse and the cost of remedial measures grows with each month of postponement. I can no longer guarantee to keep the line running as it is now for any definite period. It is quite likely that under adverse weather conditions one or both of these slips will get out of hand, necessitating the imposition of severe speed restrictions and possibly the interruption of traffic at any time.'

He also pointed out that the heavy load of main line modernisation would make it difficult to catch up on arrears of maintenance on the branch. This brought matters to a head.

In the event, the BTC abandoned the idea of mass closures, partly because of the fiasco over the illegal closure of the Bluebell line[14] and partly because of the optimism created by the Modernisation Plan, which BR thought could improve the fortunes of many lines. In its September 1956 review of its financial situation[15], the BTC set out as one of its objectives for passenger traffic: 'To recast entirely the form of the feeder and secondary

A view across the deserted goods yard at Westerham on 13 July 1957, showing 'H' class No 31548, unusually running bunker first, at the country end of pull-push set No 482. This was formed of the carriage portions of two SECR railmotors dating back to 1906. From 1934 this and sister set No 481 were the regular rolling stock on the branch. Both sets worked on the branch every day until the 1955 cutbacks after which only one was used each week. *Author's collection*

On 15 April 1961, 'H' class No 31500 arrives at Dunton Green to take over the Saturday afternoon train service. After 1955 Monday–Friday trains were withdrawn during the middle of the day but on Saturdays the service resumed at midday to cater for commuters who worked a 5½-day week. *Author's collection*

One of BR's new diesel railbuses, introduced in 1958, seen at Swindon. W79978 was one of five built by AC Cars for the Western Region but was later transferred to Scotland, before being withdrawn in 1968. A meeting to discuss railbuses was held on 10 August 1958 at which all regions were represented. For the Southern, Mr F. P. B. Taylor said that most of their hopelessly loss-making branch lines had been closed but they could run a pilot scheme on the Westerham and Hawkhurst branches, using three or four vehicles based at Tonbridge. However, they needed parcels space and their capacity was probably insufficient for some of the Southern's passenger loads. No railbuses were ever allocated to the Southern though ex-Southern lines in the West Country did make use of them. *Author's collection*

Despite the deteriorating state of the branch track, 10 November 1957 saw a visit by ex-SER 'O1' class 0-6-0 No 31064 to Westerham on the 'Kentish Heights Special', a half-day ramblers' excursion from Greenford in West London to Westerham branch stations. It travelled via Kensington Olympia and Clapham Junction. This was the second special over the branch in 1957; on 15 January 'West Country' Pacific No 34017 *Ilfracombe* worked an 11-coach children's special train to Kensington Olympia. *Author's collection*

An unusual visitor. 'N' class 2-6-0 No 31828 ventures onto the Westerham branch at Dunton Green with a southbound freight train on Wednesday 22 April 1959. The headcode implies that the train was bound for the Tonbridge and Ashford line, so the photographer thinks it may have been shunted onto the branch to allow other trains to pass it. Given that the shunting movement to allow this would have been time-consuming, it hints that there may have been a problem in the Sevenoaks area. *Bluebell Railway Museum – Alan Postlethwaite*

line services by substituting for the infrequent stopping steam train a smaller, cheaper and more attractive diesel or electric unit. This will eliminate one of the most serious drains on the economy of the railway system, whilst providing at the same time an improved service.'

In the light of this, although Westerham remained on the list for review, it seemed unlikely that the Branch Lines Committee would give the go-ahead for closure in the near future so, in December 1956, the Southern's commercial manager, Mr W. H. F. Mepstead, was asked to review the situation. He concluded that the branch generated passenger revenue of £9,300 a year, of which £2,100 represented the branch share. Parcels and freight earned some £13,000 a year, but freight was light, averaging only a wagon of coal a day to each of Brasted and Westerham[16]. The previous Branch Lines Committee report showed that savings from closure would be far in excess of earnings and it seemed likely that complete closure would be recommended one day. On the other hand, the line connected with an electrified line offering a fairly intensive service to London.

Regions had been asked to recommend lines on which to try diesel railbuses. The Southern had chosen Westerham over the Hawkhurst branch because it was already worked by a single train but a fair trial would not

'H' class 31520 propels pull-push set No 482 away from Brasted on its way to Dunton Green on 13 September 1959. It is hard to believe, looking at this sylvan spot, that there are now eight lanes of motorway here. *Bluebell Railway Museum – Alan Postlethwaite*

The Westerham branch train rounds the curve towards Dunton Green on 13 September 1959 with pull-push set No482 leading. These vehicles, already over 50 years old by that time, had only another 6 months to go before withdrawal. *Bluebell Railway Museum – Alan Postlethwaite*

be possible if the line was hampered by speed restrictions.

Looking ahead, though, the usage of the branch was well within the capacity of a bus service. Even if BR had to subsidise buses, it would still make savings and the subsidy would merely be a transfer of money from one part of the BTC to another.

A handwritten addition to the report concluded that 'we shall have to incur the £16,000: the case is not yet open and shut'. A longer note in the same writing (most likely McKenna's) summed up the situation:

'I doubt whether the fate of the Westerham Branch can really be settled until cheaper methods of traction have been tried and we will probably be pressed to await the traffic results of the line with the main line electrified.

'£16,000 at this juncture could be justified: it is really part of the costs of keeping the line open. If in due course this line is closed a substantial part of this expenditure is still recoverable in materials.

'While it might be cheaper to use a bus rather than any form of train, the BTC have committed themselves with the Consultative Committees that we won't withdraw services if "per se" they can be made to pay by modernised rail transport. The argument in the last part of [the report] cannot be pressed to its logical conclusion.'

This was a fudge. The idea that much of the £16,000 could be recovered if the line closed was far-fetched. Money spent on repairing slips was lost forever as was the labour cost of track renewals.

* * *

The Branch Lines Committee papers on the Westerham branch do not appear to have survived but a reference to them tells us that in October 1957 it supported the branch being retained. The renewals proposed in 1956 were finally approved and were belatedly carried out in 1958.

Under the BTC's new approach, closure was seen as a last resort if, despite modernisation, a line still didn't pay. Indeed, the BTC argued that widespread closures

Pull-push sets Nos 481 and 482 were built from the carriage portions of SECR railmotors that were introduced in 1907 and even in 1959 they were redolent of the Edwardian age in which they were built. This is the former first class saloon of Trailer Third carriage No 915, previously Trailer Composite No 5581. In 1941 all London area suburban trains (including the Westerham branch) became third class only. In 1952 the coaches were retrimmed with third class upholstery and renumbered. *Bluebell Railway Museum – Alan Postlethwaite*

wouldn't actually save much money. Of its £40 million deficit in 1956 (equivalent to about £2.5 billion today), only £3 million would be saved by closing lines. The rest would come from modernised working[17]. Even as late as July 1958, the then Minister of Transport told the House of Commons that closure of loss-making services was not an automatic outcome:

'. . . the British Transport Commission does not advocate removing services in cases where there is some eventual hope of their paying, or providing necessary feeder services to other parts of the railways[18].1'

The people of Westerham must have taken heart at this – what was their railway if not a necessary feeder? Unfortunately, that way of thinking soon fell out of favour when, despite the Modernisation Plan, BR's losses grew. The mood changed as the government found itself funding not only BR's massive investment but its increasing deficits too[19]. New faces appeared at the Ministry of Transport and BR found itself faced by a phalanx of much less supportive masters. The changes began in April 1959 when James Dunnett arrived as the Ministry's new permanent secretary, with a vision of a smaller, more cost-effective railway. Next, in the role of deputy secretary, came David Serpell, previously at the Treasury[20]. (Serpell was to become infamous when, in the 1980s, he produced a report on options for further dramatic cuts to the railway network, one of which envisaged the retention of only 1,630 miles.)

Finally, after the October 1959 election, prime minister Harold Macmillan appointed Ernest Marples as Minister of Transport. In 1951 Marples had been a junior minister in the Ministry of Housing when Macmillan, his boss, had been given the career-threatening target of building 300,000 new homes a year. Marples is widely accepted as being the man who rolled up his sleeves and got the job done, while Macmillan took the credit. Now, in 1959, Macmillan saw Marples as the man who would sort out Britain's transport systems.

Controversially, Marples was also the founder of the road building firm of Marples, Ridgeway & Partners so it wasn't hard to guess the direction in which he was going to steer transport policy. The M1 was being built before Marples arrived at Transport but he arrived just in time for its official opening in November 1959 and quickly became the face of the motorway revolution.

The car and the lorry gave the public new freedom but the growing number of vehicles demanded more roads. However, the government could not afford new roads while paying for railway modernisation and carrying BR's losses too. The new masters at the Ministry of Transport made it clear that there was to be a price for continued railway modernisation – loss-making lines were to go. This was compounded in 1960 when the Guillebaud Inquiry

The third class saloon of carriage No 915 in pull-push set No 482. After conversion from the SECR railmotors in 1924, sets 481 and 482 were sent to the Isle of Wight but only stayed there until 1927. They arrived on the Westerham branch in 1934. *Bluebell Railway Museum – Alan Postlethwaite*

'H' class No 31520 propels its pull-push set away from Tonbridge on its way to take up its duties on the Westerham branch. *Author's collection*

An unidentified 'H' class 0-4-4T propels its train away from Tonbridge. Pull-push set No482 was one of two sets (the other was No 481) which were regulars on the Westerham branch from 1934 until early 1960. *Author's collection*

Westerham branch pull-push set No 482 at Tonbridge, where it was officially based. The unusual inward-opening passenger doors can clearly be seen. The third rail has been laid through Tonbridge as part of the Kent Coast electrification scheme but it doesn't seem to be seeing regular – if any – use. The train's steam heating is turned on (although much of the steam seems to be escaping) so this scene probably dates to the winter of 1959-60. Set 482 was withdrawn in March 1960. *Author's collection*

'H' class 0-4-4T No 31512 at Dunton Green in the second half of 1959 or early 1960 with one of the former SECR railmotor pull-push sets. The locomotive was transferred from Gillingham to Tonbridge in May 1959. *Author's collection*

recommended substantial pay increases to bring BR staff into line with other industries. The government accepted Guillebaud's conclusions but used the opportunity to tighten the noose around BR's neck. It was no longer willing to invest in lines simply to reduce their losses. Loss-making lines that needed investment were to close.

Speaking in the House of Commons in March 1960, Macmillan said that he would not allow BR to become an intolerable burden on the economy[21]. The railway system was to be remodelled – a euphemism for cuts. Those working in the industry had to accept this and the public also had to accept the need for change. He gave a stark warning – there would be a reduction in services and for some people that would mean the sacrifice of convenience.

Little did the passengers on the Westerham branch train know, as they read Macmillan's words in their newspapers, that, just a few days earlier, they had been chosen to make that sacrifice.

2

The Fight Begins

The Westerham line had been living on borrowed time throughout the 1950s but it was Kent Coast electrification that struck the final blow. Phase 2 of this scheme, covering the main line south from Sevenoaks to Ashford and Dover, was due for completion in 1962. Facilities for steam locomotives were to be abolished[22], which meant that unmodernised lines had no future as, in BR's worsening financial state, there was no money to electrify branch lines.

A different sort of closure

2,000 miles of railway, mostly rural, had closed during the 1950s but Westerham was different. It was relied on by London-bound commuters, many of who had bought homes on the basis of having trains to get them to work. However, the line was losing money and was unlikely to cover its costs even if it was modernised. It was exactly the sort of line that would have to go if the new masters in Whitehall had their way.

It is often claimed that the Westerham line was the first commuter line to be closed but that is untrue. Commuter lines in London and elsewhere had closed long before the Westerham branch (in south-east London alone the Crystal Palace High Level branch closed in 1954 and the Greenwich Park branch went as far back as 1917) but most of those had alternative transport close by, which could not be said of Westerham.

What brought Westerham into the limelight was that

'H' class 0-4-4T No 31533 approaches the summit of the line at Combe Bank as it heads for Brasted and Westerham. It is hauling ex-LBSCR pull-push set No 723, comprising a composite and a driving brake third. It replaced the former SECR railmotor sets in 1960 but was itself withdrawn in September of that year. ***Author's collection***

A 'Battle of Britain' Pacific passes Dunton Green signal box with an express bound for Folkestone and Dover. The date is late 1959 or 1960 and, while the number of the locomotive cannot be made out, it is one of the class that had its plaque lowered to make room for the arrow when working the 'Golden Arrow'. The track in the foreground is the connection between the Westerham branch and the main line with the branch headshunt curving off to the left. ***Author's collection***

many of the line's passengers were well-connected, capable of organising a fight and getting themselves noticed. They had also had a rehearsal at the time of the 1955 cutbacks. BR should have learned from the furore then, but it seems it didn't. If it had forgotten, it was about to get a sharp reminder.

Weaknesses

The problem with the Westerham branch was that it suffered from crippling weaknesses:

*The junction at Dunton Green was served mostly by stopping trains, which meant long journey times. Even with a swift connection at Dunton Green, the most popular train of the day, the 7.38am from Westerham, did not give an arrival into Charing Cross until 8.43, 65 minutes for 25 miles. Ironically, the fastest journeys were by trains that were too late for anyone who had to be at their desks by 9am.

*The villages of Brasted, Sundridge and Chipstead were situated on the main road, some way from the branch stations.

It is 1960 and the writing is on the wall for steam in Kent. 'Schools' class No 30921 ***Shrewsbury*** **rushes down the gradient into Dunton Green with an express for the Kent Coast. The connection to the Westerham branch is on the left.** ***Author's collection***

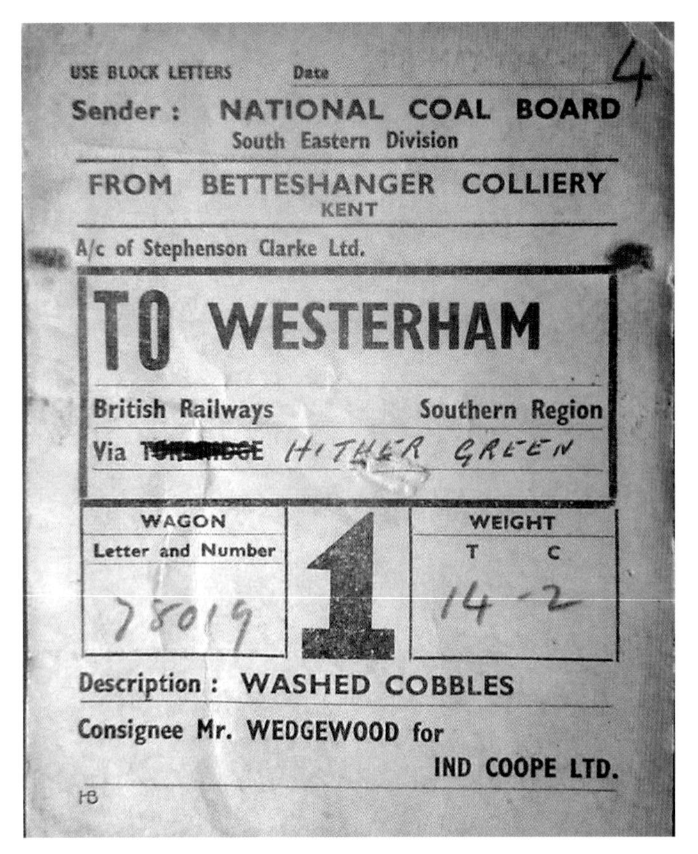

USE BLOCK LETTERS Date 4

Sender : NATIONAL COAL BOARD
South Eastern Division

FROM BETTESHANGER COLLIERY
KENT

A/c of Stephenson Clarke Ltd.

TO WESTERHAM

British Railways Southern Region

Via ~~TONBRIDGE~~ HITHER GREEN

WAGON Letter and Number	1	WEIGHT T C
78019		14 2

Description : WASHED COBBLES

Consignee Mr. WEDGEWOOD for
IND COOPE LTD.

HB

A wagon label for a delivery of some 14 tons of coal – of the type known as washed cobbles – from Betteshanger Colliery near Dover for the brewery at Westerham. The date is probably 1960 – Ind Coope did not take over the Black Eagle Brewery until 1959, two years before the line closed. The brewery was probably the only recipient of coal delivered to Westerham at that time. *Author's collection*

*The 1947 Town & Country Planning Act placed Westerham in the London Green Belt, limiting development and depriving the line of new sources of traffic. When the line closed in 1961 Westerham had a population of 4,228, an increase of only 141 in 10 years.

*Little effort was made to run the branch efficiently and it didn't receive much attention from management.

The first two weaknesses were a consequence of the route chosen for the line by the South Eastern Railway in 1864 and adopted by the local Westerham Valley Railway company. It might have helped if fast trains had stopped at Dunton Green but that would have been difficult in steam days as the station was in the bottom of a dip with challenging climbs in both directions. Some potential branch passengers drove elsewhere to catch faster trains.

The third weakness was a result of government planning policy, even if it was one which many Westerham people backed – they did not want their valley becoming suburbanised. Even the bus service lost money, so it was in LT's interests as well as BR's that the line should close and its passengers switch to the buses.

On the other hand, the final weakness was entirely within BR's control and it was one that the branch users were to exploit to the full as they fought against closure.

Battle commences

There were mixed feelings among BR managers about closing the Westerham line. Some expected rapid rejection of the proposal because it affected a commuter line; they gave the impression of merely going through the motions. Others saw it as a clear-cut case and expected closure to be approved with little debate. Neither group saw any need to support the case with more than basic financial and traffic information[23]. The line lost money and there was no point in going to a lot of effort to prove the obvious. The real question was whether you could close a commuter line, even if it did lose money.

BR's poor preparation of its case was to be hugely damaging. The Westerham line carried financially astute businessmen who were more than capable of taking BR to task. Once the objectors began demanding detailed figures, the inadequate management of the line was cruelly exposed. BR found itself playing catch-up with demands for ever more detailed information while inconsistencies between different sets of hastily-produced figures undermined its case. It became an object lesson in how not to go about a closure.

* * *

Preparing the case for closure was one of the first tasks that fell to Mr T. R. V. Bolland when he became Line Traffic Manager of the Southern Region's South Eastern Division in 1960. Bolland was a hawk. To him the Westerham branch was irrelevant; it lost money and it stood in the way of progress. However, just as Beeching was to do, he mistakenly believed that he only had to explain the cold facts and everyone would accept them. He failed to understand the practical and economic dependencies, never mind the emotional links, that tied the people of Westerham to their branch line – or the extent to which they would fight to keep it. He failed to see how people would react when they were told that, not only was their daily routine to be upset, but their journeys to work would take longer and they were to pay a substantial amount extra for the privilege.

On that basis, Bolland must shoulder much of the blame for the protracted battle that was to follow. He handled the closure badly and, according to Gerry Fiennes[24], it seems that he didn't learn the lesson and went on to repeat the same mistakes on the Eastern Region.

* * *

C. P. Hopkins, Southern Region general manager (left), and Sir Philip Warter, Chairman of BR's Southern Area Board. They are seen inspecting Kent Coast electrification work in a still from the 1957 film *Bringing The Sea Closer.*
British Pathé

On the face of it, the case for closing the Westerham line was overwhelming. The branch itself earned just £3,518 a year while its direct costs were nearly £30,000, resulting in a loss of almost £26,500 a year and that didn't include the contribution that the branch was supposed to make towards BR's overheads or the interest on its £75,000 assets. However, closures had to be justified not by a line's losses but by the savings BR would make if it closed.

The distinction is crucial. The savings achieved by closing a railway were inevitably less than the loss it made because some costs continued even after the line was shut[25]. For example, rolling stock costs included a contribution towards the overheads of the railway workshops but they would not be reduced by scrapping one engine and two carriages. Similarly, fencing, bridges and culverts had to be maintained until the land was sold. Fares were lost when a line closed and it might be necessary to provide alternative services to replace the trains. These sums had to be set against the headline losses.

BR expected to cut costs by almost £20,000 a year by closing the Westerham line but lost revenue, subsidies for extra buses and other costs reduced that to £8,900. On the other hand, BR would avoid repairs which would average £2,740 a year over the following five years. In total, BR would be better off by £11,600 a year by closing the line, as the figures in Appendix 2 show.

The two different figures – losses of £26,500 and savings of £11,600 – caused confusion. People could not understand how a 'loss' of £11,600 had suddenly grown to £26,500. Marples liked to quote the higher figure because it made the case for closure appear more compelling but he was wrong to imply that BR's losses could be reduced by £26,500 by closing the line.

The figures in detail

BR figures showed that the branch earned a total of £25,678 a year from passenger and freight traffic but much of that was payment for journeys beyond the junction.

Only a small part paid for travel on the branch itself – a season ticket passenger to London, for instance, contributed just over a shilling (5p) a day to the branch accounts[26]. The branch share of the total earnings, passenger and freight, was just £3,518, as Figure 2.1 shows.

	Local to branch		Through traffic				Total		Branch
	Jnys	Receipts	Forwarded		Recieved		Jnys	Receipts	Share
	No	£	Jnys	£	Jnys	£	No	£	£
Passenger (exc STs)	11,272	417	17,832	2,703	9,076	1,554	38,180	4,674	1,448
Seasons	-	-	59,697	6,124	2,904	312	62,601	6,436	1,072
Parcels (no).	4	1	1,272	436	4,780	1,598	6,056	2,035	178
Total passenger		418		9,263		3,464		13,145	2,698
			Tons	£	Tons	£	Tons	£	£
Goods cl 7-21	-	-	8	40	301	988	309	1,028	121
Goods cl 1-6	-	-	237	444	302	601	539	1,045	121
Coke, coal etc	-	-	139	52	4,736	10,351	4,875	10,403	546
Total goods			384	536	5,339	11,940	5,723	12,476	763
Misc	-	57	-	-	-	-	-	57	57
TOTAL		**475**		**9,799**		**15,404**		**25,678**	**3,518**

Figure 2.1: Westerham branch annual traffic receipts (year not stated, assumed to be 1958)
Source: BR Southern Region/TNA file reference AN 177/246

It would have needed half the population of Westerham to use the railway on a daily basis for it to break even but, as Figure 2.2 shows, average train loadings figures had increased only slightly over the years.

Train	March	November	December	April
am	1953	1955	1959	1960
6.10	4	4	6	6
6.59	20	15	14	16
7.43/7.38	84	56	58	52
8.10	-	42	41	42
8.44	31	26	28	39
TOTAL	**139**	**143**	**147**	**155**

Figure 2.2: Average daily loadings up morning trains 1953-1960
Source: BR Southern Region/TNA file reference AN 177/246

'Schools' class No 30927 *Clifton* passes Dunton Green with a short special parcels train from the Kent Coast. The Westerham branch platform is to the right of the photograph. The footbridge was originally at Grove Park but became redundant there when the line was widened. The bridge originally had a roof but this had gone by 1960. ***Author's collection***

These figures tally with BR's claim that an average of 167 passengers used the seven up trains each morning, including 14 scholars travelling to Tonbridge. Being a commuter line, the passenger figures didn't vary over the year as they did on lines to holiday resorts, so the passenger censuses weren't challenged as being unrepresentative, but were BR's revenue figures correct?

There were 140 season ticket holders on the branch, almost all of whom travelled to London. However, the season ticket revenue of £6,436 claimed by BR represents only 90 passengers. What about the other 50? The likely explanation is that they bought their season tickets in London. Those who travelled from the unstaffed halts at Brasted and Chevening are almost certain to have done so and the limitations of the ticketing systems of the time meant that their purchases might not show up in the branch accounts.

Such questions are often raised in books about railway closures, with the implication that BR cooked the books – that lines were closed which were, in fact, profitable. But to be fair to BR, getting the figures precisely right wouldn't have made much difference in the Westerham case. With costs of £30,000 a year, it hardly mattered if the branch earned £4,500 rather than £3,500.

BR claimed that it would lose little revenue since most passengers would still have to travel to work in London. The branch share of fares would be lost and, because some people would get a job nearer home, move house or drive to work, 10 per cent of the contributory revenue to the main line might go too. The uncertainty was the number of passengers who would be deterred by the replacement buses and would look for another way to travel or place to live.

Freight earnings would be unaffected by closure; coal and any other wagonload traffic would be delivered to Oxted, Dunton Green or Sevenoaks instead. 'Smalls' – loads bigger than parcels but less than wagonload – were already handled by road under zonal arrangements.

Doubts about closure within BR

The proposal to close the line was discussed at BR's Southern Area Board on 3 March 1960. The document is reproduced in Appendix 3. The minutes of the meeting state blandly that the proposal was approved but a memo from the general manager, C. P. Hopkins, reveals the debate that went on.

As early as May 1960 BR began to consider electrification to Westerham. The scheme would have included the building of a new 2EPB unit for use on the branch. A few years earlier, brand-new Southern Region 2EPB unit No 5759 is seen at Wimbledon on a West Croydon service. It was built at Eastleigh in 1956 and lasted in service until 1995. It has now been preserved on the East Kent Railway. ***Mike Morant***

Bulleid Light Pacific No 34035 ***Shaftesbury*** **hurries a coast-bound express past the branch junction at Dunton Green in August 1960. The locomotive was undergoing draughting trials at that time, hence the 'hooded' shape of her front end. New conductor rail, to upgrade the line for fast electric trains, has been dropped between the rails. The replaced conductor rail would have been ideal – and close to hand – for electrifying to Westerham.** ***Author's collection***

The board was in two minds about the closure. To make matters worse, the chairman, Sir Philip Warter[27], revealed that he had made a promise three years before that no major changes would be made to the line. This caused consternation among the managers present, no-one being aware of any such promise. It turned out that Warter had made the promise in a letter sent privately to Patrick Burgin, a partner in a firm of London solicitors. Shortly after the board meeting, Warter wrote to Burgin, reminding him of their previous correspondence and explaining that BR had found it necessary to take another look at the line and would be proposing its closure. Luckily for BR, Burgin had moved from Westerham to live in Hertfordshire. If he had still lived in Westerham it could have caused problems for a prominent solicitor to have such a promise in his hands.

The board wondered if it was right to go ahead with the closure but Hopkins pointed out the problem of retaining an island of different traction in an area that would become all electric. Warter suggested sounding out the local authorities before going to the TUCC and withdrawing the proposal if it met with opposition. Hopkins said that if they felt like that, they should drop the proposal. For his

Westerham pull-push set No 610 at Sevenoaks in around 1960-61. After completing its morning's work, the branch train returned to Tonbridge. On the way back in the afternoon, it formed a passenger train from Sevenoaks to Dunton Green. In 1961 this was the 4.11pm from Sevenoaks. As noted in a BR report (Appendix 5), the local lines were served by platforms on both sides, which was both dangerous and wasteful of space. *Author's collection*

part, he would not object to being turned down by the TUCC – at least they would have tried. On that basis, but reluctantly, the board agreed that the proposal should go forward. McKenna noted:

'Spoke [to] GM. If we fail we shall just have to make the best of it.'

There was clearly no great faith on the part of the Southern's senior managers that the closure was going to be approved, nor much enthusiasm for it. There were even thoughts that the closure might only be short term and that BR should hold on to the trackbed. Douglas Ellison, from the general manager's office, made a note that:

'If we get closure approval, I think we ought to hold on to the right of way indefinitely. We may well need it if the Green Belt "caves in" and development is allowed in the future.'

This seems to rule out the theory, at least as far as BR management is concerned, that the purpose of the closure was to allow the South Orbital Road to be built.

Concessions and subsidies

The closure proposal included two unusual features aimed at increasing its chances of being approved –a concession to season ticket holders to reduce the higher fares they would incur when the line closed and a proposal to subsidise the replacement bus services.

The question of increased fares was a real one. Fares from Sevenoaks to London were slightly less than those from Westerham[28] but passengers faced the extra cost of bus fares to Sevenoaks, amounting to two shillings a day – an extra 10 or 12 shillings a week (LT did not offer return or season tickets on its buses) at a time when the average weekly wage was about £12. Passengers from Westerham to London faced an increase of 30 per cent in their travel costs so there were bound to be objections about the increased journey times and costs that closure would bring. Not much could be done about the times but the costs could be tackled. Bolland proposed that, for one year after closure, passengers holding monthly or longer season tickets to destinations beyond Dunton Green would be allowed to renew them at existing railway fares and use them on the bus to Sevenoaks.

Southern Region Oxted line demu (later Class 207) No 1304 on a down train at Mayfield on the now-closed Eridge–Polegate 'Cuckoo' line. A similar type of unit was considered for the modernisation of the Westerham branch. Although this particular design was not introduced until 1962, after the Westerham line had closed, their narrow (8ft 6in) bodies would have enabled a unit to get from Westerham to the fuelling point at Tunbridge Wells West via Tonbridge. *Ian Nolan*

This concession, which was described as 'unorthodox and unprecedented', was agreed by BR's Southern Area Board but it was to be kept secret and only offered at the TUCC hearing if the case appeared to be going against closure. By holding back the concession, it would appear that BR was responding to complaints about the increased costs of travel while the TUCC would be able to claim that it had wrung a concession out of BR. Everyone would come out of it looking good and, of course, there was a chance that BR might not need to offer the concession at all.

Subsidies for buses

BR had agreed to subsidise 10 extra buses in each direction between Westerham and Sevenoaks to replace the Monday to Friday train service. This, it was quickly pointed out, was against the rules and there were doubts as to whether it would be allowed – the BTC wasn't keen on replacing loss-making trains by loss-making buses. Ellison, who took a censorious phone call, later reported to McKenna:

'I said [it] was a 'bribe' to try to get the branch closed – we had no hope otherwise. To get the extra bus services we had to pay, BTC or otherwise. It was only for a year in the first instance.'

Whether it was against the rules to pay for replacement buses or not, there was confusion over BR's obligation to provide alternative services at all. BR did not officially have to provide alternative services but the TUCCs were supposed to ensure that alternative services were

A BRCW 1550hp Type 3 diesel (later Class 33) hauls a Folkestone Harbour to Victoria boat train past the junction with the Westerham branch at Dunton Green, probably in 1960 or 1961. The locomotive has yet to receive its yellow warning panel. One of the options that BR considered for the modernisation of the Westerham branch was to use one of these locomotives hauling a two-coach pull-push set. *Author's collection*

Westerham signal box. Apart from morning and evening freight shunting, there was no need for signalling at the terminus. A scheme was put forward to close it in 1955 but was deferred because of electrification work and other 'more worthwhile' projects. *Author's collection*

available and might reject a closure if they were not. If buses would only be provided if a subsidy was paid, BR had no alternative but to pay, whether headquarters liked it or not. Muddle is the best way of describing the situation[29].

In the first year BR would have to pay extra subsidy since season ticket passengers would pay no bus fares but BR expected that passengers would eventually find other ways of getting to work – particularly when the concession expired – and the need for the extra buses would disappear along with the subsidy. It didn't work out like that, though. As we shall see in Chapter 4, the bus subsidy was to cause BR long-term problems.

The first draft of the closure proposal included a timetable for the replacement buses but BR feared it might commit itself to the operation of specific buses so it decided to say only that a number of extra buses would be provided. This, of course, created problems because objectors had no idea how their journeys would be affected. Some of the objections might have been less vociferous if the new bus times had been revealed from the start.

Closure announced

BR submitted the closure proposal to the TUCC on 30 March 1960. It was made clear from the start that diesel operation of the line was not an option. The branch would become an isolated diesel pocket and it would be difficult to service the trains. The cost of an hourly diesel service had been worked out at £10,000 a year and there would be station and track costs on top of that. No extensive development was likely in the area and any potential increase in traffic from dieselisation would not be enough to eliminate the loss.

The case was that even the limited service operated since 1955 made a loss. The loadings of the trains were light and even the busiest morning and evening trains did not average more than 30 to 50 passengers, with a maximum of 80 each way.

There were two separate versions of the closure submission (see Appendix 4). One contained the full breakdown of savings and was for TUCC eyes only. The public version gave much less detail, hiding bus subsidies among 'extra costs' since BR regarded them as a 'domestic issue' between itself and LT. More pertinently, it probably

The SECR goods starting signal at Westerham in August 1961. This would have been swept away had any of the various plans for resignalling the line come to fruition. In the background is the lower quadrant home signal – also a rarity by this date. To the left are the houses of Madan Road, the gardens of which have now been extended across the trackbed. ***Author's collection***

feared that rail users would ask why it was acceptable to subsidise buses but not the more convenient trains.

Protests flood in

The closure was announced publicly on 5 April and protests immediately flooded in. A letter from Mr M. R. Mathews to the local MP, John Rodgers, summed up the views of many local people:

'...All of us in this country realise that little used and totally uneconomic branch services of British Railways will have to be abandoned, but I am sure you will agree that it is quite absurd that this Branch line should be brought into this category. In spite of its present obsolete equipment and methods of operating it is extensively used and if it shows a loss this is the natural result, which would occur in any business, endeavouring to operate without any modernisation over a period of at least fifty years.

'It is inconceivable to me, and many of your constituents in Westerham will agree with me, that with imagination and modern equipment this line should not operate at a profit. We trust that you will interest yourself in this problem to ensure that the facts are brought to light.'

Mathews was a joint general manager of Trust Houses Ltd, then the UK's largest hotel group. He had introduced his managers to the concepts of profit-and-loss accounts and budgeting procedures and it was he who brought the budget hotel idea to the UK, so he was clearly a formidable opponent. He proved to be a tenacious one too and it wasn't long before it dawned on BR just how hard the fight against this closure would be.

Mathews expected to be given the full costs of operating the line with modern equipment and he wasn't the only one. Mr H. R. M. Farmer, a senior clerk at the House of Commons, demanded a breakdown of the figures and told the TUCC that he would be formally applying for a postponement of the closure hearing scheduled for 9 June. Sevenoaks Rural District Council also asked for the hearing to be postponed to give it time to get expert financial advice to contest the figures. It wanted more information about dieselisation – it queried BR's conveniently-rounded £10,000 – and complained that the passenger census figures did not make sense. (BR later had to admit there were problems with the figures.)

When George Tippett, the secretary of the London TUCC, received the request for a postponement he wrote back to Ellison warning that, if it was granted, the CTCC would not be able to consider the case until September, instead of in July. He clearly expected the TUCC to approve closure – perhaps because he had been meeting BR about the closure – and so doubted whether a postponement was worthwhile.

Hearing postponed

If BR thought that a logical explanation of the case would settle the matter, it was mistaken. Even the TUCC chairman was surprised by the opposition and supported the idea of postponing the hearing. When the TUCC asked if a postponement would cause serious embarrassment, BR replied that it had no reason to refuse an extension of time – the last thing it wanted to do was to give the impression that it was trying to rush the matter. In private, though, Bolland was furious that, having submitted the proposal on 30 March, he would not be able close the line at the start of the winter timetable on 12 September. He accepted the postponement with bad grace. However, an unsigned, handwritten BR note includes a telling comment: '...In view of public interest and small savings in the case, it does not seem to be worth while making an issue of this request for more time.'

We should remember BR's reference to 'small savings' in view of later comments about its reasons for the closure.

'H' class 0-4-4T No 31324 at Westerham with Maunsell pull-push set No 610. These sets were formed in 1960 to replace the Southern's ageing mixture of pull-push rolling stock, although the carriages used dated from the 1930s. Even so, they brought main line standards of comfort to branch lines all over the south of England. Passengers changing to an austere suburban electric unit at Dunton Green would have noticed the difference. ***Author's collection***

Complaints about the inadequate information given in the proposal were also building up and the TUCC asked if the more persistent protesters could be given the detailed figures. Ellison agreed but insisted that the figures had to be passed on by the TUCC – other BR Regions would object if the Southern did so directly – and he wondered if even the more detailed figures would satisfy the objectors. However, Ellison did accept that the cost of dieselisation (which turned out to be the result of a quick 1956 estimate updated for inflation) was unsatisfactory and promised better figures.

Within a fortnight of the closure being announced, a Westerham Branch Railway Passengers' Association (WBRPA) had been formed with Farmer as its chairman. Its first meeting was held in Westerham on 2 May. By the end of the evening it had recruited 90 members and won valuable publicity in both local and national press. The fight was well and truly on.

Behind the scenes

While BR maintained a steadfast public face over the closure, behind the scenes thoughts turned to the possibility that it might lose. The day after the WBRPA held its meeting, McKenna wrote to his colleagues:

'The opposition to this closure is becoming very great indeed. If the decision goes against us at the TUCC and, as has been the Commission's customary practice in the past, we accept the ruling, then I think we shall have to be ready with our plans for working the line in the future.

'Presumably diesel working is out of the question and, obviously, we cannot continue with steam. Would you, therefore, have a look at a scheme involving a form of electrification, and let me have a rough idea of the financial details. I have in mind something along the following lines:

Closure of the branch to freight traffic.

Provision of conductor rail along the branch, fed from the Dunton Green end.

Maintenance of the present service by a shuttle, consisting of one standard two-car electric unit.

Isolation of the branch (other than for stock transfers) at the Dunton Green end and elimination of the signalling.

'Whilst I realise that electrical conditions at the Westerham end would be difficult, perhaps we might just get by.'

The regional accountant had reservations about this exercise – mainly because of the difficulty of producing

Driving Motor Brake Second SC79998, one vehicle of the battery electric railcar set used on the Scottish Region's Ballater branch. It is seen out of use at Inverurie Works on 20 May 1961 still carrying its original livery. The set was returned to service in June 1962 with a new form of battery but, following a series of breakdowns and minor fires, it was withdrawn in August 1962. The batteries, weighing over 8 tons in each of the two cars, can be seen here between the vehicle's bogies. However, they do not appear to be to the original design so they may have already been replaced by this date. ***Author's collection***

costs that were truly comparable – and it took a formal instruction from the general manager to get him to do the work, now extended to compare the costs of using a diesel-hauled pull-push set, electrification using a 2EPB unit, and a diesel multiple-unit.

While the passengers stepped up their fight and senior BR managers got ready to lose the fight, the line's staff resigned themselves to closure. Interviewed by the *Sevenoaks News*, leading porter Arthur Johnson said that he was waiting to go to a new job with promotion, so he would be better off. Signalman E. R. Warwick told the reporter that he was not really worried. 'They intend to close it, and that's that.' At a consultation meeting the staff-side representatives agreed that no objection could be raised against the closure and no difficulty was expected in finding positions for the redundant staff.

Visits to the line

On 12 May 1960, Ellison, accompanied by two colleagues, visited the branch. It was almost certainly the first time in a long while that anyone in authority had visited the line. His report, reproduced in Appendix 5, paints a good portrait of the branch in its final couple of years[30]. On 20 June members of the TUCC visited the line, though they didn't actually travel on the branch as trains did not run at the time planned for their visit. Instead, they caught the train to Sevenoaks and made a two-hour coach tour of the area, followed by lunch at the Grasshopper Inn at Moorhouse, to which BR officers – but not objectors – were invited.

There is no surviving record of the visit but the TUCC members came back full of interest in the economies suggested by the protesters and the possibilities of diesel traction. BR must have had some figures to hand because TUCC members were concerned about the £43,750 cost of a two-coach diesel-electric multiple-unit (demu) and wondered if such an expensive solution was necessary. Some members even suggested that a diesel shunter might be used, as it would not need to travel to St Leonards for servicing, or a small diesel that could be serviced and fuelled by a local contractor.

The TUCC also made it clear that they were concerned about inconvenience that would be caused to those passengers who had to use the replacement buses and they insisted on seeing details of the proposed new bus timings and the train connections they would provide.

Dieselisation

It was mid-June 1960 – after the originally-scheduled date for the TUCC hearing – before BR finally produced the detailed dieselisation figures, somewhat undermining its earlier claims that the costs were the result of careful study. However, the bare summary given to the TUCC, shown in Figure 2.3, scarcely reflects the effort that went into compiling the new figures. They were intended to limit the opportunity for further questioning.

	1960 timetable		Hourly interval service*	
Costs	as at 1956	as at end 1959	as at 1956	as at end 1959
	£	£	£	£
Rolling stock				
Interest	3,200	3,500	3,200	3,500
Renewals	1,900	1,900	1,900	1,900
Repairs	1,400	1,200	2,000	1,800
Train Crews				
Drivers	1,300	1,300	1,300	1,300
Guards	1,000	1,100	1,000	1,100
Other Costs				
Fuel	1,100	900	1,500	1,300
Lubricants	100	100	100	100
TOTAL	**10,000**	**10,000**	**11,000**	**11,000**

*Hourly during the day with extra trains during morning and evening peaks. Sunday service to run March to September.

Figure 2.3: Summary of costs for dieselisation (two-car demu) as given to the TUCCSource: BR Southern Region/ TNA file reference AN 177/246

Behind this raw summary were far more detailed figures (see Appendix 6), developed in case the decision went against closure. They were based on two two-car demus, one in use and one spare. This underlines an important distinction between the costs that BR used in closure cases, namely full and marginal costs[31]. The TUCC required that it be given full costs, so the figures had to allow for a spare unit for the branch[32]. However, if BR had been forced to keep the line open, costs would have been worked out on the marginal basis of a single branch unit, spares being shared across the fleet.

As it happened, the distinction didn't matter much. The units were built with two cars but by 1960 were having a third added. This should have increased the costs by nearly 50 per cent but BR, possibly to avoid accusations of inflating the figures, ignored it at this stage[33]. Despite the odd results that these costing distinctions may have produced, the TUCC was surprised and delighted by the information that BR provided. BR, in turn, explained that it was trying to atone for the paucity of the original information.

BR's first attempt to update the figures was a mess. It assumed an hourly-interval, all-day service that seemed to involve little more train mileage than the peak-only service – less than one extra round trip a day[34]! This was later corrected to a more realistic 22,000 additional miles a year. Even so, the figures showed that running the all-day service would cost only £1,000 a year more than the peak-only service. Although the figures weren't strictly comparable with the steam service, they showed that the 1955 cutbacks had almost certainly lost BR money; crews and stock cost much the same whether they were being used or sitting idle for much of the

'H' class 0-4-4T No 31523 propels a 1922-built LBSCR pull-push set away from Westerham, a change from the routine ex-railmotor sets, nos. 481 and 482. The LBSCR sets had a large luggage van so perhaps there were a lot of parcels to be handled that day. Westerham despatched a lot of locally-made lampshades which were light in weight but bulky. The train has just crossed the small bridge over Beggars Lane and is passing the fixed distant signal for Westerham. The photograph is undated but No 31523 was withdrawn in January 1959. This scene has changed considerably. The bridge has long been demolished and Beggars Lane is now an eastern bypass for Westerham, but this stretch of embankment survives, albeit overgrown. *© Mike Morant Collection*

day[35]. The main extra was the cost of fuel for the off-peak trips. It came as a shock to BR managers to discover that the costs of the off-peak trains were so small – and a lot less than the revenue they had earned in 1955. BR kept this quiet; to have admitted that they got it wrong in 1955 would have invited claims that similar mistakes were being made in 1960.

The neat way in which the new dieselisation figures matched the original £10,000 should have rung alarm bells and, indeed, considerable manipulation of the unit mileage was needed to achieve the required result. It mattered because the substantial costs of fuel and servicing were based on it. The figures only took account of mileage on the branch itself. The original idea was that the unit would be refuelled at Tonbridge but the final figures assumed that this would somehow be done on the branch. Trips to St Leonards for maintenance were also ignored. BR was aware it was a fiddle, as a handwritten note attached to the papers revealed:

Annual mileage (branch trips only) 66,314
Annual mileage (incl. start & finish at Tonbridge)*72,481
Annual mileage (stabled on branch overnight but 2 return trips weekly to St Leonards (West Marina) for fuel and maintenance) 77,695
Annual mileage (incl, start & finish at Tonbridge and 2 trips weekly to St Leonards (WM) and return for maintenance)* 83,861
*Author's note: add another 4,200 miles a year if the units had been stabled overnight at Tunbridge Wells West depot rather than at Tonbridge.

Modernisation – the alternatives to closure

While work was underway on the dieselisation figures for the TUCC, BR was separately working on the options for modernising the line. The results were completed early in July 1960 and compared three different schemes with the costs of steam working. Once again, both peak-only and all-day services were included.

Scheme I was based on a Type 3 1550hp diesel-electric locomotive (later Class 33) hauling a two-car pull-push set. The type of set to be used was never defined but the costs included £6,000 to convert suitable coaches (and presumably the locomotives). Maunsell steam pull-push set No 610 had, in fact, started work on the branch in July 1960 so maybe it was intended to adapt this for diesel haulage[36]. Scheme 2 was for the electrification using a 2EPB electric multiple-unit (emu) while Scheme 3 was based on a three-car demu.

The results of these comparative figures are shown in Appendix 7 and a more detailed breakdown, showing exactly how the figures were arrived at, can be found in Appendix 7A.

Not surprisingly, using a brand-new main-line diesel to haul a two-coach train did not make sense but there was little difference between the costs of electric or diesel working with multiple-units. Both would have saved nearly £6,000 a year compared with steam but electrification offered simpler and cheaper operation once the third rail had been laid, even when its high initial costs were included[37]. The major differences between electric and diesel were the cheaper cost of 'fuel', the lower maintenance costs of the electric unit, and the fact that it didn't need to travel unnecessary miles to take on fuel. It could also be maintained locally, not at distant St Leonards.

The immediate thing that stands out is how similar the results are. There was no massive reduction in costs compared with steam working, partly because the interest charges on motive power and stock were based on their original cost, which was a lot less for 50-year-old equipment than for new stock.

There were also differences in staff costs between the methods of working. The steam service had been worked without a guard, a junior porter travelling on the train to issue and collect tickets. A diesel or electric unit would have required a guard so that, in the absence of a fireman, there were still two qualified crew on the train to carry out safety duties. It was expected that the guard would issue tickets though this was not a widespread practice in 1960. It had been introduced on some diesel railbus operations in 1958, albeit with a few union grumblings, and the lack of corridor connections between the vehicles of a suburban electric or diesel unit would have made it difficult.

Flawed figures

These comparative figures show the 'real' costs of keeping the Westerham branch open. Unhelpfully, the new figures were not comparable with earlier ones – especially the 'corrected' dieselisation figures prepared for the TUCC. Despite this, and against the advice of the regional

'Battle of Britain' class Pacific No 34067 *Tangmere* rushes a London-bound train from the Kent Coast past the signal box and the connection to the Westerham branch at Dunton Green. The locomotive crew will have taken advantage of the falling gradient from Sevenoaks to give themselves a good start to the hard climb to Polhill Tunnel. ***Author's collection***

'H' class No 31530 hauls a Sunday train along the branch on 18 June 1961. It is hard to believe that this leafy scene was photographed less than 20 miles from the heart of London. ***Bluebell Railway Museum – Colin Hogg***

accountant, a summary of the figures was given to the TUCC without any caveat or explanation, in an attempt to show that modernisation would do little to stem the line's losses.

Differences between these new figures and the figures given to the TUCC just weeks earlier included the cost of crews for the peak-only service, which had leapt from £2,400 to £3,981 and, whereas the earlier figures said that the crew costs would be the same for an all-day service as for a peak-only service, the new ones said that the all-day service would cost an extra £1,200[38]. The reason was that drivers were now entitled to a half-hour break between their third and fifth hours of work. Even if the service were confined to peak hours only, a relief driver would have been needed at some point during the morning and evenings. Presumably the same would have applied to the steam service, though the figures do not show this. In addition, four drivers would have been needed on Saturdays and Sundays, dashing any hope of those services being profitable.

However, the latest figures were flawed, though this was not apparent from the summarised results. Far from being a straight comparison between steam and the alternative forms of traction, as BR claimed, the exercise was like comparing chalk to cheese.

The modernisation schemes – but not the steam service – assumed the closure of Westerham signal box, the conversion of the line to 'one engine in steam' working, and some reductions in staff at Westerham. However, the revised signalling costs assumed that the sidings and freight service would remain but, whereas the steam figures included the costs of running the freight trains, none of the modernisation figures did, muddying the waters. Simplified signalling might have been expected to reduce costs but, because of the new equipment that BR insisted was needed, costs would in fact increase.

The suspicion is that, while everyone else assumed that freight would be withdrawn, the signal engineer's department simply resurrected an old scheme to close Westerham signal box while retaining freight facilities. This, of course, made nonsense of the figures. It may have saved time and effort but it resulted in a shoddy piece of work.

Objections

By the end of May 1960 over 60 objections to the closure had been received and they were still flooding in, including detailed arguments against closure from the Passengers' Association, Kent County Council, Sevenoaks Rural District Council, and other local authorities.

A number of themes ran through the letters of objection. The branch was an essential service and should be subsidised if it could not be made to pay its way. There was development in the area and traffic on the branch was increasing. Closure would increase congestion on the roads and, in any case, there was inadequate car parking at Sevenoaks station. The alternative buses could not compare to the train service – the costs to the passenger would be higher, the journey time longer, and the waiting facilities more spartan.

The Passengers' Association said that morning passengers would have to leave home up to 28 minutes earlier and would get home later too, while suffering increased fares. Bus connections at Sevenoaks were sometimes too tight – buses leaving one minute after the train from London was due to arrive – meaning either a long wait or paying even more to travel by a Green Line coach. There were fears that the buses would be unreliable in bad weather and the trains might be delayed, missing the connections.

The existing buses were already overcrowded and passengers were often unable to get on their intended bus because it was full. Many of the trains carried more than a bus load and the situation was likely to worsen as development around Sevenoaks continued.

The branch was essentially part of the London suburban system and its economics should be considered not in isolation but as part of the whole system – the closure of a feeder to the main system was not a solution. Comparison was made with the four-mile Bexhill West line, which carried a similar volume of commuter traffic but had just been reprieved from closure, even though Bexhill had an alternative rail service to London[139].

Many protesters drew attention to the economies that could be made. Steam should be replaced by diesel or electric traction, signalmen were not needed, and staff should be removed from Westerham.

BR produced an internal report in which it sought to dismiss the objections. This is reproduced in Appendix 8.

Despite the objections, Tippett, the secretary of the TUCC, still thought that closure would be approved. In a phone call to BR on 16 June he said there was a reasonable chance of getting it through. When Ellison said

Westerham near the end, a solitary wagon in the yard being the only sign of freight activity. ***Author's collection***

that, even with modern traction, the loss was likely to be £16,000, Tippett agreed that it seemed a high price to pay.

BR fights back

In mid-July 1960 BR wrote to the TUCC, challenging the objections. They also revealed the proposed new bus times. The document is reproduced in Appendix 9. It claimed that the proposed new buses would provide sufficient capacity and would meet the needs of most branch passengers. However, it warned that the extra buses would lose money and their use would need to be monitored, though it promised to come back to the TUCC if it wanted to withdraw them. It rejected suggestions that half a dozen extra buses and the cars of those who preferred to drive would add materially to road congestion. There was car parking space at Dunton Green for about 20 cars, it said, and 70 new spaces had just been provided at Sevenoaks.

BR admitted that the bus could not compare favourably in journey time with the train. On the other hand, passengers would be able to catch fast trains from Sevenoaks and for many the bus would be handier for their homes. Passengers would indeed have to pay more but the branch was losing money and that could not continue. BR rejected the idea that development in the area would help to improve the line's fortunes. It also pointed out that car ownership was higher than average in this prosperous area.

BR said that it had considered using diesels but the savings would not make the branch profitable. Electrification could be carried out relatively cheaply as the branch was short and would not require any sub-stations but the same considerations applied – the savings weren't enough to make the branch pay.

Despite the fact that its modernisation schemes planned to do so, BR dismissed the idea of removing signalmen at Westerham as it would need expensive changes to the track and signalling at Dunton Green, a job which had been deferred in 1955 because of the pressure of electrification work and other more worthwhile projects1[40]. (Even if the changes at Dunton Green had really cost as much as the claimed £4,000, BR would have saved over £5,000 in signalmen's wages between 1955 and 1961 – a better return on investment than most railway projects at that time.)

BR also insisted that, apart from the signalmen, Westerham station was worked as economically as possible, bearing in mind that the staff dealt with passengers, parcels and freight traffic. The staff might possibly be reduced if freight and parcels were transferred elsewhere but the savings would not make a noticeable difference.

Many objectors pointed out that, if the branch closed, revenue would be lost from the weekend ramblers and tourists who used the line. BR countered that, despite the provision of an hourly service on Sundays from March to October, the traffic was light – indeed, BR noted that other objectors had suggested that these trains be cut to save money. (On the other hand, when an open day was

'H' class No 31308 propels its train away from Westerham on its way to Dunton Green on 7 August 1961. Like the station building and goods shed, the signal box does not seem to have had the attentions of the painters for a few years. ***Author's collection***

'H' class 0-4-4T No 31324 waits in the branch platform at Dunton Green on 13 August 1961 before departing on another 11-minute trip to Westerham. *Author's collection*

held at Sir Winston Churchill's home at Chartwell on a Wednesday in July 1960, rather than trying to boost traffic by running a couple of extra round trips on the branch, BR issued a staff circular saying that intending passengers would have to book to Sevenoaks and continue by bus.)

At the end of its response, BR made an interesting statement:

'With the coming elimination of steam traction in the South Eastern Division of the Southern Region this branch cannot continue to be operated as at present. If the branch were retained modernisation capital would be needed. There is a limit to the amount of money which is available and any such investment as is made must be directed to projects which will show a reasonable return on the capital invested. None of the alternatives for keeping the branch open meet this requirement.' This made it clear why the branch was being closed – not so much because of its losses but because it needed investment[41]. It was based on the fallacy, inspired by government, that there should be no investment in railways that did not make a profit, even if the result was to worsen the railway's deficit. If the concept of no investment in unprofitable services had been translated to other fields, today's rural postal deliveries would still be made on foot, civil servants would write with quill pens, and there would be no modern roads. Investment to reduce costs is not only worthwhile but necessary, even if the activity does not make a profit. However, the opposite became a mantra among politicians and railway managers[42]. Whether it would have been possible to reduce the costs of the Westerham line is something we will look at in Chapter 4.

The case considered

The Westerham closure was finally considered by the London area TUCC at its meeting on 21 July 1960. In those days, TUCC meetings were not the lengthy public inquiries they were later to become – indeed, TUCCs often discussed a number of matters, not just a single closure, during a day's meeting. On this occasion the meeting went on all day, which was to have an ironic outcome. During the meeting, an LT representative assured the TUCC of the care it took to ensure connections were maintained between trains and buses at Sevenoaks. However, when

The Westerham line's final summer is almost over as 'H' class 0-4-4T No 31177 tops up with water at Westerham on 27 August 1961. The photographer is standing on the site of the engine shed, the brick bases of its walls, latterly topped by iron railings, being its sole remains. The houses in the background are in Madan Road and some of their gardens have now been extended across the former trackbed. ***Author's collection***

the home-bound objectors arrived at Sevenoaks at 6.55pm they were just in time to see the 6.57 bus set off as they ran up the station approach! Further complaints resulted.

Despite the length of the meeting, most of which was taken up hearing objections, the TUCC had concerns about some of BR's information and adjourned the decision until its October meeting to give BR time to answer a number of questions about:

• track renewals;
• the costs using (a) a diesel railbus and (b) a battery railcar as used on the Ballater branch in Scotland;
• the signalling costs and an explanation of why they had increased despite the signalling being simplified;
• and the breakdown of the branch engine mileage.

It had become clear that this was not going to be one of those decisions that the TUCC could simply rubber-stamp but the further delay caused BR concern. In August 1960, the Southern's Electrification Committee considered the Kent branches that were up for closure – Westerham, Allhallows and Hawkhurst – and decided that if closure of any of those lines was refused, it might not be possible to modernise them before steam had to be withdrawn in 1962. It suggested that draft proposals for electrification should be put through the BTC approval system on a 'just in case' basis.

Answers for the TUCC

During the summer of 1960 BR worked hectically to meet the demands of the TUCC for more information. The subject of track renewals was a particularly sensitive one as conflicting evidence had been given at the July hearing. One BR manager had said that the whole line needed renewal while another conceded that some track had been replaced but most had not. The objectors had insisted that most of the line had been relaid – and they were right.

The urgent repairs that had caused so much concern to the Southern's civil engineers a few years previously had finally been carried out in 1958. Nearly 1/4 miles of track from Dunton Green to a point just west of Chevening Halt had been resleepered. The next mile in the direction of Brasted had been relaid with new sleepers and second-hand rails, as had another mile or so on the approach to Westerham. The intervening 1/4 mile length through Brasted still required renewal. BR hoped to avoid the expense of this, together with further work to deal with earth slips, by closing the line.

To find out about BR's sole battery-electric railcar, Hopkins, the Southern's general manager, wrote to his opposite number in the Scottish Region, James Ness. Despite being referred to as a railcar, it was actually a two-car multiple-unit, adapted in 1958 for use on the 43-mile branch from Aberdeen to Ballater as an experiment for the North of Scotland Hydro-electric Board. It was powered by lead-acid batteries with a capacity for 150 miles between charges[43].

BR used the information provided by the Scottish Region to calculate the costs of using diesel railbuses and battery railcars with the results as shown in Appendix 7B. These revealed that battery railcars would cost more than either a third-rail electric unit or a diesel-electric unit. Once again, though, BR was not comparing like with like. Unlike the earlier figures, the latest ones assumed the need for two dedicated units for the branch, one in use and one spare. (The Ballater branch was operated with just one unit, a diesel unit substituting when it was out of use.) The diesel railbus, on the other hand, proved to be the cheapest of all the various options.

In response to the TUCC, the signal engineer listed the equipment said to be needed to update and simplify the line's signalling. However, as we noted earlier, his

'H' class No 31530 waits in the platform at Westerham before starting out on another trip to Dunton Green in September 1961. The only railway artefact in this scene remaining today is the base of the yard crane. ***G. W. Sharpe/ Author's collection***

department's approach was confused. As well as assuming the continued operation of freight trains, it also proposed more sophisticated signalling than was needed for the basic operation of the branch – in particular, the junction at Dunton Green was to be signalled as though there were to be through passenger trains running on and off the branch.

The equipment, costing £4,518 (around £250,000 today), comprised:

1 x three-aspect colour light signal	£416
1 x one-aspect colour light signal[44]	£212
1 x shunt signal	£343
1 x set of electrical detection	£135
2 x locks and controllers	£170
1 x track circuit	£215
1,500 yards of concrete troughing	£1,243
Insulated sole plates	£104
Low tension cables	£655
3 x two-lever ground frames and connections	£598
8 x Annetts locks	£208
Point rodding for a facing point lock	£78
Sundries	£141

Did the signal engineers simply take an old plan out of the files and submit it in response to the TUCC's request? Were they too busy to update the plans or did they think it was a waste of time to do so? Or were they encouraged to submit unnecessarily high costs?

TUCC resumes its hearing

The TUCC resumed its consideration of the Westerham closure at its meeting on 4 October 1960 but this time there were no objectors present. The chairman, Mr L. G. Burleigh, a transport adviser with ICI, opened the proceedings by saying that the issue could not be decided on the simple basis of the savings that would come from withdrawing the steam service. The committee had to decide whether there was a cheaper way of running the line.

The meeting started with a lengthy but unenlightening discussion on the branch's engine mileage. It was followed by a debate on signalling costs that descended into confusion when one of the BR representatives, Mr J. Hancock, admitted that the goods yard at Dunton Green was to stay open and therefore the junction would have to be retained in any case. However, this would cost a lot less than if the branch itself was to be retained, which, he claimed, would require new colour-light signals at Dunton

'H' class No 31263 at Dunton Green on 30 September 1961. On the far right is the main station building, abutting the London-bound platform. Between it and the goods yard can be seen the corrugated iron roof that shelters the steps to the subway that runs beneath the branch platform and tracks. On the far left is concrete troughing that was dropped as part of the scheme to electrify the branch. Unlike the branch stations, all the buildings at Dunton Green had recently received a coat of paint. *Author's collection*

Green. Hancock did not try to justify this and BR's cost of simplifying the signalling raised doubts in the mind of at least one TUCC member.

Discussion was brought to a halt when the chairman, fearful of getting bogged down in another long technical debate, said that if members were unconvinced by the costs or did not understand them, they would have to ask BR for a fuller explanation. Another member then suggested that BR should simply be asked how much of the signalling costs would be saved if the branch closed and this curtailed questioning of the figures.

Needless to say, the TUCC was unimpressed by the track renewal saga. As one member commented, the passengers had been proved right on this point and BR wrong when it said that most of the branch track needed to be renewed. Now BR said that it would cost £7,300 to renew just 55 chains of track and he doubted the accuracy of this figure. (In fact, it was on a par with the costs of the work carried out earlier but it illustrates the problems that BR created for itself by giving poor information.)

Once the discussion moved away from the detail and on to the broader questions, it became clear that the members were divided. Some thought that BR could reduce the costs of running the line and that closure would cause a great deal of inconvenience. They were opposed by those who felt that the TUCC would not be justified in expecting BR to keep a loss-making line going when it would need significant capital expenditure and when buses offered an alternative. Much of the discussion hinged on the timings and loads of the replacement buses, and there was a good deal of second-guessing what branch passengers would do in the absence of their trains.

The chairman summed up the situation when he said that many members felt there was a strong case for closure but he wanted to be sure that the users were treated fairly. The objectors had not seen the new information that the TUCC had received from BR so he suggested that the committee should postpone its decision to give objectors a chance to comment on it at another meeting. Other members disagreed and wanted to reach a decision that day. One even suggested that they could tell objectors about the new information when they informed them of their decision. Another felt it would be wrong to involve the objectors again without telling them that the committee members' minds were already made up.

TUCC supports closure

One of the members cut discussion short by moving that the committee recommend closure. It was approved, nine votes for and one against, with the proviso that BR be asked to grant the season ticket concession for one year with a review at the end of that year. It was also agreed that the main objectors be sent copies of BR's new evidence.

The minutes recorded a long list of reasons to support the decision, though it is unclear how many were actually raised during the meeting. They included:

*Steam working had to be abolished by 1962 when, because of the introduction of colour light signalling, steam working through Sevenoaks Tunnel would no longer be allowed for safety reasons.

*A diesel railbus would reduce the cost of working the branch by £8,752 a year but the committee rejected the idea that this was virtually the same as the £8,860 that BR would save by closing the line. With costs of £20,900 a year to run the line and revenue of only £3,500 a year, the railbus would still lose money and it had to be judged on that basis.

*Since there were alternative bus services, it would be wrong to ask BR to invest £32,822 or more in a line which would still lose money – which ignored the fact that the bus service would also require capital investment and would lose money.

*There was unlikely to be any substantial extra traffic on the branch.

*Concerns about longer journey times arose from not knowing about the additional bus journeys. The maximum increase in journey time would be 19 minutes in the morning and 20 minutes in the evening and few passengers would be affected by both. For many passengers, bus stops would be closer to their homes than the railway stations.

*The extra cost to passengers would be between £16 and £18 a year. This was described as 'not unreasonable when related to the loss that BR would incur in maintaining the branch line service'. It was hoped that BR would ease the extra cost by issuing road/rail season tickets to the existing season holders for at least a year. (A note in the red ink of Ellison's handwriting reveals that one of the BR representatives on the committee had announced the concession to help sway the discussion.)

*The closure would aggravate the car parking problem around Sevenoaks station but anyone who could not find space there could use the car park at Dunton Green or use the buses.

* * *

This 'judgment' says a lot about the role that the TUCC had taken upon itself. It clearly felt that its job was to improve BR's financial position; it did not believe that it should encourage the continued operation of a loss-making line and it refused to ask BR to invest in one. Without doubt, the presence of BR representatives on the committee had an impact on their thinking and deliberations. The consultative procedure was widely criticised as working too much in BR's favour but this was largely based on the proportion of closures that the TUCCs approved[45] and the fact that, until 1958, the BR

'H' class No 31263 at Westerham on 30 September 1961. This engine was purchased from BR as part of the branch preservation scheme. It is now on the Bluebell Railway in Sussex. ***Author's collection***

members even took part in votes. Here, though, we see evidence of a TUCC positively disregarding inconvenience to passengers on the grounds of the line's financial burden on BR and rejecting moves to reduce its losses.

Short-lived delight

It was reported to BR's Southern Area Board at its meeting on 3 November 1960 that the proposal to close the Westerham branch had been agreed, as had its proposals to close the Hawkhurst branch and the Kent & East Sussex line[46]. The following day, Ellison wrote to the Secretary-General of the BTC about the TUCC's hope that BR would issue road/rail season tickets for one year after closure.

'We had always been prepared to make this concession in order to assist our case,' Ellison reminded him, 'and it is recommended we should do so. It might be helpful at the next meeting of the Central Transport Consultation Committee next Tuesday if the Commission's representatives were able to say that the concession would be granted for a period of one year.'

* * *

No doubt there were celebrations within BR over the success of the Westerham closure proposal, but they were to be short-lived. Scarcely a month after the TUCC made its decision, the whole thing was back in the melting pot.

3

Closure in the Balance

When it met on 8 November the CTCC rejected the TUCC's recommendation. It felt that the TUCC had taken insufficient notice of the legal requirement that the BTC had to provide an adequate and properly co-ordinated system of passenger transport for the London Passenger Transport Area, within which the Westerham branch ran. It also thought it was wrong that objectors had not been given the opportunity to respond to the new information provided by BR. It noted particularly the TUCC chairman's view that the objectors should have been heard again before a decision was reached.

There are hints that the CTCC was critical of the way in which the TUCC had weighed up the evidence. For example, the TUCC had dismissed concerns that some trains carried more than a bus load of passengers by saying that some people would travel by car. But it also accepted that there were problems with car parking at Sevenoaks and, in a circular argument, said that anyone who could not find room to park there could use the buses. As an alternative – having extolled the benefits of the faster trains from Sevenoaks – anyone who could not find room to park there could drive to Dunton Green and catch a stopping train instead.

The CTCC seems to have recognised that there was bias in favour of BR in the TUCC's deliberations. It therefore decided to refer the matter back to the TUCC so that it could consider the points raised by the objectors.

One of the Western Region's AC Cars railbuses waits to leave the former Southern Railway terminus of Bodmin North on a shuttle service to Boscarne Junction. There it will connect with trains between Bodmin Road and Padstow. The station is still fully signalled and staffed; BR seemed to have little idea how to run branch lines economically. It is hardly surprising that Bodmin North closed in January 1967. ***Author's collection***

One of the Scottish Region's railbuses waiting to leave Crieff for Gleneagles on 1 July 1963. This railbus was one of two built by Bristol Commercial Vehicles with bodywork by Eastern Coach Works, a combination well known in the bus world. Although their use on the Gleneagles–Crieff–Comrie line resulted in passengers increasing from 277 a month to 715 despite poor main-line connections at Gleneagles, they were unable to save the line. *Author's collection*

'This is serious'

Southern Region managers were stunned by the news. Ellison noted on the file: 'This is serious'. An urgent meeting concluded that no firm steps should be taken towards modernising the line until the TUCC reached its final decision. This was accompanied by a warning that, if the eventual decision was to retain the line, steam might have to stop before the branch could be electrified, leaving it with no services. McKenna, the Southern's assistant general manager, told colleagues: 'If it ever comes to it, I do not think we should be pressed into resorting to special measures to bridge the gap.' and a similar message was sent to the TUCC.

Not all of the Southern Region's top ranks accepted this view, though. The assistant general manager (traffic), Mr P. A. White, asked the general manager to approve the preparation of a formal submission to modernise the line in case the decision should go against BR. His proposal (see Appendix 10) reiterated the three options considered previously but went into more detail about the way the line would be worked. He recommended electrification, using a two-car unit based at Orpington. Simpler signalling, based on one-engine-in-steam working, would be introduced, with a ground-frame giving access to the branch at Dunton Green.

* * *

One BR manager, probably Bolland, complained that the situation was the fault of the consultative machinery and did it no credit.

'Submission 31st March
Should have been heard by London Cttee in early June
Deferred at objectors' request (and with our agreement) until 21 July
Decision reached by London Cttee 4 Oct
Referred back by CTCC 8 Nov'

A handwritten note from McKenna to the general manager, dated 25 November 1960, was blunt.

'I see no reason to take positive steps to order any equipment or works before a final recommendation of the CTUCC. If we find that the decision goes against us and after withdrawing steam in June 1962 we cannot maintain the service, it is just too bad.'

BR intended to push the consultative committees into making a swift decision but it ignored the fact that many of the delays were the result of BR's inadequate and inaccurate information. BR had become used to closure proposals being rubber-stamped by the TUCCs and had become complacent. That was foolish because BR itself had long recognised that Westerham would be a difficult case. BR really had no-one else to blame but itself – it is difficult to come to any other conclusion.

Hopkins, the Southern's general manager, who had always been uncertain of the outcome, did not support the approach urged by some of his team. His response, dated 6 December, was reasoned:

'Little though we like it, we should be prepared for an adverse decision from the Area TUCC on the Westerham Branch and go through all the motions of putting through a scheme for the continued operation of the branch service when electric services in the Phase 2 area are fully introduced.

'We are agreed that Scheme B (two-car electric unit) is the scheme to go for and perhaps you will let me have a submission.

'In putting this forward – and it must go as far as BTC level – we shall include comments calculated to bring to a head at the highest level at the BTC, and possibly the Ministry, their attitude towards a planned branch line closing that is clearly justified on the grounds of economics but that may go against us on social grounds[47].'

'H' class 0-4-4T No 31324 at Westerham with the branch train on 13 August 1961. The station building shows a lack of painting and maintenance, as does the detached downpipe on the corner of the goods shed. ***Author's collection***

No more pipe-dreams

On 12 December 1960 Ernest Marples met the prime minister, Harold Macmillan, to discuss the White Paper on the Reorganisation of the Nationalised Transport Undertakings[48]. For Macmillan, the overriding point was that BR was making huge losses which had to be stopped. Marples said that the railways had been incompetent, technically and financially, and had failed to take a proper approach to their job. For him, the railways' main role lay in their ability to deal with commuter traffic in large population areas and he was sure that Beeching – whose appointment as the new BR chairman Macmillan had just approved – would concentrate on the realities of the situation and not on pipe-dreams[49]. The future was clear. Ending the railway's losses outweighed social considerations. The size of the railway network was to be drastically reduced.

Back to the TUCC

The agenda for the TUCC meeting on 8 December was already full so it was decided to set up a working party of TUCC members and BR representatives to take things forward. The working party would report to a special meeting of the TUCC on 8 February 1961 at which the Sevenoaks Rural District Council and the Passengers' Association were to be invited to attend, along with the local MP.

The TUCC secretariat went through the notes of the committee's October meeting and drew up a list of 31 questions that BR needed to answer. This, at last, was a sensible approach – BR's failure to give proper answers to the TUCC was probably one of the reasons why the CTCC had rejected its conclusions.

Bolland drafted answers to the 31 questions in time for the first meeting of the working party. He also added a few comments in answer to the objections from the Sevenoaks Rural District Council and the Passengers' Association. There would, he said, be no hardship to branch rail passengers, only inconvenience, pointing out that many towns larger than Westerham had no rail links. There would be no extra cost to passengers in the first year, thanks to the season ticket concession, and the maximum extra travelling time would only be 40 minutes a day.

Ellison hastily pointed out to the working party that there had not been time to 'tidy up' the answers to the questions and asked that they be restricted to its

Bernard Walsh, barrister and railway enthusiast who did much in his attempt at preventing closure, he is seen on the balcony of Chappel Station signal box at the East Anglian Railway Museum. *East Anglian Railway Museum*

members. Southern Region headquarters clearly did not see eye to eye with Bolland.

The 31 questions were whittled down to 24 at the working party's first meeting; the resulting questions and answers are shown in Appendix 11. Most of the eliminated questions concerned the timing and capacity of replacement buses. Bolland's hard line came over in his answers to these – he did not intend to provide buses on which the fares collected did not cover their operating costs, even if that meant that some train journeys had no equivalent bus.

The working party reports

The working party's one-sidedness cannot be ignored. It demonstrates the problems that existed in the consultative machinery at the start of the 1960s. The TUCC members were not railway experts and did not have the skills to challenge BR's specialists[50]. In addition, some TUCC members and staff had a close relationship with railway managers and regarded themselves as being part of the railway hierarchy with responsibility for the future of the industry. The working party itself seems to have been dominated by its BR members and its bias is shown by the difference of approach taken in the two parts of its report. In reviewing the BR evidence in Part I railway managers' explanations were accepted without question while in Part II the objectors' comments were simply rejected.

Part I of the report grouped the questions and answers by topic. Questions 1 and 2 were about the savings that would be made if the line closed. The report concluded that:

'The explanations given appear to be reasonable . . . We do not think there remain any reasonable grounds to doubt that annual savings of this order [£8,860] would be achieved by the closure and also that expenditure on capital renewals, amounting to £13,700, during the next five years, would be avoided.'

Had they been involved, the objectors would no doubt have pointed out that some of the savings could have been made without closing the line.

Questions 3 and 4 related to the continuing liabilities and costs that BR would incur if it closed the line. The questions threw little light on the subject but the working party used the answers to compare the costs and revenue if the line was closed against the costs and revenue of a railbus service.

Questions 5 and 6 looked at the costs to passengers if the line closed. The objectors had estimated that regular passengers would pay about £2,550 a year extra. The report recognised that passengers would have to pay more than they first expected because bus fares had risen faster than rail fares but this was countered by a comment that the additional fares would fall far short of meeting the cost of the extra buses.

Using BR's figure of an average 167 passengers a day on the line (113 from Westerham, 20 from Brasted and 34 from Chevening), the working party calculated that the maximum additional cost to passengers would be £3,813 a year if everyone used the buses. Increased crew wages meant that the cost of the additional buses had increased from £8,500 to £9,300 a year, though this would be partially offset by increased fare income, up from £2,000 to £2,300[51]. The report noted that passengers would be allowed to travel at branch season ticket rates for a year after closure. Because of this, BR had to pay the full cost

Diesel railbus No W79978 at the Tetbury branch terminus on a service to the main line junction at Kemble. These vehicles operated over the main line from Kemble to Swindon every day for refuelling, although they were not allowed to carry passengers on those trips. ***Author's collection***

of the additional buses in the first year after closure. The subsidy would fall to £7,000 in the second year once branch passengers started to pay bus fares – an increase from the £6,500 given in the original closure proposal.

The working party wondered whether passengers might be willing to pay more in fares but the report concluded that it would be impossible to ask users of the branch to pay £104 a year each to cover the full costs of running the line with a railbus. What it did not do, however, was ask to whether passengers might be willing to pay enough extra so that the cost of keeping the line open would be no more than that of closing it. Like the government, it was fixated with the idea that there should be no investment in lines that did not cover all their costs, even if it cost BR more to close them than to keep them open.

Alternative traction

The TUCC had taken the view that, since steam had to end anyway, it was pointless to compare the costs of modernised working to the costs of steam[52]. It insisted that any modernised operation had to be judged by whether it would make the line profitable. For this reason, the TUCC refused to compare the costs of railbus operation against those of a replacement bus service.

The TUCC had thought that the costs of a railbus service were high, particularly as far as signalling, staff and interest costs were concerned; with touching naivety, the working party wanted to know whether BR's answers to its questions supported that view, noting that BR had reduced the cost of new signalling from £4,690 to £4,145 since part of the money had to be spent at Dunton Green even if the line closed. Inevitably, the working party accepted the revised figures without question.

The only idea for reducing the cost that BR was prepared to consider was that of converting Westerham station into an unstaffed halt. However, the working party doubted whether the 'relatively small saving' of £448 a year would justify the practical disadvantages of not having a member of the railway staff on duty at Westerham. It did not ask why the saving was so small, nor did it explain what the 'practical disadvantages' were.

Despite the figures showing that it would make a small

profit, the working party said there was nothing to be achieved by reinstating the day-long train service. Little off-peak traffic would be stimulated by a railbus, over and above that which was already fed to the railway at Sevenoaks by the existing bus service. The working party gave no justification for this assumption and there is a hint that it was worried that a better rail service might take passengers away from the unprofitable buses.

Replacement buses

The TUCC had noted that three trains carried more passengers than a single bus could handle. In its view, there would be no problem because some passengers would travel by car and others would change their travelling times to take advantage of the faster trains serving Sevenoaks station. However, the working party decided to check the three cases, just in case.

It dismissed one of them straightaway – a train was heavily loaded one evening during the census because of late running on the main line and therefore gave an untypical result. It did not ask, though, whether late-running occurred on a regular basis, as some objectors had alleged. It accepted that one of the morning buses could be held back by a few minutes to relieve the load on later journeys and it noted that LT was prepared to lay on additional bus journeys if necessary at little or no extra cost without the need for a third new vehicle. The report concluded that the risk of the alternative bus service proving inadequate was low and was safeguarded by the new assurances.

Objections dismissed

Part II of the report considered the objections made to the closure, beginning in a way that verged on the surreal. In its submission the Sevenoaks Rural District Council had quoted BR's reason for wanting to close the line – and it had nothing to do with it losing money. As we saw in Chapter 2, BR had said that:

'. . . If the branch were retained modernisation capital would be needed. There is a limit to the amount of money which is available and any investment as is made must be directed to projects which will show a reasonable return on the capital invested. None of the alternatives for keeping the branch open meets this requirement.'

In other words, the line had to close because there were no funds for investment in its modernisation. In contrast, the council said that investment in the branch was justified and that the TUCC should not judge it by the losses it was currently making. However, the working party turned this inside-out, implying that the council supported the TUCC's approach that the line should, indeed, be judged by its losses:

'. . . the case for the retention of the branch line must finally be judged on the basis of the full costs of its operation with a diesel railbus, and not on the basis of the savings that can be claimed by the Commission under the [TUCC] formula.'

Shortly before closure – the closure poster is displayed on one of the boards attached to the railings – 'H' class No 31308 pulls into Brasted station. *Author's collection*

The working party said that, because the line needed investment, the TUCC was right to ignore its own rules that the case should be judged only on the basis of the savings that BR would make by closing it.

Buses, traffic and parking

The report rejected the objectors' claims of increased journey times, saying that they took no account of the extra buses, which was hardly surprising given that BR had deliberately kept the times of the extra buses secret. The report decided that the increase in journey times would be much less than the objectors had feared. However, it ignored the practical problems that would arise.

To take one example, the popular 7.38am train from Westerham gave an arrival at Charing Cross at 8.43, in reasonable time for a 9am start. The replacement bus left Westerham eight minutes earlier at 7.30am and, because it gave an arrival in London eight minutes earlier, the report claimed that there was no increase in journey time. In practical terms, though, passengers would have to leave home earlier to get into work for the same 9am start. If the TUCC truly represented passengers, it should have picked up on such points and not sought answers that supported the case for closure.

There was dispute over the impact of the closure on traffic congestion. The objectors had claimed that the A25 and the A21 were already overcrowded and the extra traffic would make the situation worse. The working party rejected this, as BR had done before, saying that the figures were based on a 1954 traffic count which had been updated by applying average traffic increases over the intervening years. The working party also decided that the heaviest traffic on the area's roads was at summer weekends, not on weekdays.

The working party dismissed concerns about car parking at Sevenoaks station, saying that the replacement buses could carry all the displaced rail passengers. If they chose to drive instead of catching the bus then car parking was a problem for them to solve. This, of course, conflicted with its acceptance that bus overcrowding could only be avoided if some passengers switched to cars.

No opportunity to challenge evidence

The working party rejected objectors' claims that they had been given no opportunity to challenge BR's additional evidence. At the end of the July TUCC hearing, the report noted, the chairman asked if the objectors had had a fair, reasonable and proper hearing. He had also mentioned that the TUCC would consider further evidence from BR before making its recommendation but the objectors had not asked for this to be sent to them. Nor had the objectors asked to comment further when the TUCC had written to them on 25 July, telling them that the case had been deferred again because more information was required from BR.

'H' class 0-4-4T No 31518 propels its pull-push train away from Brasted Halt on its way to Dunton Green on 22 October 1961, the last Sunday on which the branch service ran. This idyllic rural scene is now a distant memory. Today the photographer would be on the clockwise carriageway of the M25. *Author's collection*

That sounds like an excuse. How were the objectors supposed to decide whether or not the new information was worth commenting on without seeing it? They clearly assumed that it would be no more than points of clarification. As we know now, the new information was nearly as extensive as the original closure proposal and was an almost total re-justification of closure. In particular, it included detailed costs for modernising the branch which the objectors would have had good reason to challenge. The TUCC was wrong, once it realised how extensive this new information was, not to have passed it on to the objectors.

The Ogilvie electrification proposal

While the working party was preparing its report, an article appeared in the *Sevenoaks Chronicle*, based on the ideas of Mr J. R. Ogilvie, a local transport enthusiast. This cannot have come at a more awkward time for BR, which was already working on plans to electrify the line in case closure was rejected. The article showed that there was another way of modernising the line – other than the railbus option – and raised questions as to why BR hadn't suggested it. BR could hardly dismiss the idea out of hand (it might have to roll out its own electrification plan in a matter of weeks) but, on the other hand, if it supported the idea, it would have encouraged objectors to see it as a way of keeping the line open.

Ogilvie said that the work could be done without major alterations to stations, signals and track. He proposed that the first two coaches of 10-car trains from London to Sevenoaks should be detached at Orpington and run non-stop to Dunton Green before serving all stations to Westerham. The rest of the train would then provide a stopping service to Sevenoaks, both trains arriving at their destinations at about the same time. The two trains would set off on the return journey at the same time, the branch train running non-stop from Dunton Green to Orpington, where it would join the stopping service from Sevenoaks. BR reminded the TUCC that it had already supplied details of the costs that electrification would involve and the service proposed by Ogilvie would be even more expensive because of the need to change the track layout at Dunton Green to give direct access to the branch in the down direction. There would also be duplication of services between Orpington and Dunton Green.

The railbus question

In January 1961 BR explained why it did not favour the use of railbuses on the Westerham line. In the absence of any experience of such vehicles of its own[53], the Southern Region drew on a review of railbus operations by the Scottish Region of BR (see Appendix 12.) In a conclusion that seemed to damn the idea with faint praise, the Southern said that railbuses would be a practicable alternative to steam on the Westerham line and would, in the short term, provide the cheapest form of modernisation but they had distinct disadvantages, which were listed as:

*Reliance cannot be placed upon a diesel railbus operating track circuits, and it would be necessary to make special arrangements every time such a vehicle had to proceed to Tonbridge for fuelling or St Leonards for maintenance.
*The railbuses have a limited seating capacity varying from 46 to 56, which would be inadequate for the peaks on the Westerham line.
*The railbus is not suitable for parcels, freight smalls, etc, and it would be necessary to provide special road cartage, thus adding to the costs of operation.
*There is no scope for diesel railbus operation elsewhere in the South Eastern Division; its use on the Westerham branch would mean an isolated pocket of this form of traction and it would be necessary to maintain a spare vehicle – especially for the branch alone – which could have no useful employment elsewhere.
*Quite apart from the foregoing it must be stressed in conclusion that the operation of diesel rail buses would involve the Commission in an annual deficit of over £17,000.

The Southern's objections to the idea were hardly surprising but the long list of negatives hardly supported its claim that railbuses were a 'practicable alternative to steam'. Admittedly, the vehicles had problems on track-circuited lines because of their light weight and two-axle design but the problem was not beyond solution. The Western Region ran railbuses from Kemble to Swindon for daily refuelling and the problem was also to occur with track maintenance machines and, more seriously, with second-generation multiple-units[54], which forced the development of a solution.

According to BR's own figures, only one morning train on the branch loaded beyond the capacity of a railbus. This was the 7.38am from Westerham and, of its average 54 passengers, eight boarded at Chevening. Compared to squeezing onto a crowded bus, standing on a railbus for less than two minutes was probably not something they would have regarded as hardship.

The excuse that a railbus could not carry parcels was a poor one since BR planned to withdraw all parcels facilities from the line but, in any case, there would have been room on the vehicle for parcels on off-peak journeys.

The fact that a spare railbus would have had no alternative employment was immaterial. A spare vehicle has to be available for use when required, not being used elsewhere.

The Scottish report mentioned teething problems with the vehicles (not helped, perhaps, by the region being allocated ten vehicles of four different makes). To be fair, railbus reliability was a problem but many early diesel locomotives proved equally unreliable.

'H' class No 31533 propels its train towards Dunton Green on 15 April 1961. Concrete troughing, intended as part of the abortive scheme to resignal the line, can be seen by the trackside. *Author's collection*

The Southern's insistence that railbuses would make no difference to the line's income flew in the face of evidence that railbuses did increase traffic. When the new services were properly promoted, traffic increases of over 100 per cent were experienced. Admittedly, doubling the load on the 7.38am from Westerham may have caused problems but any other increase would have been both likely and welcome.

The negative tone of the Southern's review was clearly intended to discourage the TUCC from seeing railbuses as a means of keeping the Westerham open but someone must have thought that the draft version was too negative because a couple of paragraphs were deleted before it was sent to the TUCC. One, in particular, betrayed a lack of enthusiasm for rail as a form of local transport on the part of the original author.

'A rail bus would be the cheapest form of rail transport but the capital cost of such a vehicle is over twice that of a double deck bus having a comparable seating capacity. Furthermore, the substitution of road vehicles for the present branch service would provide a service linking more closely the present town and villages on the branch with Sevenoaks, the natural focal point of the area and from which point a better train service is available.'

As Ellison noted, when he marked this comment for deletion: 'This is a knock (or could be taken as such) at all railways.'

Whether railbuses would have provided a realistic solution for the line is another matter – those used elsewhere were withdrawn by 1968, partly because of problems with their use but mainly because the lines on which they were used were axed under Beeching[55].

Maintenance costs and other questions

In a belated answer to the outstanding Q10 of the questionnaire, BR explained that the £3,005 annual cost of maintaining the line was an estimate based on 'a number of years' experience of day-to-day repairs to roads, bridges, and buildings [on the Westerham branch] plus [essential] expenditure on making good slips in the formation and preventative stabilisation works'. (The words in brackets were added in pencil to the chief civil engineer's original memo.)

This figure was dubious in the extreme. No breakdown was provided but the £3,005 did not include staff wages, nor did it include day-to-day maintenance of the permanent way and fencing, the £532 a year cost of which was shown separately. It was later admitted that the civil engineer's department kept no records of its spending but simply estimated maintenance costs as a percentage of the replacement cost of an asset, such as a bridge or building, whether or not the money was actually spent. By BR's own admission, little was spent on the line between 1952 and 1958, just enough to keep it running. Photographs show the effect on the line's buildings, despite which, BR claimed to have spent nearly six times as much on them as on maintaining the track. In effect, the Westerham line was subsidising maintenance elsewhere.

Admittedly, some of the money was to do with earth slips. However, as the chief civil engineer warned in 1956, repairs to the slips became more costly the longer the work was postponed. It was unreasonable to use the resulting higher costs as the basis for on-going spending. In any case, a lump sum had already been included in the line's future costs for repairs to the remaining slips. This appears to be a case of double-counting by including them as both annual costs and as future capital expenditure.

A separate figure of £2,155 was given as the annual provision for the renewals of all assets, including permanent way, roads, fences, bridges and buildings, based on their future replacement cost. The money charged each year was transferred to a Sinking Fund from which renewals were to be funded. In theory, that meant that future like-for-like renewals had already been paid for from past years' renewals provisions.

The TUCC wanted to know the latest date the branch could remain open if steam traction were to continue. BR had already said that steam working could not continue once colour light signalling was installed in Sevenoaks tunnel, which was scheduled for the first part of 1962. Now BR made it clear that, to save money, it wanted to close the line at the earliest possible moment.

The second TUCC hearing

On 8 February 1961 the London area TUCC met to consider the working party's report. The chairman at the previous year's hearings, Mr Burleigh, was in hospital and unable to chair the meeting. His place was taken by Mr G. Allison-Beer. Bolland was also absent because of illness.

The meeting opened with a discussion about the working party report and differences emerged straight away. Mrs Bolton praised 'an excellent report' but one of those involved, Mr H.T. Parkin[56], made it clear that he only

On 22 October 1961 'H' Class 0-4-4T No 31518 propels its train past the Westerham home signal on its way to Dunton Green. Despite being mounted on a relatively modern rail-built post, the signal arm is a vintage lower quadrant version. Six days after this picture was taken, the residents in the houses on the left would be waving goodbye to their trains. ***Author's collection***

A quiet interlude at Brasted. During the decade after this photograph was taken unstaffed stations would become commonplace and their buildings would be demolished in short order but, amazingly, Brasted's station building was to survive until construction of the M25 began in 1977-78, more than 20 years after its staff left for the last time. ***Author's collection***

approved the report as a factual record of the information that had been obtained. The committee should not draw any conclusions from the report about the views of individual members of the working party on the case for closing the line. To have the report undermined in such a way must have been devastating and it seems to have cut the discussion short.

The users' deputations arrived at 11am, including those from the local councils and the Passengers' Association. Representatives of BR's Southern Region and London Transport also joined the meeting. This part of the meeting continued until 5.15pm, (the record of the discussion runs to over 30 close-typed pages – see Appendix 13), after which the Committee came to its decision.

After welcoming the deputations, the chairman said that he had decided not to ask the railway representatives to speak first; the committee wanted to hear what the deputations had to say about the new evidence and their reactions to the working party report. The objectors had agreed between themselves that the council representatives would deal with matters of planning, development, and traffic while the financial and railway aspects were left to the Passengers' Association, which had hired a barrister to present its case.

For the Kent County Council, deputy clerk Mr M.A. Bains, told the committee that shortage of building land was forcing many people to live outside London and commute in. The Ministry of Housing had asked councils to review the whole question of areas for development and more houses were certain to be built in the Westerham area, despite the Green Belt.

The council regarded a daily increase in travelling time of 39 minutes as definite hardship. Bains reiterated that the A25 was congested and even a marginal increase in traffic would be intolerable. Although the council wanted to see the railway service continued indefinitely, if it had to be closed, it should be delayed until the new South Orbital Road was open.

He said that a railbus service would save £8,752 a year compared with the steam service, whereas closing the line would save £8,860 a year, only £108 more. This drew an intervention from the BR member of the committee. Mr J. Hancock, who pointed out that these figures did not take account of the renewals that would be needed over the next five years. Mr G. J. Dickens, from LT, stressed that the working party had looked at the railbus idea in detail; it would need capital investment of £32,000 and would still lose up to £17,000 a year.

Bains' response was that the council wanted the branch to be dieselised and that any loss would be justified by the social need for the line. He reminded the committee that the council had never adopted a dog-in-the-manger attitude about railway closures. When BR's case was fair they had not opposed closures, but the Westerham branch was exceptional.

Councillor I. M. Forsyth criticised the working party report for its rejection of claims that the A25 was congested. He told the TUCC about his experiences of congestion on the road and described as 'feeble' the Ministry of Transport's arguments that closure would only result in a little more traffic. He also said that the replacement buses would do little for Chevening passengers, who would now be faced with a walk of a mile or two each way from their homes to the bus stop.

Evidence for the passengers

The Passengers' Association was represented by a barrister, Mr B. D. J. Walsh, but he was a barrister with a difference. Bernard Walsh was a railway enthusiast and he knew his stuff[57]. He was to prove a formidable opponent.

Walsh adopted a subtle approach, weakening BR's case step by step. First, though, he had to deal with the basic weakness of the objectors' case, which was the undeniable truth that the line lost money. He told the TUCC that BR's evidence pointed to a difference in policy between commuter and branch lines, in that commuter lines had a tendency not to make money but they met a social need. The Westerham line should be treated as a commuter line and not receive worse treatment than any other commuter service merely because it also happened to be a branch line. Any loss on the service should be accepted more readily than in the case of a country branch.

Having established that point, he then began to dismantle BR's case, the gist of which was that BR would save £8,860 a year by closing the line. Although the Association agreed with that in principle, since the additional buses would cost £11,700, the cost of two diesel railbuses would be only £20,300 more. The chairman helpfully added that, if

Dunton Green seen from a passing Hastings line diesel train. An 'H' class 0-4-4T and pull-push unit can be seen in the Westerham branch platform. Work connected with the resignalling which was part of the Kent Coast electrification scheme is underway at the end of the platform. Posts for both Up Main and Up Branch starting signals have been erected and heads were subsequently added to both signals. There is no doubt that the branch was included in the scheme. The date is some time in the summer of 1961. *Author's collection*

'H' class 0-4-4T No 31543 leaves Dunton Green with a Westerham train, seen from a passing train on the main line. Noticeable in the scene are piles of concrete cable troughing for the resignalling scheme. The timber fence in the background divides the station approach from the goods yard while the roofed stairs down to the subway leading under the branch tracks can be seen on the right. *Author's collection*

the line closed, BR would also have to spend £1,006 on an extra road goods vehicle.

Having begun to undermine BR's financial arguments, Walsh then looked at BR's claimed savings if the line closed. He rejected the idea that BR would save £2,922 a year on interest by closing the line. This interest was based on a notional valuation of assets, some of which were very old. BR would not save any of this unless they could sell the whole of the line's assets for their original value of £70,000. It could not avoid the interest merely by abandoning the line, any more than someone could avoid paying the interest on their mortgage by burning their house down.

Walsh said that the cost to passengers of using the replacement buses, after allowing for 1961 fare increases, would be £3,840 a year and he revealed that the members of the Association had agreed to pay that amount in higher rail fares if the line were kept open. Mr Parkin asked why, if passengers were willing to pay more for their train service, they should not pay for the replacement buses. Walsh replied that the railway gave them a service that they wanted, which they needed, and for which they were prepared to pay extra whereas they would be charged more for a worse service on the alternative buses. He also pointed out that the buses were going to lose £500 a year more than previously expected which was not allowed for in BR's claimed savings of £8,860.

Social need

Walsh warmed to his theme. The Westerham line was a classic example of a line which served a social need. It would not be right to ask the passengers to meet the full costs of running the line when BR was prepared to lose £8,000 a year on replacement buses. It should accept a similar loss on the train service.

He condemned the working party's conclusion that the TUCC should take into account the total losses of a modernised service. BR had agreed with the TUCC that only actual savings should be taken into account in closure cases. To abrogate that agreement would revive the interminable wrangles that had occurred in earlier cases. While certain figures might be useful for BR's internal purposes, they were unreal when assessing the closure of a line.

An important principle was involved, Walsh insisted. He accepted that there were difficulties because an alternative form of traction was involved – nobody believed that steam-working should continue – but that did not justify abandoning the agreed formula. Parkin interrupted to agree that the formula was binding upon the TUCC and he did not accept that they had abandoned it. The TUCC had added something to the formula because they had to allow for the capital cost of introducing a new sort of service. In considering the annual costs, they had to reconcile the formula with the railbus alternative, which raised the practical difficulties of comparing two dissimilar things.

Walsh agreed that the TUCC's task was not easy but they could not jettison the principle. They had to work out the difference between the costs of the two operations, based on the savings from closing the line but excluding savings that were purely notional. The working party suggested that a railbus service would lose up to £17,000 a year but that loss included £6,000 of notional interest charges, many of them for buildings and structures that had been in use for years[58]. The capital involved had been paid back or paid out and interest on it should no longer be charged.

Saving money

Walsh was in full flow as he turned to the other costs of working the line. The working party had mentioned the possibility of saving £448 a year by converting Westerham station to an unstaffed halt. There must have been a smile on his face as he turned BR's argument for not removing the Westerham staff on its head. The practical disadvantages to passengers of not having station staff at Westerham, he said, were as nothing compared with the practical disadvantages of not having a station.

Walsh criticised the working party's dismissal of the off-peak service, saying that the additional cost of operating an off-peak service with a diesel railbus was £1,838 a year. The branch receipts from the off-peak service before its withdrawal in 1955 were £1,850 a year – at 1961 fares they would be £2,322, giving a profit of £484 even if there were no increase in traffic. Whether or not there would be an increase in off-peak traffic did not depend upon the number of new people coming to live in the area in the way that commuter traffic did and on practically every line there had been an increase in traffic following dieselisation.

Comparing the costs

Walsh then produced his master-stroke. During the lunch break, he and the Passenger Association's financial adviser had compared the costs that would still exist if the line closed and the cost of keeping the line open with a railbus. When they totalled the 'unsaveable costs' that would continue even if the line closed –the notional interest on the assets of the line and the loss on running the replacement buses – the line would still cost BR £14,785 a year after closure. A diesel railbus service would lose £17,400, ignoring any increased income. The extra loss of £2,615 had to be balanced against the social need for the line. Even so, it could be reduced by another £448 by converting Westerham to an unstaffed halt and a further £484 by restoring the off-peak service. The passengers were ready to pay higher fares for the rail service, and that would make up the difference.

The chairman then asked for the Association's views about electrifying the branch. Walsh said that they were not wedded to any form of traction – they only wanted the branch to continue and to be operated at the lowest cost. BR had said that railbuses offered the cheapest form of modernisation. However, one of the disadvantages of the railbus was that it could not be relied upon to operate track circuits when it had to go to Tonbridge for fuelling or St Leonards for maintenance. On the Eastern Region empty railbuses regularly ran on the main line, Walsh told the committee. BR had got over the problems by issuing instructions to signalmen as to how they should signal the railbuses. These were not instructions given for individual journeys but were permanent instructions.

The chairman pointed out that the Southern Region was going to have automatic colour light signalling with track circuits and it was suggested that a railbus would not correctly operate these signals. Walsh replied that the Eastern Region had automatic signalling on part of the line between Stratford and Colchester yet empty railbuses still operated over the line. For BR, Hancock interrupted to say that he could not comment on the Eastern Region's practices there and then, but he could not accept that statement[59]. He asked if Walsh had any evidence that railbuses were allowed to run into Stratford under their own power. Walsh replied that he did indeed and he explained the regulations involved.

The chairman still thought that there might be problems as there was to be a signal box at Orpington and another at Sevenoaks. He did not see how the railbus was going to be controlled coming off the Westerham line if the track circuit operation was not 100 per cent effective as the signal box at Dunton Green would only operate at special times. Walsh explained that the box at Dunton Green would only be required when it was necessary to take the railbus to Tonbridge, or up the main line for maintenance. He would have thought it could easily be arranged for the railbus to move when traffic was light and Dunton Green signal box was open.

Parkin said that the TUCC had previously listened to a great deal of discussion about the signalling at Dunton

Green and he hoped the point could now be disposed of. Everybody agreed that a railbus had to be operated in different conditions from a heavy train and special arrangements would be needed. Walsh thought that by 'special arrangements' BR was implying special mechanical or electrical alterations. What he had described on the Eastern Region could not be called 'special arrangements' – they were permanent regulations, not just for special occasions.

BR tries to fight back

Rupert Shervington, traffic superintendent of the Southern Region's South Eastern Division, covered for the absent Bolland. Perhaps he had too little time to prepare for his appearance; his performance was poor and he stuck unyieldingly to BR's original justification for closure. That was a mistake, given the evidence that had been raised in the meantime, but perhaps he was simply following instructions. Everyone agreed that steam could not continue and therefore its costs and losses were irrelevant, but Shervington stuck to the line that withdrawing the steam service would save £20,000 a year immediately and, even with the extra £7,500 cost of providing replacement buses and a road cartage service, there would be a net saving, short term, of £9,000 a year. He ignored the savings that could have been made earlier if BR really had been concerned about reducing losses. We are left with the inevitable conclusion that BR allowed unnecessary costs to continue to justify closing the line and that the real reason for closure was to get rid of a line that sat awkwardly in the Southern's electrified world.

Shervington reiterated that BR was willing to soften the blow of closure by allowing the use of rail season tickets on the bus service for one year – even if BR expected passengers to desert them before long.

He said that BR had examined the idea of introducing modern traction and had considered all other possible economies but, he said, even if alternative traction was introduced, signalling was abolished, and all station staff withdrawn, the branch would still run at a loss. However, he failed to explain why it was acceptable to subsidise loss-making buses but not loss-making trains.

Silly claim

He then went on to suggest that the line was unprofitable because of the high cost of maintaining the permanent way. The cost, he said, was no more than the cost of maintaining a road but no highway authority would dream of providing a road for the benefit of 170 passengers in five or six buses a day. That, of course, was a silly thing to say – there were country lanes all over Kent that carried fewer than 170 people a day and no-one thought of closing them because they needed resurfacing.

Dunton Green in the summer of 1961 with the post for a colour light signal in place at the London end of the Westerham branch platform. The signal had already been partly dismantled; subsequent photographs show that it had been removed by the time the line closed. The main line up starter signal is already in place but not yet in use. *Mike Morant Collection*

Mr Forsyth had referred to the possibility of the closure being deferred. Shervington reminded the committee that the proposal had been before them since March 1960, and BR would be sorry if a decision was postponed any longer, as the line was losing between £750 and £1,000 a month, which it could ill afford. Once again, this was a hollow protest given the lack of any previous efforts by BR to reduce costs on the line.

The chairman asked what BR would have to do as far as signalling and the like was concerned if closure was postponed. Sidestepping the question, Shervington replied that there would be considerable costs in keeping the branch open and they would rise with each month of postponement. It had been suggested that the reason for wishing to close the branch was because of main line electrification but that was not the case, he said. The fact that a pocket of steam operation would be left in the middle of an electrified area was serious but it was incidental. The real reason for wishing to close the line was because BR could not afford the loss but he did not explain how this matched up with BR's original description of the 'small savings' to be had from the closure.

Shervington then turned to the points made by Walsh who, he said, had suggested that this line should be treated differently from other branches. BR's only consideration was that the line was unprofitable, whatever the nature of its traffic, and therefore it wished to withdraw the service[60].

Westerham station could be turned into an unstaffed halt but, from an operational point of view, it was unacceptable to have such an isolated unstaffed station and, even if the staff were withdrawn from Westerham, the service would still not be profitable.

Third driver

Shervington then explained why a third driver would be needed for the service. All of BR's costings took account of this, with the exception of the steam service – under steam, the duty could be married in with other work – but for an isolated operation a relief man would have to be provided[61]. A guard would also be needed as a second man in case of accident or breakdown.

Turning to the off-peak service, Shervington said that it had been withdrawn because passengers did not use it. It would bring in only £1,800 to £2,000 a year so its re-introduction would make no difference to the financial position. This drew another intervention from Parkin, who said that even at 1955 fares it would reduce the loss by £12 a year. Shervington was forced to agree.

Shervington then turned to the signalling at Dunton Green. If the branch closed, all branch signals could be withdrawn but if the line remained open, signals would be needed to protect the junction. The fact that railbuses did not operate track circuits reliably would require block working, a form of signalling that would end when new signalling was introduced between Hither Green and Dover in 1962. To reintroduce block working would reduce the capacity of the line considerably. The chairman interrupted to say that there was no question of reducing the capacity of the line for 24 hours a day, only when the railbus came off the branch for servicing. There was already block working at Dunton Green for the sidings.

Closure is nigh – and all signs of the branch being included in the resignalling scheme have been hastily removed.
Author's collection

Shervington agreed, but said that the box at Dunton Green would only be opened if a freight train was scheduled to call. The railbus would need the box to be opened twice a week, which would be difficult and expensive. In addition, block working required only one train to be in section between Sevenoaks and Tonbridge, instead of the four or five allowed by colour light signalling. The movement of the railbus would reduce the headway on the main line to that extent, though he accepted that this would only occur twice a week[62].

With Shervington's evidence complete, Walsh said that confusion remained. Why, he asked, when BR was prepared to bear a loss of £8,000 a year on the replacement buses, was it not prepared to accept a similar loss on the branch? Why did BR insist that the passengers must pay the whole of the loss on the railway? When Shervington replied that the offer made by the Passengers' Association was not nearly enough to offset the line's losses, Walsh repeated his question but Shervington insisted that his assumption was wrong. BR was not prepared to accept a loss of £8,000 a year on the bus service; that was why they were proposing to close the branch line. Costs of £7,500 to £8,000 would be incurred in providing the alternative services but he did not agree there would be a loss of that order. It was not a choice of losing £8,000 on the road, or losing something less on the railway.

No long term bus subsidy

Shervington was clearly floundering. It fell to Mr C. H. Jones, the Southern Region's assistant chief accountant, to explain why BR did not expect the replacement buses to make an on-going loss. He conceded that, in the short term, BR would have to subsidise the alternative buses to the extent of £7,000 a year but the subsidy was not expected to continue for ever. The additional buses would, he said, 'be rationalised in the normal bus services, which would be so organised that they would become paying services' and BR would not have to keep paying the subsidy.

His implication was that the extra buses would be withdrawn, leaving only the basic service once more. The fares from the former railway passengers who did not drive would help make the remaining buses profitable. It was almost as if there was an agreement between BR and LT to close the railway to turn two loss-making services into one profitable bus service.

Crewing the trains

Walsh accepted that a railbus could not be manned by a driver alone. He argued that the steam service was being worked with a junior porter as a quasi-guard. Why, therefore, on a single line of this kind, with a diesel railbus, would it be necessary to have a person of superior qualification, bearing in mind that the train did not have to be protected?

'H' class 0-4-4T No 31324 waits to leave Dunton Green with the branch train on 18 August 1961. To the left of the locomotive can been seen concrete 'saddles' to support new signalling equipment and on the far side is concrete troughing for signal cables. The number 238 on the headcode disc indicates the Tonbridge shed duty that the locomotive was working. These varied from year to year but with main line electrification the number of steam locomotive duties reduced; in the mid-1950s the number would have been in the 300s. ***Author's collection***

Shervington replied that junior porters were provided on the steam trains to sell and collect tickets but they did not carry out any of the functions of a guard. Protecting a train on a single line was as important as on a double line. With a pull-push steam train there were two crews – the driver in the front with the fireman and another man at the rear. They provided protection between them. (Shervington seemed to be unaware that Westerham pull-push trains did not have a guard.) Walsh said that, on a single line where a train staff was in use, BR rules did not require the protection of the train in the rear. Shervington disputed this, saying that on a single line both ends were

CLOSURE OF WESTERHAM BRANCH RAILWAY LINE

On and from MONDAY, 30th OCTOBER, 1961 all passenger and freight train services will be withdrawn from the branch line between DUNTON GREEN and WESTERHAM. CHEVENING HALT, BRASTED HALT and WESTERHAM station WILL BE CLOSED.

British Railways will continue to provide collection and delivery services for parcels and freight sundries traffic throughout the area and facilities for truck load traffic exist at other stations in the vicinity.

Further information may be obtained from the Station Masters at SEVENOAKS (Telephone 52231), or DUNTON GREEN (Telephone 325), or from the Line Traffic Manager, Southern Region, British Railways, South Eastern Division, 61 Queen Street, London, E.C.4 (Telephone WATerloo 5151, Ext. 227).

Alternative bus and coach facilities in the area are provided by the London Transport Executive and enquiries regarding these services should be addressed to London Transport Executive, 55 Broadway, London, S.W.1 (Telephone ABBey 1234) or any local office.

Condemned! The poster that announced the closure of the Westerham branch.

the rear and it was necessary to carry out protection. Once again, Walsh was right – BR Rule 178(a) applied – and Shervington wrong.

One of the TUCC members, Mr H. L. Carey, asked whether the railbus could be used anywhere else in the country and what action BR would take if a decision to close the line was deferred until the South Orbital Road was opened. Shervington confirmed that the railbus could be used elsewhere but he was unable to answer the second question.

Jones then said that the cost of operating the branch with a railbus would be £108 a year more than the cost of closing the line but, as the working party had pointed out, this compared the savings from closure with the costs of operating the line but the figures were not comparable.

The additional cost to the passenger of using the buses would be £26 a year but this compared to the railway's loss of £104 per passenger. He accepted, as Walsh had suggested, that BR made losses on commuter lines, but they were nothing like those incurred on the Westerham branch. This was not a case where there could be any justification for keeping the branch because it was a commuter line.

Capital and interest

Shervington then announced that the extra bus services would be operated by two vehicles that would be kept on beyond their normal life. This astounding revelation suggested that either LT intended to use vehicles that were no longer fit for service or that it was in the habit of scrapping vehicles that still had useful life in them. Shervington then claimed that LT was in a different position from BR in that its buses were 'part of their ordinary working stock'. If the passengers did not use the buses, BR would ask the TUCC to relieve it of the obligation to subsidise the service and the vehicles would be absorbed into LT's other services with no capital outlay or continuing loss.

Shervington said that, even in the short term, BR would have to find £7,300 to renew a section of the permanent way and £6,000 to stabilise the track if the line were kept open. This £13,000 should rank equally with the £32,000 capital outlay to allow railbus operation. The chairman said that the work done for the £13,000 would last for 10 or 15 years and asked what the renewals would cost if spread over 20 or 25 years. Jones interrupted to say that the annual cost of renewals had already been given as £2,155. The chairman asked if £21,000 had been spent on renewals in the past 10 years[63], to which Jones replied that he could not say what had been spent in the last 10 years, because the incidence of these costs did not fall into particular years. It might be that the whole line would be renewed at the same time.

Parkin asked when the 55 chains due for renewal in 1962 would be renewed again. He also wondered whether the earth slips had already occurred or whether they were just anticipated. Jones explained that the 55 chains of track would probably be renewed again in 30 years. The material to deal with the slips was on the lineside, or was in stock for doing the work. The importance of both items was that they were immediate commitments.

Jones said that the Association had calculated that passengers would have to pay £3,840 extra in fares but BR did not expect all of them to use the buses. If they did, BR would not lose the £3,500 contributory revenue that had been allowed for in the original closure proposal because the fares from Sevenoaks were the same as from Westerham[64]. BR hoped to keep most of the contributory revenue if passengers used the buses – only if nobody used the buses to Sevenoaks would it be right to count the whole £3,500 as a loss.

Jones then turned to the comments that had been made about the treatment of interest on capital. Under

It could have been almost a normal day on the Westerham branch but this was the 12.50am train from Dunton Green on the last day of all, 28 October 1961. ***Ian Nolan***

the TUCC 'Heads of Information' formula, BR had agreed not to show renewals or interest, the reason being that, if they closed a line, they wrote it off. If a line continued in operation, it had to be renewed. BR's provisions were based on a sinking fund, which did not include any contribution to renewal, therefore it was real capital[65]. The 'Heads of Information' formula was not an appropriate basis for comparing the cost of one type of service with another, he claimed.

Jones disputed the Association figures because they included interest of £2,922 even if the line closed. That interest would not be incurred, he said, because the capital would have been written off but he did not answer Walsh's point that capital could not be written off simply because the line closed. It seems that, in the strange world of railway accountancy, that is exactly what BR did.

BR did not accept the Association's figure of £4,327 for annual maintenance and other costs which it said would continue even if the line closed. The only costs which would continue for any time amounted to £2,974 a year for the maintenance of the line and bridges until the line could be disposed of. The £1,000 cost of the parcels lorry would continue for a long time but it was hoped that £7,000 bus subsidy would eventually disappear.

Jones insisted that the figure the committee had to consider was the £17,400 annual loss the line would make if BR had to continue the service. Even if the line stayed open for one or two years, it would lose nearly £9,000 a year. If it was kept open longer, investment would be needed for rolling stock and colour light signals.

Answers lead to questions

The chairman asked Walsh if his questions had been answered but Walsh replied that the answers raised even more questions. The chairman said the committee was anxious that the deputations should feel satisfied so he would allow further questions if they were put briefly.

Walsh asked Jones if he was now saying that the 'Heads of Information' formula was not binding on BR. Jones replied that BR's statements on the closing of lines had been and would still be submitted on that basis. Walsh then asked if Jones agreed that the deficit of £17,400 included certain notional savings which the CTCC had definitely frowned upon and had said should be excluded. Jones disagreed, saying that the CTCC had given no directions as to the way in which the costs of a potential service should be shown. He accepted that the 'Heads of Information' formula should be used for a closure proposal but when the committees had to consider other factors, such as an alternative service, the full costings had to be used. This was the only basis on which costs could be properly compared. In these costings, interest, including that on the new capital for the diesel railbuses, had been shown at a less-than-realistic 4 per cent[66]. Walsh said the Association did not object to interest being included on new capital, but they did object to the inclusion of interest on old assets. He said that he would refer the committee to the TUCC's Bluebell line report on that point.

Walsh then took BR to task over the cost of the railbuses. He said that Shervington had distinguished between the capital cost of railbuses and the capital cost of buses on the grounds that the latter would be part of LT's ordinary working stock. He suggested that, if necessary, the Southern Region could move the railbuses to some other part of the Region or to another Region. Shervington told him that the railbuses were experimental and nobody was satisfied that they were a good thing. There were no other places within a reasonable distance of Westerham where railbuses could be used and the Southern Region had no plans to introduce them elsewhere.

Walsh then asked about BR's hopes of saving £7,000 by cutting the replacement bus services. Jones said that none of the buses would be cut without reference to the TUCC.

The last 'H' class to visit Westerham. No 31518 after arrival at the branch terminus with the 1.50pm train from Dunton Green on 28 October 1961. *Ian Nolan*

Walsh then repeated his earlier (but unanswered) question as to whether the earth slips, on which it was planned to spend £6,000 in the following five years, had yet occurred or if any of the money had been spent. Jones replied that the slips had not occurred. The money was to pay for steel piling to prevent slips from occurring. None of it had been spent.

Turning to the interest that Jones had said would not apply if the line closed, Walsh asked whether this interest was actually paid and how it was saved if the line closed. Jones replied that the Southern Region was debited each year with interest on its proportion of BR's capital. If the line were closed, the assets would be finished with but when a capital item was in service, it must produce a return and it was to correct to include this at 4 per cent. Parkin agreed and said that this was normal commercial practice. Walsh said that he would be happy to take the interest out of all the costings but he could not accept that it should be ignored only if the line closed. It was a paper transaction – BR's interest bill did not change when a line closed.

Jones said that if the line closed the interest charge would no longer be relevant, but as soon as assets were used something had to be earned on them[67]. Walsh responded that, in essence, what BR was doing was adding in a profit margin to the costs of running the service, which was a laudable aim. In practice, it simply made the line lose (more) money. The interest charge was based on assets which were not worth their book value and should have been written off[68]. Walsh was right: while those assets were still shown on BR's books – and until they were sold off for full book value – interest was due on them, whether the line was open or shut.

The chairman said the committee appreciated both sides of this argument.

Conversion into a road

The chairman said there had been a suggestion that the line might be converted into a road and he asked Mr Bains if he could comment on this. Bains replied that the county council did not want the branch to be closed but, if it were closed, part of it might be used for the South Orbital Road. This is the first indication that there was a Plan B for the use of the line if it were to close, but it does seem that the council genuinely wanted to keep the line open and fought hard for its retention. However, as we shall see later, the Kent roads department was actively planning at the same time on the basis that the line would close.

Mrs Robinson asked what the Passengers' Association would consider a fair loss to be incurred on the branch and to be borne by other people. Walsh replied that there was a difference of only £2,615 a year between the loss which would be incurred on railbus operation and the continuing liabilities to be incurred if the line were closed and an alternative bus service provided. This difference of

Pull-push operation of trains had become synonymous with the Westerham branch. 'H' class 0-4-4T No 31518 and Maunsell pull-push set No 610 form the last such train to leave the terminus – the 2.23pm departure on 28 October 1961. ***Ian Nolan***

£2,615 had to be balanced against the £3,840 which the passengers would have to pay for a worse service. In view of the hardship of having to wait for a bus in the open and having a less reliable service, the difference could properly be made up by the public. Alternatively, if the committee could not accept that view, the passengers were prepared to pay, in increased fares, a sum which would more than cover the difference.

Walsh said that it would not be right to ask the passengers to bear the complete loss, since BR were budgeting to run a bus service which would involve them in a loss of nearly £15,000 a year. If BR were prepared to lose that amount they ought to be prepared to lose a similar sum by keeping the line open if the passengers made up the difference. Mr Adcock suggested that Walsh was distorting the position a little. LT would initially provide sufficient bus capacity for all the passengers who used the line. LT might find that it had over-provided and could, with the committee's approval, reduce the capacity and the costs. He did not think it was right to base everything on the full cost of two buses and four crews.

In a final word, Forsyth, for the Sevenoaks Rural District Council, said he hoped it would not be forgotten that there were people without cars; people who made journeys to London, to visit friends in hospital, and school children who had to go to Tonbridge.

The decision

After the deputations left the meeting it was down to the members of the committee to make up their minds. Most of the discussion simply reiterated points made earlier and do not need to be repeated here.

Parkin led the way in the discussion, saying that a railway to Westerham was a social necessity which should be maintained. People who had decided to live in the area knowing there was a train service to London might not have any absolute right to that service but they were justified in expecting something equivalent to get them to work on time each morning. Their jobs depended on a service that could be relied on. The replacement buses could not do that and, because they would lose £7,000 a year, they would be ripe for withdrawal from the outset. Comments made during the day showed that BR did not intend the additional buses to be permanent.

Other members were divided. While many supported Parkin, one said that, with so few residents travelling on the branch, Westerham was hardly a commuter area. Passengers from this type of district usually reached the nearest main line station by bus. Another, though, said that they had heard nothing about efforts to stimulate traffic. The branch had been allowed to drift and the right course was to improve the service and give the line a chance.

Carey said that BR had put up a good case for closure

and asked the committee to think of the line as a business proposition. However, BR was intent on the success of the main line electrification and seemed to be worried about the impact on it of railbus movements. He thought that BR had not got the full measure of the possibilities of a railbus. When they had, they might want to use them more extensively. If railbuses were introduced on the Westerham line, there was nothing to prevent them being used elsewhere if the experiment failed. On the other hand, he noted that Kent County Council were anxious that work on the South Orbital Road should begin without delay and it might well be that, if the road were built on the alignment of the branch, the rail traffic could be carried satisfactorily on an express bus service.

The LT member, Mr G. J. Dickens, said that there simply weren't enough people living along the line to support a train service. The committee had to decide on the facts and the facts showed that the replacement of the steam service by railbuses could not be justified. The working party had gone into the costs and the facts in its report still held good.

The BR member, Mr Hancock, said that the Westerham line was a single-track railway and could not be regarded as a commuter line. The branch was used by only 4 per cent of the town's population and the prospects for future traffic on the line were poor. A 600 per cent increase in traffic would be needed to make the line pay. The objectors wanted to spend £32,000 on modernising the branch when that money was needed for more promising schemes. Even then, the line would still lose £17,000 a year and the investment was unjustifiable in view of the bus service which BR had agreed to provide.

Dickins said that the working party's report supported closure and the subsequent discussion had done nothing to invalidate the committee's original recommendation.

With that, Parkin returned to the fray, saying that BR had misled the TUCC in the early stages of the case about its reason for wanting to close the line. It had only arisen because of the inconvenience of keeping the branch going when the main line was being electrified. The revenue from off-peak trains, before they were withdrawn in 1955, was greater than the cost of running the trains with a railbus and the situation justified an experiment.

Parkin referred to the inconsistency in the treatment of interest charges on the line's fixed assets. He accepted that the line would still make a loss but that was true of all London lines. The Passengers' Association had contrasted the costs of closing the line with those of running a railbus and he was convinced this was the right approach to the problem. He then moved that the TUCC recommend the Westerham branch remain open.

Hancock opposed this. He denied that the committee had been misled, or that BR's reason for closing the line was electrification of the main line. The heavy losses on the branch could not go on. He denied that all London lines made a loss – some electrified lines in the London

The 'H' class bids farewell to Westerham. Its morning duties on the branch over, 'H' class No 31518 leaves Dunton Green for the run back to Tonbridge on the last day of service, 28 October 1961. The 'H' class had been the normal motive power on the branch from 1952. *Bluebell Railway Museum – Colin Hogg*

area were paying their way, he said, but the Westerham line lost five-sixths of its total costs.

The motion was put to the vote. Six members voted that the line should be retained, with one against. Another member, plus the two BR members, abstained. It is remarkable that the conclusions of the working party – which were firmly in BR's favour – were almost completely rejected by the committee.

BR soon claimed that the reversal of the decision was due to different members of the committee being involved on the two occasions, with the implication that the second hearing had got it wrong. It never crossed its mind maybe the first hearing got it wrong. BR stuck unyieldingly to its original figures and arguments despite the doubts stacking up against its case. In the end, the TUCC was convinced that BR would lose almost as much money by closing the line as it would by keeping it open, while subjecting branch passengers to a considerable degree of inconvenience, if not hardship.

Despite BR's insistence that the buses were an adequate alternative to the branch line, their assurances were shown to be worthless when they made it clear that they expected demand for the extra buses to fall away quickly, leading to their withdrawal.

Back to the CTCC – the final decision

The TUCC's decision produced a flurry of activity within BR. Having spoken to the General Manager, Ellison noted on his copy of the papers that: '. . . our future cannot rest on unstable decisions and "hit and miss" methods like this!!' BR's only hope was to persuade the CTCC to reject the TUCC's decision. Ellison was asked to write a paper for Mr M.A. (Archie) Cameron, one of the BTC representatives on the CTCC – 'very short, using brutal arguments and language, two foolscap sheets the maximum, preferably one'. The letter that accompanied Ellison's finished paper was blunt:

'I hope you will be able to do something about upsetting their latest decision, which was in effect made by a different Committee from the one that decided in our favour last October. The financial figures could not be seriously challenged, but under a biased Chairman they went against their previous decision, and against the recommendation of their own Working Party, purely on social grounds.'

The paper itself opened with a continued attack on the consultative committees:

Open day at Westerham on the final day of service. Note the wagon by the goods shed and others further down the goods yard. There must have been a special train after the line closed to collect them but no photographs of it have come to light. ***Ian Nolan***

'D1' class 4-4-0 No 31739 takes on water at Westerham on 28 October 1961 before working one of the last day trains to Dunton Green. ***Author's collection***

'This is not a case which reflects credit on the Consultative machinery. It has been in hand for 12 months, has involved us in a large amount of detailed work and is not settled yet.'[69]Perhaps it was as well that an even more arrogant addition to this introduction was deleted before it was sent off:

'I do not consider that the TUCC for London's latest decision should be regarded as superseding their earlier one.'

BR failed to see that its poor handling of the case had contributed substantially to the problem. There was no mention that its corrected costs for dieselisation were not ready by the date originally set for the closure hearing. A postponement on that basis alone would have been inevitable. Nor was there any mention of the unnecessary objections caused by the decision to withhold timings of the replacement buses or the doubts caused by its inaccurate and inconsistent figures.

Ellison complained that the case was only referred back to the TUCC on 'procedural grounds', but it was BR's release of so much detailed information after the first hearing that was the real cause. If BR had prepared its original case properly, the problem might have been avoided. Ellison also complained that, while the working party had supported the closure case (perhaps not too surprisingly, given the extent to which BR dominated its work), the full TUCC had disregarded its report. That should have told him something. The paper then refuted the TUCC's reasons for rejecting the closure. BR had raised many of these points before, of course, and the TUCC had disagreed with them. BR was simply trying to have the last word.

One of the claims in Ellison's paper cannot be allowed to pass without comment – that two additional buses and one lorry could provide the same facilities as two railbuses for less than half the investment. This ignored the fact that BR's costs of £28,000 included a spare railbus to cover maintenance. The comparable costs did not include spare road vehicles even though the two buses and the lorry would need maintenance and would be at as much risk of breakdowns as the railbuses. The TUCC rules also required spare vehicles to be included in the costs.

Ellison then went on to repeat Shervington's strange contention that the cost of the buses could be ignored because the replacement service would use life-expired buses. This flew in the face of BR's own arguments about the way that capital costs should be treated and, as we have noted, it suggested that LT was wasting money by buying new buses before the old ones were unfit for further service. On the other hand, did it not occur to BR to use the same principle to reduce the cost of electrifying the Westerham line by using one of the life-expired electric units that were being scrapped in 1961 instead of ordering a brand-new one?[70] In his book *BR First Generation Diesel Railbuses*, Evan Green-Hughes reveals that the cost of the railbuses was inflated by major changes demanded by BR even while they were being built – such as moving the driving desk from the centre to the left-side of the vehicle and adding retractable steps. BR's final specification was not sent to the suppliers until two months before the vehicles were due for delivery, which pushed the cost up from the £10,000 to £14,000 each. Had BR ordered two railbuses in 1960, they could have been built for something like the original £10,000 each. On that basis, a railbus and spare would have cost £20,000, not £28,000, whereas two buses and a lorry, plus spares, would have cost £23,400. This is a clear example of BR taking the worst possible case for retaining the line and comparing it against the most favourable case for closure.

* * *

One BR manager who thought that the closure should have been handled better was the Southern Region's chief accountant. In February 1961 he sent out a letter to all departments, stating how financial information in support of closures was to be provided in future to avoid the problems that had occurred in the Westerham case.

* * *

Despite its shortcomings, Ellison's paper was well-received at BTC headquarters. However, it transpired that the CTCC would not be able to consider the Westerham closure at its meeting on 21 March as the agenda already included some contentious cases. Instead, a sub-committee of two members would consider the case, as had been done with the case of the Barnard Castle–Penrith line and the Allhallows branch. Cameron at the BTC reported optimistically:

'I have little doubt that we will get the right answer from the CTCC in both these cases, and I think the same will apply in due course to Westerham, particularly when the members of the sub-committee have read your document.'

At the CTCC's March meeting Cameron welcomed the Westerham case being referred to a sub-committee but if he thought he could get whole case reheard, he was to be disappointed. The chairman stressed that the sub-committee simply had to decide whether the TUCC had dealt with the case properly.

* * *

The sub-committee completed its report by the end of April 1961. Cameron asked Hopkins, the Southern's general manager, for comments which might help him to press the case at the CTCC's May meeting. Hopkins was under no illusion as to the way things were going. Across the foot

'Q1' class 0-6-0 No 33029 hauls a train tender-first past the entrance to Brasted goods yard on the last day of service on the branch, 28 October 1961. ***Author's collection***

of the letter he wrote: 'Let the Minister decide.' He had previously authorised that a submission be prepared for a two-car emu for the branch. We also know that work to resignal the line had started by this time.

The sub-committee accepted that new information and issues had indeed been put forward at the second TUCC hearing. The proposed bus service was likely to be less dependable, punctual and certain than the trains and would cost the passengers more. The bus service to Sevenoaks was not an adequate or co-ordinated substitute for the train service and the fact that BR was getting ready to withdraw it supported that view.

The sub-committee refused to attach any weight to the question of journey time as it depended on combinations of circumstances, none of which could be calculated with certainty. Some passengers might take longer, some not. In any case, passengers could calculate more exactly how long their journey might take with the branch train service. The increased cost of travel was 'an onerous burden on the former railway passengers' and BR had admitted this by offering the season ticket concession. However, if the line stayed open BR should increase the branch fares.

Having dealt with these questions, the sub-committee then turned to a more detailed consideration of the branch finances. The loss that BR might make by running a modernised service was not the issue. As the objectors had argued, what mattered was a comparison between the cost of running the branch with a railbus and BR's on-going costs if the branch closed. The TUCC failed to take this into account at the first hearing. The capital needed to modernise the line with a railbus was about £19,500 more than the cost of buying new buses. The annual loss would be about £5,000 more than that of operating the buses, a loss that was justified in view of the economic and social hardship that would be avoided.

The sub-committee also considered the way that BR included interest in its costs. BR couldn't have it both ways – interest was either an on-going cost that would continue until the assets of the line were sold for their full book value or it should be ignored in all the comparisons. On the other hand, the sub-committee did accept that interest should be charged on new investment if the line was kept open. This included the cost of new rolling stock and signalling, the £7,300 needed for track replacement, and the £6,000 to be spent on repairing bank slips. The real cost of operating a modernised service included spending on track renewal as well as buying railbuses.

The sub-committee thought that a modernised service would attract extra traffic and supported the idea of

A: Closure and Augmentation of Bus Service		**B: Operation of Diesel Railbus**	
Capital Outlay	£	*Capital Outlay*	£
2 buses	11,700	2 Railbuses	28,000
1 road motor	1,006	Removal of water crane	132
		Signalling	4.145
		Track renewals	13,700
	12,706		45,977
		Difference = £33,271	
Annual Cost		***Annual Cost***	
Bus operation (inc interest)	8,500	Civil engineering costs (inc 6% interest)	9,341
Parcels cartage	1,036	Signalling (inc 6% interest)	482
Continuing liabilities	1,985	Train working costs (inc 6% interest)	1,985
Loss of main-line revenure	1,600	Other Costs	1,649
	13,121		19,655
Annual Receipts		***Annual Reciepts***	
Bus passengers	2,000	Passengers, parcels & freight	3,500
Parcels	200		
Freight	750		
	2,950		3,500
Net annual loss	10,171	***Net annual loss***	16,155
		Difference = £5,984	

increasing fares on the branch to match what it would cost passengers to travel by bus via Sevenoaks. The extra £3,800 would, they said, virtually wipe out the remaining difference between the cost of operating a railbus service and that of closing the line. It then went on to draw up its own comparison between the costs of closing the branch and those of running it with a railbus, showing that the impact on BR's finances of keeping the line open was just £6,000 a year. If branch fares were increased, the difference in loss would be reduced to about £2,200 and this would be reduced further still if modernisation and the operation of an off-peak service increased traffic.

As we have already seen, these calculations were based on unreliable BR figures, such as the inflated costs for the railbuses and signalling and the failure to include the cost of spare buses. We will look at these figures in Chapter 4 to decide whether BR did actually save money by closing the Westerham line.

* * *

The sub-committee posed four questions for the full CTCC to consider:

*Would it be justified in recommending the closure of the line which would inflict substantial inconvenience, possibly amounting to hardship, on the regular passengers?
*Had BR satisfied the obligation placed upon it to provide an adequate bus service between Westerham and Sevenoaks?
*Should the CTCC recommend that the Government provide capital for investment in the modernisation of this branch even though the return on investment was questionable?
*Did the CTCC believe this was a marginal case where the difference between the economic justification for the retention of the line and the social need for retaining it should be bridged by an annual subsidy to cover the loss on operation?

* * *

Hopkins wrote a pessimistic letter to Major-General Wansbrough-Jones, the BTC's secretary-general, on 4 May:
'There are several points of detail which we could take up but I do not feel that a further series of detailed comments is called for at this late stage. I would just make the point that the railbus costings which we put forward were adopted because this was the cheapest possible alternative, but for practical reasons the form of traction which would in fact be adopted (if we had to retain the branch) would be third rail electrification, like the main line. This would not increase the annual costs very much but the capital outlay would be quite considerable.

'In general, the report does not alter our case and we remain firmly of the view that to inject new capital into the line for the benefit of only 167 passengers and only to go on losing money is not justified, and therefore the line should be closed. In view of the indecision of the London TUCC it is now a matter for the CTCC to decide; if they think it should be closed all well and good; if not, then clearly there is a dispute between us and it will be for the Minister of Transport to adjudicate.

'We do not see this line as part of our future network and clearly there are certain other similar branches falling into the same category, on which, if the Minister decided they had to be kept open, we would be obliged to accept the revenue losses in the Regional accounts. This would be a pity, but we should, I feel, be unwise to raise the question of subsidies in these relatively small cases; when we come to larger issues such as the Isle of Wight or the West of England, however, we should have to consider the matter of a specific subsidy very carefully indeed.'

The final paragraph of this letter is telling. Westerham was the first of a number of closures in the pipeline which would cause hardship to the users. If the CTCC refused to close a line carrying just 167 passengers, it could hardly do otherwise in cases affecting vastly more users, leaving BR with substantial losses. There was little sign of Whitehall enthusiasm for paying the resulting bill.

There was a risk for BR in raising the issue of subsidies for socially-necessary services on the back of a case which involved only a small loss. Marples might refuse a subsidy and insist that BR carry the loss, setting a precedent for later cases involving losses that BR could not afford to carry. If the Westerham closure was refused, it would open a can of worms.

The CTCC decides

When the full CTCC met in Lincoln on 8–9 May 1961, General Whitefoord reported that the Westerham sub-committee was satisfied that the figures of savings and costs were correct at last. It accepted the TUCC's view that closure of the line would cause inconvenience, amounting to hardship. However, to modernise the line would cost £33,000 more than providing a bus service and even a modernised train service would lose more money than the buses. As a result, BR was unlikely to see any return on the investment.

It was for the CTCC to weigh up whether a modernised service on the line was socially necessary, taking into account the hardship, the cost of modernising the line, BR's continuing costs if the line closed, and the special

Westerham sunset: with the setting sun behind the train, Bulleid 'Q1' class 0-6-0 No 33029 leaves Westerham with a late afternoon train on the final day of service on the branch, 28 October 1961. *Author's collection*

duty which the BR had under the 1953 Transport Act to provide an adequate transport service in the London Passenger Transport Area.

Cameron tried to press BR's case, reminding the committee that the TUCC had reached contradictory decisions, the second when the case had been referred back on a point of procedure. The committee that had reconsidered the case had been a different body to that on the first occasion and the objectors had also had the benefit of an experienced advocate[71]. The secretary retorted that the case had been sent back because, after the first hearing, the TUCC had considered further evidence in private, denying the objectors the chance of commenting on it. When they were finally able to do so, the objectors' comments had been very effective.

The chairman told members that if they endorsed the TUCC's decision, it would involve substantial expenditure for a problematic return. Nevertheless, he thought the feeling of the meeting was that they should do so. One of the members said that they had to balance hardship against costs and they should come down on the side of hardship. The committee agreed to recommend that the Westerham branch should be retained, on the grounds that to close it would involve undue social hardship. Not surprisingly, both BR members dissented from the recommendation. One asked that the sections of the sub-committee report that set out the financial implications should be included with the minutes that were sent to the minister.

The aftermath

The practice of the time was that if the CTCC agreed that a line be retained, BR (and the Minister of Transport) simply accepted the decision. Recognising this, BR stepped up work on the plans for the electrification of the branch. A formal request to order a two-car emu for the line was sent to the Southern Region's general manager on the same day that the CTCC announced its decision but, at the same time, the Southern Region asked the BTC to put its case to the Minister. In an exchange of handwritten notes on 12 May, McKenna asked Hopkins if he had got any joy out of Cameron at the BTC. 'Modified joy', replied Hopkins, but he feared that headquarters might wilt. McKenna's final comment said: 'IN FACT all we can do now is hope the BTC do put the case to the MOT and do not "cave in".'

On 30 May the CTCC wrote to the Ministry enclosing the minutes of its meeting. Behind the scenes, questions of niceties tested the minds of senior civil servants; they wanted more information from BR but was it proper for them to invite BR to comment on the CTCC's recommendation? In the Allhallows line case there had been concern about the propriety of the Minister entertaining representations from BR after the CTCC had made its recommendation. Since the CTCC was not a legal tribunal, there was no reason why this should have been a problem but there were fears that people might draw a parallel with the so-called 'Chalkpits' case[72]. The civil servant handling the matter, Mr E. C. V. Goad, simply wrote to the BTC on 2 June saying:

'I refer to the minutes of the Sixty-second Meeting of the Central Transport Consultative Committee, and in particular to Minute 1083 in which the Committee recommended that the Westerham branch line should he retained. Under the procedure recently agreed, the Ministry have undertaken within ten working days of receipt of the Committee's Minutes to inform you when it is probable that more time will be required for consideration of a recommendation. Accordingly, I am to inform you that the Minister is giving special consideration to the above recommendation by the Committee.'

BR was clearly unaware of the niceties of the situation because on 6 June Hopkins wrote again to Wansborough-Jones at BTC headquarters:

'There is clearly a dispute between us and the Consultative Committees. May I take it that the BTC will now pursue the matter with the Ministry in order that a final decision be reached at the earliest possible moment. For ourselves, we are still firmly of the opinion that the Branch should be closed.'

We'll close it anyway

This approach got an immediate response, for a note records that Cameron rang Hopkins from BTC headquarters the same day to say that the matter was to be considered at the BTC's next railway meeting. It was proposed that BR should simply tell the Ministry that they were going to ignore the consultative committees and close the line anyway. With Dr Beeching having taken over the chairmanship of the BTC on 1 June, Cameron felt there was every reason for thinking that he would back this idea. The only way the closure could then be stopped would be if the Minister intervened and directed that the line should not be closed. BR was attempting to force the Minister's hand.

Legally, there was nothing to stop BR from unilaterally closing the line but it would have been political dynamite. The whole point of the consultative committees would have been destroyed and we can imagine mass resignations of their members, coupled with leaks revealing how badly BR had handled the case.

What the episode proved was that the ad-hoc closure procedure that had developed during the 1950s was no longer fit for purpose. It may have worked for simple closures but Westerham had tested it to its limit. It was sure to fail in future cases involving extensive hardship – the consultative committees would be unable to avoid recommending against closure in case after case. The government could not risk such a situation and, as we shall see in the next chapter, Westerham was to change the way that railway closures were handled during the Beeching era.

'D1' class 4-4-0 No 31739 at Westerham on the last day of the branch, 28 October 1961. ***Author's collection***

Debate in the Ministry

On 12 June, an unidentified civil servant noted that:

'In both the Allhallows and the Westerham Branch line closures we have noted how the Committees have yielded to pressure that the hardship caused by the closure should be weighed not against the expected savings but against the difference in the loss incurred in operating a diesel service and the loss incurred when the line is closed . . . It seems likely that whenever proposals are strongly opposed, the question of modernising the line is likely to be raised by objectors. From our point of view the important thing is that the CTCC should not lose sight of the capital expenditure which modernisation will involve.'

Yet again, we see that the government was more concerned about cutting capital expenditure on railways than the losses that a line might make. The following day, Goad noted that:

'. . . the proposal to close the branch line Westerham to Dunton Green; a special submission is being forwarded [to the Minister] on this and as [BR] has been told that they should not take any further action on this line for the present, there is no immediate urgency on this recommendation in the present context.'

What did 'further action' mean? Had the Ministry warned BR not to go ahead and close the line unilaterally or had it told BR to hold back on electrification plans? There must have been contact between civil servants and BR but no record of it survives.

On 15 June Wansbrough-Jones wrote to the permanent secretary at the Ministry of Transport, referring to the Ministry's letter of 2 June and pointing out that BR wanted to close the line as soon as possible, ideally to coincide with the introduction of the winter timetable on 11 September 1961. Goad replied indirectly a few days later by telling the secretary of the CTCC that the Minister was still considering the matter. Beyond this, we do not know how Marples reached his final decision or what advice he was given by his civil servants – Part 1 of the Ministry's file on the Westerham closure decision is missing. We can make an educated guess, though, at the ideas that must have been at the heart of his thinking.

A decision to close the line would, for the first time, go against the recommendation of the CTCC. This was never the outrageous, undemocratic step that many have claimed but it did threaten to undermine the purpose of the consultative committees. To go against the committees inevitably meant that the government would have to rethink their future role.

The closure case had been an all-round embarrassment. Marples must have felt that it justified his view that railway management was incompetent and had to be rescued from its own failings. BR had run the line inefficiently and when its figures were put under scrutiny they were found to be wanting. However, he had no intention of reprieving Westerham just because BR had got it wrong and the prospect of BR getting it wrong in hundreds of future cases did not bear thinking about.

Marples never saw Westerham as part of the core commuter network that was, in his eyes, BR's only essential function. Even if the line could be modernised and run efficiently it was not worth the time, effort and money.

The line could only be retained if significant investment was put into it and this contravened the government's insistence that it would not invest in marginal or loss-making services.

In the absence of the relevant ministerial file, was the potential use of the trackbed for road building a consideration? We will look at this later but for now we can say that Marples had enough other justification for the closure without the road question affecting his decision.

The 'misfired' question

At 6.10 in the evening of 27 July 1961 Hopkins received a telephone call telling him that Marples had agreed that the Westerham closure should go ahead. By ignoring the CTCC's recommendation this decision would give the case its status as one of the most controversial of all railway closures. Hopkins seems to have understood this if his note of the precise time of the call is anything to go by. An era ended at that moment.

The announcement had been spurred by the tabling of a parliamentary question by the Sevenoaks MP, John Rodgers, who asked the minister if he had reached a decision. The question was due for answer in the House of Commons on Wednesday 2 August, only a day or two before the start of Parliament's summer recess.

The puzzle is why Rodgers chose that particular moment to ask his question. It had been nearly three months since the CTCC had made its recommendation and Marples seemed to be in no hurry to make up his

The End. 'Q1' class No 33029 after arrival back at Dunton Green with the final passenger train from Westerham. *Ian Nolan*

mind – surprisingly so, given that the case was later said to be so clear-cut. If Rodgers had not intervened when he did, might the announcement have been delayed, forcing BR to press ahead with modernising the line?

An intriguing clue is offered by Hopkins' hurried pencil notes of the call that told him of the ministerial decision. A word that seems to be 'misfired' appears alongside the note about the parliamentary question. After three months, did Rodgers think that Marples was wavering and hope that by pushing for a decision – with the deadline of the recess looming – he would get a favourable response? Given his subsequent reaction, he was obviously not expecting Marples to approve closure. The real reason will always be a mystery but it remains one of those fascinating 'what-ifs'.

To help frame an answer to Rodgers' question, the Ministry needed to know when BR proposed to close the line and when the replacement buses would be available. The Ministry wanted the line closed before Parliament re-assembled on 25 October, presumably to avoid the possibility of a debate in the House. That suited BR, which still wanted the closure to coincide with the start of the winter timetable.

Hopkins passed the news to McKenna, who telephoned Bolland, stressing the need for secrecy. Bolland thought he could arrange the closure for 11 September and promised to call McKenna back the next morning. McKenna and Bolland were, in fact, on the phone to each other repeatedly the following day. Bolland discovered that LT was planning to reschedule its local bus services from 25 October and it hoped the closure date could fit in with that. McKenna told Bolland that the October date would not really be satisfactory and asked him to go back to LT to ask if it could provide substitute buses on an ad hoc basis, at BR's expense, until the new schedules started. However, no official request could be made until the closure had been formally announced.

Hopkins sent a message to Wansbrough-Jones to tell him of progress. He planned to say something to the effect that the date that the Southern Region had in mind for closure was 11 September to coincide with the beginning of the winter timetable, but this would depend on the introduction of the bus service. Wansbrough-Jones said that this would give the Minister an escape route if things went badly in the House of Commons.

* * *

There was relief in the Ministry when Rodger's question had to be dealt with by a written answer, presumably because of time limitations. A furious row in the House, with a backbench MP attacking a minister of his own party, had been avoided. In his answer, published on 2 August, Marples said:

'I have carefully considered this case but I am unable to agree with the Central Committee's conclusion that closure of this line, and adoption of the railway's alternative proposals, would cause undue social hardship. I have therefore informed the Chairman of the British Transport Commission that he is free to proceed with the closure as soon as arrangements have been made for the necessary augmentation of the bus service. This will not be before the introduction of the winter time-table on 11 September and may be later.'

The news made the front pages. 'THE PUSH-AND-PULL LINE IS TO CLOSE', the *London Evening News* told its readers: 'Plea to save controversial railway track rejected – but MP keeps up fight'. Referring to the controversial planning case, Farmer, chairman of the Passengers' Association was quoted as saying:

'This looks like another Chalkpit case. The Minister's decision was given as a written reply to a Parliamentary question at a time which gives no opportunity for further negotiation. I think this is the first time the Minister has decided to close a line in the face of a recommendation of the National Committee.'

Rodgers immediately tabled a motion in the House of Commons, deploring the decision, viewing with concern the Minister's 'unprecedented action' in rejecting the advice of two consultative committees, and calling on him to instruct BR to take no action about the closure until the House could debate it when it reassembled at the end of October.

This put Marples in a difficult position. If the line closed in September, it would look as though he was trying to avoid a debate on the closure. On the other hand, he was critical of the delays that had occurred and now he was going to add his own.

The Times was supportive of the minister. In its leader column it said that the charge against the Minister was that he had rejected the advice of the CTCC. It was an all too common mistake to assume that, just because there was an advisory body, a Minister had to accept its conclusions. The responsibility was the Minister's, it continued. He was answerable and his position would be impossible if advice were mandatory. The newspaper was taken to task over this view in a subsequent letter from the chairman of the Westerham Conservative Association, pointing out that the real problem was that the decision would come into effect before Parliament had the opportunity to debate it.

In its issue of 11 August, *The Times* carried a light-hearted piece written by an anonymous but knowledgeable Brasted resident – maybe Sir Charles Pym. The writer noted the motion tabled in Parliament and the letters in the papers but was not optimistic:

DUNTON GREEN

To be carried out on Saturday, 2nd December, commencing at 12.5 a.m.

The Westerham Branch single line will be put out of use except for the portion between the connection with the Up Main line and the connection leading to the Goods Sidings, which will in future form part of the Goods Sidings. The points leading to and from the Loop line, 36 yards and 247 yards Westerham side of signal box together with the trap points in the Loop line 83 yards and 201 yards Westerham side of signal box will be disconnected from the signal box clipped and padlocked in the 'normal' position.

The points in the Westerham Branch single line (facing for Down movements) leading to Goods Sidings 146 yards Westerham side of signal box together with the trap points in the Goods Sidings will be disconnected from the signal box and clipped and padlocked in the reverse position.

The following signals will be abolished:—

Running Signals

Description	Yards from Signal Box
Down Branch Starting	182 yards Westerham side
Up Branch Starting	64 yards Westerham side
Up Branch Home	307 yards Westerham side

Shunting Signals

Controlling Movements	Yards from Signal Box
From Dead End Siding to Branch or Loop	36 yards Polhill side
From Branch to Dead End Siding or Up Main	84 yards Westerham side
From Loop to Dead End Siding or Up Main	85 yards Westerham side
From Branch to Goods Siding or single line	129 yards Westerham side
From Goods Siding to Branch	183 yards Westerham side
From Loop to Branch	199 yards Westerham side
From Branch to Loop	307 yards Westerham side

A new shunting signal controlling movements from Goods Sidings to Up Main line will be provided 23 yards Westerham side of signal box.

The shunting signal 43 yards Polhill side of signal box controlling movements from Up Main to Down Main and from Up Main to Branch or Loop will in future apply for movements from Up Main to Down Main and from Up Main to Goods Sidings only.

(R/Z.1000/43/51/1)
(P/EW No. 45 S.E.D., 1961) (R/SB.784) (1)

'Few branch lines similarly in extremis of recent years have lived to tell the tale: and ours, a mere four miles and 56 chains long, was never of a particularly robust constitution. Dunton Green with its main-line connexion is probably not unduly perturbed, but Westerham, for all I know, is organizing a last-ditch resistance, and Chevening Halt a march on Westminster. At Brasted, the only other station on the line, some of us are quietly resigned and already sentimentally nostalgic.

'. . . Until they 'fell to pieces', as the guard puts it, the rolling stock consisted of two pull-and-push coaches from the old South-Eastern and Chatham Railway. The two in use now for the 11-minute trip still carry the S.R. monogram within. One is a compartmented, corridor coach—necessary, since the guard both collects and issues tickets in addition to performing his other duties. The other has a central gangway, and what can only be described as an entrance hall, complete with coconut doormats. An exhortation to "Travel by Golden Arrow" seems somehow anachronistic. Apter in the context is a framed reproduction of a Kentish oast house, which has been upside down for as long as anyone can remember.'

Bearing in mind what was to replace the line within 20 years, the final passage of the article was even more of a valediction for a way of life than the author intended:

'The line, threading the ancient Vale of Holmesdale, chalk downs on one side and sandstone hills on the other, crosses some of the most delectable countryside to be found within 25 miles of London—or anywhere else in England, for that matter. Apart from visitors who ride the summer Sunday trains the 180 season-ticket holders are the ones who will suffer most immediately from a closure of the line. But those of us who dwell in the valley or on the facing hills will face a subtler loss. With the mellowing years the line has become as much a part of the landscape as the Pilgrims' Way that runs a race with it higher up the hillside, the white plume of smoke rising above the tree tops as natural a phenomenon as the clouds over the Downs or the evening mists that rise from the water-meadows. Yes, if it goes, we shall miss the Westerham Flyer.

'British Railways, obviously, cannot afford the luxury of being sentimental. All the same, we cannot help it—hope seeps in. After all four miles and 56 chains is such a very little railway. Dr. Beeching would hardly notice it . . .'

While these words were being penned, Bolland had spoken to Ellison on 8 August saying that arrangements could be made to close the line on 11 September. The following day the BTC officially instructed the Southern Region to go ahead with the closure and asking for it to be carried out on 11 September if possible.

Electrification work in progress

This was followed by a potentially embarrassing revelation. Cameron heard that passengers had seen conductor rails, insulators, and other equipment stacked at Dunton Green and had assumed that the line was to be electrified. He imagined all sorts of consequences that might flow from this. The Southern Region assured Cameron that this was, in fact, second-hand material removed from the main line, which had been relaid with heavier conductor rail for fast electric trains. The station master at Dunton Green had been given an appropriate answer for any passenger who asked.

In fact, the Southern's answer was completely false. As one of the photographs shows, the conductor rail on the main line was replaced a year earlier and would long since have been removed, not gathered up and dumped at Dunton Green. It is hard to believe that it wasn't kept to enable the Westerham line to be electrified cheaply using second-hand material.

It is clear that, since the CTCC's rejection of the closure proposal in May, the Southern had assumed that the line was to remain open and material was gathered for its electrification. How much of this was officially sanctioned is another matter though.

Concrete troughing for signal cabling had been dropped off beside the first mile of track from Dunton Green, and can be seen in many of the last day photographs. A new three-aspect colour light signal was erected at the

The London-bound platform at Dunton Green showing the passage leading to the Westerham branch platform. ***Author's collection***

London end of the branch platform at Dunton Green and the base (at least) for a distant colour light was installed between Dunton Green and Chevening. The signal at Dunton Green was hastily removed when closure was announced. So, too, was the redundant conductor rail. The author has also seen a photograph of a branch train showing insulators dropped along the trackside. There was also a rumour that an electric multiple-unit had been hauled along the line to test clearances, though it is possible that an unknowing observer saw the branch pull-push set which, from the front, did resemble an electric unit.

These developments did not get the publicity they undoubtedly deserved. Had they done so, it would have been extremely awkward for both BR and the Ministry; there would have been accusations not just of waste and muddle but also that the decision to close the line was neither expected nor as clear-cut as Marples had made out. Had Rodgers revealed this in the debate in Parliament, the effect could have been devastating. It would have made both BR and the Ministry look incompetent and it would have embarrassed Marples. Rodgers must surely have been aware of the news – or did no-one think to point it out to him – so it is hard to understand why he did not make use of it.

Closure postponed

With preparations under way to close the line on 11 September, things started to go wrong. A note dated 11 August reveals that:

'The Secretary-General telephoned and said that due to political difficulty arising from the Written Answer given by the Minister recently in the House on this matter – apparently a Motion has been put down and the Minister finds himself in some difficulty – the Ministry have requested that any announcement about the date of closing of the Branch should be delayed for a day or two until the difficulties at the Ministry have been ironed out.'

The Southern immediately stopped any announcements about the closure and held up the distribution of posters. The following day Hopkins wrote to Wansbrough-Jones:

'I am sorry I had left just before you telephoned yesterday evening. Sir Philip [Warter – chairman of the Southern Area Board] had told me of the Permanent Secretary's conversation with him and it was at my insistence that he told the Permanent Secretary that the Region had had its instructions from the BTC and was proceeding.

'I have now told our people that they must ensure that nothing is publicized about the closure until further advice it received. Meanwhile, however, I have said that the arrangements for the closure on the 11th September should continue to go ahead but quietly.'

Two days later, on 14 August, Hopkins took a phone call from Serpell, who wanted to know the position as regards the closure arrangements. He needed to know if 11 September was already set in stone. Hopkins explained that:

*The Westerham Branch service remained in the winter timetable but could be deleted by notice.
*References to Westerham had been left out of the Winter Departure Sheets for London Stations. (They were at the proof stage with printing held up.)
*The coal merchant concerned had been informed that after 11 September he would get his coal at another station.
*LT had approached their staff about operating the ad-hoc bus service from 11 September onwards.
*Serpell asked about road licences and the purchase of buses but it was explained that this was a matter for LT, not BR.
*Public notices and letters to interested parties were ready but were being held back.
*Local people knew what was proposed as regards September 11th.

Ellison checked on the situation with Bolland, who confirmed that local staff were aware of the plans, the coal merchant at Brasted had been told and bus crews at Dunton Green garage were being consulted about working overtime to cover the additional buses from 11 September. Bolland added that the news was bound to leak out and, in any case, they would have to know something definite by the end of the week. Ellison told him that he should not be too concerned for a few days yet – the difficulties at the Ministry might resolve themselves by then. The implication is that pressure was being brought to bear on Rodgers to drop his demand for a debate.

There will be no public service on it

The following afternoon, Serpell telephoned Derek Barrie, the assistant secretary-general at the BTC. (Wansbrough-Jones was on holiday.) The Ministry had decided that, to avoid political upset, the end of October would be a better date for the closure. For the time being, though, the Ministry was not going to issue a directive on the issue but preferred to rely on BR's co-operation.

Barrie passed the news on to Hopkins. Hopkins explained the previous day's events to him and said that he could agree to 30 October but he had to be told quickly what the BTC wanted him to do. He wondered whether Beeching should be informed, which Barrie promised to do.

Why couldn't BR simply do as the Ministry requested? The answer is that the Ministry of Transport was not supposed to interfere in day-to-day railway affairs and it was coming perilously close to it. The Ministry had given permission to close the line – now, to avoid embarrassment, it was trying to interfere in operational matters.

At this point, Sir Philip Warter became involved again. Hopkins told him that he needed a formal decision from the BTC varying its original instruction. Warter talked to both Beeching (who knew nothing of the matter) and Serpell. By the end of the afternoon Beeching had agreed that 30 October should be the date for closure and Barrie said that a formal letter would be in Hopkins' hands by the following morning. He was as good as his word. The letter read:

'. . . informal representations have been made to us by the Ministry of Transport that some Parliamentary difficulties might be avoided, and the Region would have greater assurance of being able to proceed with their arrangements to close this line without further intervention, if the official date of closure were postponed until about the end of October, which it is understood is the period which you originally had in mind.

'While there is no question as yet of any directive from the Ministry to adopt any particular date, the Deputy Secretary of the Ministry has asked that if the Commission and yourself still consider it necessary to close the branch earlier than 30th October, the Ministry should be officially informed at once, as in these circumstances the Minister would probably wish to reconsider the position.

'I understand from our conversation that firm public notice of the intention to close with effect from September 11th has not yet been promulgated, and that so far as you are concerned there is no practical difficulty in effecting the closure on and from Monday, 30th October. If such is the case, the Commission will be grateful if you will proceed accordingly and confirm that this is being done.

'... the Chairman of the Commission has been informed of the circumstances of the request made by the Ministry and is in general agreement with the terms of this letter.'

Hopkins issued his instruction to his colleagues:

'As agreed, we now proceed to make effective the closure of the line so that on and from Monday, 30th October, there will be no public service on it.'

On the bottom of his copy, Ellison made a note that he had spoken to Bolland, who was to carry on as though this was a normally agreed case.

Now that it had got the decision for which it had waited so long, BR wasted no more time. On 17 August letters were sent to the local authorities and other interested parties, including Rodgers, telling them of the closure date. Posters had been ordered and would be displayed on stations within a week. A press release was issued the following day.

Debate in Parliament

The last hopes of saving the line now rested on the debate in Parliament which eventually took place on 19 October (the recess ended early). It was not a good day for Marples. Earlier that afternoon he had faced a barrage of MPs demanding his resignation when he announced that Cunard had deferred its order for a new ship to replace the *Queen Mary*, which had been a central plank of the Government's shipbuilding policy. The fate of the Westerham branch must almost have come as light relief.

The debate[73] opened with Rodgers, the Sevenoaks MP, reiterating the events of the closure proceedings and the issues it raised. He said that the Minister's decision was unprecedented. While Marples had acted within his powers, to act within one's powers was not necessarily to be right. No real explanation had been given to the House or to his constituents as to why this line was to be closed.

Rodgers had sent the minister a petition signed by nearly 2,500 people living in the area affected and literally hundreds of letters he had received. He said that the majority of people who used the line commuted all the way to London. They were not rich people. They were the daily bread winners. Their jobs depended, in large measure, on their ability to be punctual at work and there could be no guarantee that the buses would arrive in time to connect with the trains. Up to three-quarters of an hour would be added to his constituents' journeys each day and the cost would go up by 10s a week. He wondered whether the season ticket concession was the result of BR's guilty conscience.

Rodgers realised that the Minister's argument hinged on BR's astronomic losses and the impossibility of making this line pay but the closure would save only £11,600, compared with the line's losses of about £20,000 with steam traction. A diesel railbus would reduce the loss to less than £3,000. And, in addition, the passengers had offered to pay higher fares in line with the bus fares. The extra £3,600 would wipe out any loss. He asked the minister to postpone the closure of the line until that experiment has been tried for two or three years.

Marples began his reply by congratulating the MP for the way he had worked diligently and skilfully for his constituents, who themselves were not without ability when it came to presenting a case. They had marshalled their forces with great tenacity. Their petition, signed by 2,400 people, was impressive he said, but alas, only 167 people used the line regularly. He would have preferred to get a petition signed by 167 people with 2,400 travelling on the railway.

He said that the alternatives to steam were either a diesel railbus or road buses. The railways had offered to augment the existing bus service. The steam service lost £26,000 a year.

'That is over £150 for each regular passenger. In other words, the ordinary taxpayer is paying £3 a week out of taxes for every person who travels regularly on this line. Taking a five-day working week, it is 12s a day paid by the taxpayer for every passenger on the service between Westerham and Dunton Green ... It is an enormous loss.

When we look at it in perspective, it is terrific.'
The cost of running the line was £29,700 per annum and the receipts £3,500. The people who used the line paid 12 per cent of what it cost. A railbus service would help a bit but it would not be a great deal better. The loss would still be £17,500 and this was still an enormous figure. If increased fares were authorised, it might cause a loss of traffic. People said they would pay but, when it came to the point, a lot of people would not do so. If the line was closed and the bus service provided the annual loss falling on the taxpayer would be about £11,000.

He then turned to the investment which the line would have needed. Capital for a railbus service would be £46,000 and for new road buses, £12,700. Neither of those sums would produce an economic return. He asked if closure would really cause undue hardship and suggested that Rodgers should go to the North of Scotland to see how the situation there compared with Westerham.

Marples revealed that he had taken the decision himself after careful consideration. The procedure established by Parliament placed the final responsibility upon his shoulders. He had rejected the CTCC's recommendations because he was unable to agree with the committee's view that closure would cause undue hardship.

'I know that certain people will be inconvenienced. I know that there is a sentimental attachment to these two coaches which chug along on a Sunday with a little steam engine drawing them, with more people in the engine than in the train. I know that it is a nice sight to see this train coming along a track with grass sprouting up between the lines, but I think that it does not play a part in this third quarter of the twentieth century in whatever transport system we are to have.

'. . . The inconvenience to users by the closure of the Westerham line is not hardship in the true sense of the word, and the Commission has taken steps to alleviate that hardship by the provision of additional bus services. The closing of branch lines is an essential part of the Commission's plan for bringing the railways towards a condition of viability.'

The last day

The final summer Sunday trains having run the previous weekend, the last day was to be Saturday 28 October 1961. It was a beautiful autumn day, something that dozens of photographers took full advantage of.

The early service was worked by Class H No 31324 powering the regular branch pull-push set No 610, but

'H' class 0-4-4T No 31308 propels its train away from Chevening Halt in September 1961. The spot on which the photographer was standing is now beneath the Sevenoaks bypass. ***Author's collection***

she gave way to sister engine No 31518, which worked the service from the 11.50am from Dunton Green until the 2.23pm from Westerham. As the day went on no 31518's smokebox was inscribed 'Flyer 1881–1961' and for the last part of the morning a Union Flag and bunting adorned the front of the engine. At Brasted, the white-painted flints that had spelled out the station name on the bank opposite the platform had been re-arranged to form the letters 'R.I.P.'.

The day started fairly quietly but crowds built up as it went on. The *Sevenoaks Chronicle* reported that people lined the cutting sides at Westerham; they and others on bridges along the length of the line took photographs of every train that came through, each one packed with people anxious to have their last sight of the scene from a train window.

BR had anticipated the crowds; for the afternoon and evening service, a seven-car train of BR Mark 1 stock – set No 277 – was sent from Bricklayer's Arms, hauled by Class D1 4-4-0 No 31739. The two trains posed beside each other for a short while before No 31518 and its pull-push set departed for Tonbridge for the last time, while No 31739 set off with the 2.50pm to Westerham.

The run-round loop at Dunton Green could not cope with such a long train, so Class Q1 0-6-0 No 33029 worked alternate services with the 'D1'. The 'D1 was chimney first to Westerham and worked the 2.50, 4.50 and 6.50 round trips from Dunton Green. The 'Q1' was chimney first to Dunton Green and worked the 3.50, 5.50 and 7.50 round trips.

The 7.50pm to Westerham should have been the last train and one of its passengers was 82-year-old Mrs Jane Graves, who had travelled on the very first train in 1881 as a babe in arms. Her brother, who had joined her on that first train, could not be on the last one as he lived in Bangalore. Mr Geoffrey Durtnell, of the Brasted building firm, whose grandfather, Richard, had been one of the Westerham Valley Railway Company's directors, took a final ride on the line with his son. Another passenger was Mr John Bunting of Chevening Road, Chipstead, who had travelled on the line every working day for 31 years. He was sad to see the train's last run but he felt he must be a passenger to 'see the old lady off'. On the Monday, he would have to walk through the village from his home, only a few yards from the halt, to be picked up by the bus on the main road.

When the last train arrived at Westerham there was no space on the platform and the whole crowd moved as one. Normally an empty working, on this occasion passengers were allowed to use it to travel back to Dunton Green. Detonators and firecrackers accompanied the emotional departure. It was supposed to run non-stop but, although it missed out Brasted, waved through by crowds on the platform, it did call at Chevening.

The reporter from the local paper recorded that people waved and cheered from every house window in Madan Road. Some stood in their gardens watching silently while others waved torches. Streamers unwound from the train windows. A carriage full of enthusiasts had obtained a bundle of luggage labels, most bearing Welsh place names, and had arranged then to read 'RIP' in one of the windows.

At Dunton Green, people swarmed on the track to have a last look at the train and take final pictures. And then the engine sounded its whistle for the last time and set off back to London to a ragged cheer from the crowd.

And that was it, although as last day photos show, there was a brake van, a van and a wagon at Westerham, and a couple of wagons at Brasted, so a subsequent train must have run to collect these, and another to recover the materials dropped by the lineside for the abandoned electrification project. No details of these workings seem to have survived, though.

A little over a month later, the branch was officially decommissioned. Points on the branch side at Dunton Green were disconnected from the signal box and clipped and padlocked to give access only to the goods yard, which remained open. No more trains were ever to run to Westerham.

4

Postscript to Closure

The last train may have run to Westerham but the story was not over. Repercussions began even as the rails started to rust. As the CTCC noted, the Westerham closure was ground-breaking. However, the way it was handled was a fiasco which showed that the existing closure procedures were not fit for handling the mass of closures that Beeching was about to unleash. Government thoughts turned to the way in which the procedures might be revamped.

Extract from Section 56 of the Transport Act 1962 limiting the role of the Transport Users Consultative Committees in considering railway closures to questions of hardship – a direct result of the time taken to decide the Westerham closure. ***Crown copyright***

(9) A committee with whom an objection has been lodged under the last foregoing subsection shall consider the objection and any representations made by the Board concerned and report to the Minister as soon as possible on the hardship, if any, which they consider will be caused by the proposed closure, and the report may contain proposals for alleviating that hardship.

Where objections with respect to any proposed closure have been lodged with more than one Area Committee, the committees in question—

(*a*) may report to the Minister jointly, or

(*b*) may agree that the consideration of objections and representations relating to the closure and the making of a report to the Minister shall be delegated to any of those committees appearing to them to be principally concerned;

and copies of every report under this and the next following subsection shall be sent to the Central Committee and to the Board concerned.

(10) The Minister may require an Area Committee to make a further report; and if in any case the Minister considers that a report or further report has been unreasonably delayed he may, after consulting the committee concerned and making such enquiries as he thinks fit, consent to the proposed closure without awaiting the report or further report.

(11) In any case in which a closure requires the consent of the Minister under this section, the Minister may give his consent subject to such conditions as he thinks fit and may from time to time vary those conditions; and the Minister may in connection with the closure from time to time give such directions to the Board concerned as he thinks fit.

Where a condition attached to a consent, or a direction, requires the Board to provide or assist in the provision of alternative services, the Minister may refer to an Area Committee any matter relating to those services, and the committee shall consider and report to the Minister on that matter.

60

BR's hopes that the replacement buses – and the subsidies it paid for them – would be short-lived were to be dashed, undermining much of the financial case for closure. On the other hand, the Ministry of Transport regarded the closure as important. It demanded that BR review the savings it had actually made from the closure to prove that the planned Beeching closures would have the desired result of reducing BR's losses.

We will look at all these issues in this chapter. We will also look at the savings that the closure of the Westerham branch actually achieved and show how, with modernisation, BR would have been better off keeping the branch open.

Changes to closure proceedings

The bitterly-fought closure of the Westerham branch led the government to introduce a new procedure as part of the 1962 Transport Act in time for the publication of the Beeching Report. The 1958 Bluebell line closure changed the way in which BR had to present its figures to the TUCCs but there was still no clear understanding of the committees' role. It did not help that BR paid for the TUCCs, provided their accommodation, and even seconded staff to them.

The TUCC's approach changed at the second Westerham hearing when it considered the impact of the closure on passengers and wondered whether it could be justified by the likely savings. It was a watershed but one for which neither BR nor the Ministry of Transport had any enthusiasm. For the Ministry, with Beeching poised to wield his axe, Westerham and the delays experienced there, demonstrated how not to close a railway. By February 1961, just as the TUCC finally came out in favour of retaining the Westerham line, Serpell was involved in discussions on their future role. In June and July 1961, while the Westerham file sat in the Minister's pending tray, more discussions took place between BR and civil servants about limiting the TUCCs' role. Marples approved. Speaking in the House of Commons in a debate on the Annual Report of the

British Transport Commission in June 1962, and referring to the forthcoming closures, he said that:

'One thing that we must avoid is procedural delays. They have cost a lot of money. The Westerham line took from April 1960 to October 1961 to close. In that time the railways lost £40,000. We could have kept a bus service going if we had given one-quarter of that sum, and it would have saved the taxpayers money, while, at the same time, keeping the service going for the passengers.'[74]In future, the TUCCs were to limit their reports to questions of 'the hardship, if any, which they consider will be caused by the proposed closure'. They could suggest ways of alleviating hardship but they were not to consider alternative methods of working, nor were they to recommend whether lines should be closed or not. They were no longer to hear challenges to the figures that BR put forward, though it was optimistic to assume that objectors would take much heed of such a rule. The minister would decide whether the hardship caused by a closure – and hardship was not defined in the Act – was sufficient to justify retention of a line and rarely was that the case.

The changes simplified the procedures but they did not reduce the time taken to process closures. BR's proposal to close the remaining lines on the Isle of Wight, for example, was published in February 1964. The Minister's decision was finally given at the end of July 1965, more than a year after the TUCC hearing. The closures did not take place until the spring of 1966[75]. In part this was because it took time for BR to prepare closure cases. The financial information required was less detailed than before but public protest forced a retreat from Marples' original intention that BR should not have to publish any financial information at all in support of closures76. (In any case, the Ministry still required detailed figures.) Gourvish, though, is critical of the general quality of the Beeching-era closure submissions – things, it seems, had not improved much since Westerham.

The 1962 changes to the closure procedures were a hasty, kneejerk reaction to the Westerham case. By and large, the TUCCs had dealt with closures efficiently and quickly and their judgements were relatively unaffected by public opinion; once it fell to ministers to make decisions, political and electoral consequences had to be considered. Had Marples simply streamlined the TUCC procedure, rather than taking the decision-making into his own hands, few closures would have been decided differently but they would probably have been carried out more swiftly and cleanly. The loss of focus that BR suffered in the mid-1960s and the impression it gave of being an

The bus that replaced the Westerham train. Dunton Green-based London Transport RT3652 waiting to leave Westerham on a route 403 service to Sevenoaks and Tonbridge in 1962. Far from being a bus kept on beyond its normal life, RT 3652 was only nine years old when this photograph was taken. *Keith Harwood*

Wallington - Croydon - Sevenoaks - Tonbridge **Route 403**

For Complete Service between Riverhead and Sevenoaks (Direct) see Summary

MONDAY to FRIDAY (TT.119)

												SS									SS			
CHELSHAM LT Garage									06 53															
Botley Hill Cross Roads									07 02															
Tatsfield Church Hill									06															
Westerham Kings Arms		05 58			06 49		06 57		07 15	07 23				07 30		07 42		07 49					08 19	08 25
Brasted White Hart		06 04			47		07 03			29		07 34		36		48		55			08 22		25	31
Sundridge White Horse		07			50		06			32		37		39		51		58			25		28	34
Bessels Green Kings Head	D	12		D	55		11			37		42		44		56		08 03	08 07		30		33	39
Riverhead St. Marys Church	06 02	14		06 35	57		13			39		44		46		58		05	09		32		35	41
Sevenoaks Railway Station	05	17		38	07 00		16			42		47		49		08 01		08	12		35		38	44
SEVENOAKS Bus Station arr	09	06 21		42	04		07 20			07 46		51		53		08 05		12	08 16		08 39		42	08 48
SEVENOAKS Bus Station dep	11			44	06							53		57				14					44	
Sevenoaks White Hart	17			50	12							59		08 03				20					50	
River Hill Weald Turn	21			54	16							08 03		07				24					54	
Hildenborough Church	27			07 00	22							09		13				30					09 00	
Tonbridge Star and Garter	34			07	29							16		20				37					07	
TONBRIDGE STATION	06 38			07 11	07 33							08 20		08 24				08 41					09 11	

			B					D		D			SS											
WALLINGTON Belmont Rd.																								
West Croydon Bus Station	07 54		09 00	10 00	11 00	12 00	13 00		14 00		15 00			16 00				17 00					18 03	
South Croydon Swan & S.L.	08 01		07	07	07	07	07		07		07			07				07					10	
Sanderstead Church	12		18	18	18	18	18		18		18			18				18					21	
Warlingham The Green	20		26	26	26	26	26		26		26			26				26					29	
Chelsham LT Garage	22		28	28	28	28	28		28		28			28				28					31	
Botley Hill Cross Roads	31		37	37	37	37	37		37		37			37				37					40	
Tatsfield Church Hill	35		41	41	41	41	41		41		41			41				41					44	
Westerham Kings Arms	46A	09 24	49	49	49	49	49		49		49	16 19		49	17 18	17 33	17 43	51C		18 19	18 35	18 40	52	19 19
Brasted White Hart	52	30	55	55	55	55	55		55		55	25	16 41	55	24	39	49	57	18 11	25	41	46	58	25
Sundridge White Horse	55	33	58	58	58	58	58		58		58	28	44	58	27	42	52	18 00	14	28	44	49	19 01	28
Bessels Green Kings Head	09 00	38	10 03	11 03	12 03	13 03	14 03		15 03		16 03	33	49	17 03	32	47	57	05	19	33	49	54	06	33
Riverhead St. Marys Church	02	40	05	05	05	05	05	14 35	05	15 35	05	35	51	05	34	49	59	07	18 21	35	51	18 56	08	35
Sevenoaks Railway Station	05	43	08	08	08	08	08	38	08	38	08	38	53	08	37	52	18 02	10	D	38	54	D	11	38
SEVENOAKS Bus Station arr	09	09 47	12	12	12	12	12	42	12	42	12	42	16 58	12	41	17 56	18 06	14		18 42	18 58		15	19 42
SEVENOAKS Bus Station dep	14		14	14	14	14	14	44	14	44	14	44		14	43			16					17	
Sevenoaks White Hart	20		20	20	20	20	20	50	20	50	20	50		20	49			22					23	
River Hill Weald Turn	24		24	24	24	24	24	54	24	54	24	54		24	53			26					27	
Hildenborough Church	30		30	30	30	30	30	15 00	30	16 00	30	17 00		30	59			32					33	
Tonbridge Star and Garter	37		37	37	37	37	37	07	37	07	37	07		37	18 06			39					40	
TONBRIDGE STATION	09 41		10 41	11 41	12 41	13 41	14 41	15 11	15 41	16 11	16 41	17 11		17 41	18 10			18 43					19 44	

A–Arrives 08 43. B–From Beddington *The Plough* at 08 50. C–Arrives 17 49. D–From Dunton Green *LT Garage*. SS–School days only.

22 20

The January 1967 timetable for bus route 403, showing the railway-subsidised extra journeys from Westerham to Sevenoaks.

industry in decline thanks to the drawn-out stream of closures might both have been avoided.

Saga of the replacement buses

When Marples agreed to the closure of the Westerham branch, he made it a condition that BR had to subsidise additional buses on route 403 between Westerham and Sevenoaks. The cost of the additional buses was originally set at £8,700 a year, less any bus fares paid by former rail passengers. In the first year after closure BR had to pay the full subsidy because the concession to season ticket holders meant that they did not have to pay fares on the buses.

A letter from Bolland to the Ministry in February 1963 reveals what happened next. From the second year after closure the £8,700 bus subsidy was reduced to £7,150 because LT's costs had not been as high as expected and BR even received a credit of £500 for the first year. Former rail passengers paid bus fares of £1,150 a year, which were set against the subsidy, leaving £6,000 a year for BR to pay.

The question of bus subsidies was closely linked to that of the preservation scheme and is dealt with more fully in that context in Chapter 5. While it appeared that a commuter service would be part of that scheme, BR hoped it would be relieved of the need to pay the bus subsidy. It was never quite as simple as that, though, as we shall see, and when the preservation scheme collapsed, BR was forced to consider the future of the replacement buses.

In any case, BR had expected that, after a year or two, use of the replacement buses would have fallen to such an extent that it could withdraw the extra journeys. Indeed, the case for closure only really made sense if BR did not have to pay the bus subsidy.

BR had promised to consult the TUCC before making any changes to the replacement buses but the Transport Act 1962 changed the rules on this. If a replacement bus was being subsidised by BR when the Act came into operation, only the Minister of Transport could approve changes to the service and only the Minister could ask the TUCC to consider the matter. As a result, on 1 August 1963, almost two years after closure, Wansbrough-Jones at BR headquarters wrote to C. P. Scott-Malden at the Ministry of Transport:

'Recent checks on the use made of the subsidised bus journeys between Westerham and Sevenoaks have revealed that the 5.58 am service from Westerham to Sevenoaks is only carrying a maximum of four passengers, only one of which completed the journey to Sevenoaks Bus Station, and none of whom had used the train service before the closure of the branch line.

'It has also shown that the 6.18 pm, 7.08 pm, and 8.0 pm services from Sevenoaks are much more lightly loaded than the remaining services, and if these four journeys (including the 5.58 am journey from Westerham) were withdrawn, the present subsidy payment of £6,000 per annum could be reduced by £510.

'As will be seen from the timetable enclosed with my letter of 11th March last, the withdrawal of the 6.18 p.m., 7.08 p.m., and 8.0 p.m., journeys would still leave journeys from Sevenoaks at 6.28 p.m., 6.57 p.m. and. 7.21 p.m., none of which are subsidised.

'We should, therefore, be glad to have the Minister's consent to withdrawing the four journeys mentioned above in order to reduce the subsidy paid by £510 per annum.'

This must have created difficulties for the Ministry. With replacement buses being promised in place of rail services threatened by Beeching, it would have been embarrassing if the buses that had replaced the Westerham trains just two years earlier were to be cut. At the same time, the Ministry did not want BR agreeing to pay for extra buses simply to get rid of loss-making trains, in the hope that the buses themselves could be cut back after a year or two.

The Ministry was still mulling over the problem three months later. In October 1963 Scott-Malden wrote to Mr E. G. Whitaker, transport adviser to Unilever Ltd and a member of the CTCC:

'I mentioned to you the other day the awkward problem with which we are faced in advising the Minister about a proposal by the British Railways Board to reduce the additional bus services provided in replacement for the Westerham/Dunton Green railway passenger service. The question is whether or not the Minister should consult the London T.U.C.C. . . . 'In view of the history, of which you are well aware, a request to the T.U.C.C. for advice might attract a somewhat dusty answer. On the other hand, if the Minister acted without consulting the T.U.C.C., the Committee might perhaps feel aggrieved.

'I understand that you are seeing the Minister next Tuesday about publicity for closure decisions, and I expect to be present. I wonder if we could have a quick word on this subject after that meeting?'

A hand-written paper in the file details the impact of the proposed changes. Withdrawal of the 5.58am bus from Westerham would mean that the first bus would be the 6.41. The Ministry noted that the 5.58 was a replacement for the 6.10 branch train which carried an average of 6 passengers, while withdrawal of the evening buses would add another 10 minutes to the journey times for some passengers.

In November 1963 the Ministry finally wrote to the TUCC asking it to advise the Minister on the hardship that would be caused by the withdrawal of the buses. The Ministry also mentioned further (unspecified) information which it thought the TUCC would want to consider. If the TUCC agreed, the Ministry would ask BR to send the information direct. Given the timing, this must have referred to the collapsing state of the preservation scheme's attempt to run commuter services.

The TUCC decided to write to the main objectors in the Westerham case but it was not until July 1964 that it finally got round to writing to the Passengers' Association and to the Westerham Valley Railway Association (WVRA) asking for their views.

Mr C. D. A. Cohen, who had been Secretary of the Passengers' Association, replied to say that the organisation no longer existed and that its former chairman, Mr Farmer, had moved away. He therefore replied on a personal basis. He found it odd that the withdrawal of the least-used 40 per cent of the subsidised services should save only 8 per cent of the total subsidy. He did not agree that the 18.18 bus should be withdrawn. The 18.05 train arrival

Fig 4.1 The signalling at Dunton Green was replaced by colour lights soon after the closure of the Westerham branch.

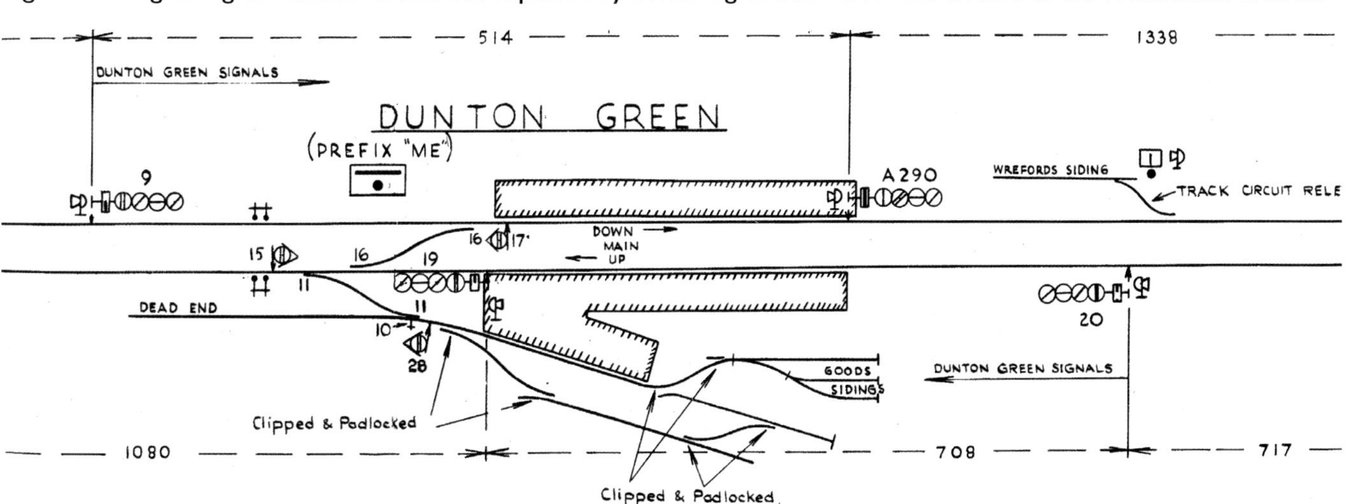

was often late; if its passengers were unable to catch the 18.13 bus they had to catch the 18.18 instead. He could see no objection to cancelling the 19.08 bus, but not the 20.00 one. If that was taken off, the next was not until 20.28, unless a passenger was prepared to pay extra to use the Green Line coach. He could see no objection to withdrawing the 05.58 bus from Westerham.

Cohen also commented on the broader outcome of the closure:

'... you might be interested to learn that, in my opinion, very considerable hardship has been suffered by all concerned due to the closure of the Dunston Green/ Westerham branch line, as the bus service is not really a reasonable substitute, particularly when one has to spend long periods standing without any form of shelter at all at Sevenoaks in the winter months. I can assure you – as I have always used the bus service myself – that the winter of 1962/63 was extraordinarily unpleasant, and therefore any steps which can be taken to alleviate the inconvenience to passengers, should be taken.'

For the WVRA, its secretary, Mr R. D. G. Ranson, said that it viewed the proposed withdrawal of the subsidised buses with alarm. Any reduction in the services would increase the hardship for people travelling to work. Most travellers had found the buses next to useless, especially during the winter, and many people travelled by car to Sevenoaks or even Bromley, Catford or Orpington. Others had been forced to leave the district. This was why some of the buses were so poorly used.

The effects of the closure were beginning to show, he continued. People were being dissuaded from moving into the area because few jobs existed locally compared with the prospects of those in London. The reluctance of people with families to live in the area meant that Westerham was becoming a retreat for retired people, with a reduced level of income. This had inflicted a serious loss to the local traders at a time when new bypasses would take away even the passing trade.

In December 1964 the TUCC rejected the withdrawal of the buses, advice which the Ministry accepted. There the matter rested until, in January 1966, BR wrote to the Ministry, reporting that the bus subsidy was to increase by £1,800 a year because of LT's increased operating costs. The letter ended with a plaintive request:

The allotments behind the platform at Westerham. This triangle of land was bought to enable the building of the Oxted extension, proposed in 1875 and again in 1885. A single track serving a new platform could have been built here, allowing the existing station and yard to be sold off for development to help pay for electrification. ***Ian Nolan***

'There seems to be no alternative but to accept this, but I would be glad if you could confirm that for the time being the bus services must be maintained.'

The reply to this letter and some later correspondence has not survived but on 1 September 1st the Ministry wrote to BR summarising the situation. It said that, if the loadings recorded in June 1967 were typical, there was little change from the situation on which the TUCC had reported in December 1964.

The Ministry was concerned about LT's practice of superimposing subsidised services on its existing timetables with no attempt to co-ordinate them. The Ministry was also concerned about the high rates of subsidy being charged, noting that the Westerham subsidy had increased from £6,000 to £8,328 a year. The Ministry then washed its hands of the matter, suggesting that BR should take it up with LT through the normal liaison channels between the two bodies.

In the end, the matter was only settled when Barbara Castle's 1968 Transport Act created the National Bus Company (NBC), which took over LT's country buses, including those serving Westerham. The NBC became responsible for railway replacement bus services outside Greater London and the financial burden was finally lifted from BR.

Review of savings

In November 1962, a year after closure, the Ministry of Transport asked BR for details of the savings actually achieved by the closure of the Westerham branch. We must assume that this was tied in to the planned publication of the Beeching Report on 27 March 1963, the intention being to show that BR could actually achieve its predicted savings from closures. BR promised an answer by the end of January 1963 but it was 11 March before figures were finally sent to the Ministry. They showed a difference of just 5 per cent between the estimated savings and those actually achieved. Cynics may suspect that it took BR a long time to produce figures that would give the Ministry the answer it wanted!

BR explained that, because of the season ticket concession, there were no bus fares to offset the subsidy payments to LT in the first year of closure. However, while this increased the subsidy payment, it encouraged passengers to travel via Sevenoaks with the result that the loss of main line contributory revenue was lower than expected. When the concession expired the subsidy fell from £8,700 a year (£8,200 in 1960 values) to £6,000, thanks to bus fares paid by former rail passengers and a reduction in LT's working costs. However, this conflicted with BR's own evidence that, a year after closure, only 48 passengers were still taking advantage of the season ticket concession[77].

It was impossible to identify which buses were used by former branch passengers since they mingled with existing passengers on both subsidised and non-subsidised services. BR said that it would monitor bus use carefully and carry out a further review two years after closure.

The overall loss of fare income as a result of the closure was said to be £3,300, compared to the estimate of £3,500 given in 1960. This, BR said, was based on a 'broad appraisal' of the savings made on the branch but no explanation was forthcoming as to how the figure had been arrived at!

It is not clear whether the Ministry ever made use of these figures. Perhaps it had hoped that BR would be able to show that it had saved more than it had originally expected. Far from reassuring the public, the figures would more likely have reopened the debate into the accuracy of BR's accounting.

Should Westerham have been closed?

Had the Westerham closure been refused, many of the succeeding Beeching closures would have been in doubt and therefore it played a significant part in shaping today's railway network. It also demonstrated weaknesses in BR's management, both financial and operational. Inevitable questions arise – should the branch have been closed and could it have been made to pay? On that hinges a great deal. If it could have been made to pay, why did BR and the Ministry of Transport want it closed?

The second part of the question may be easier to answer than the first. The contemporary view was that the line had to close was because it needed investment for modernisation if it was to continue through the 1960s and there is much to support that conclusion. As BR itself had admitted, the actual savings from closure were 'small'.

The alternative – that the branch was closed because of its losses, as Marples was to claim – begs the question that, if saving money was so important, why were simple opportunities to do so ignored for so long? Why was the branch freight retained when its usefulness had passed? Why was signalling retained at Westerham? Why were the off-peak services cut in 1955, worsening the situation? The fact is that, by 1960, government transport policy was squeezing funds for modernising the railways. The bill for Kent Coast electrification was £62 million and there was pressure to cut that, so there was never any prospect of electrifying further branch lines. In fact, the return on the Kent Coast electrification was later estimated to be just 4.85 per cent, less than the cost of borrowing the money and way below the Ministry's 8 per cent benchmark[78]. If the same rules had been applied to the Kent Coast system as to the Westerham branch, much of it would have been shut down as parts of it were clearly making substantial losses.

* * *

We must now ask whether the Westerham closure was justified. There is no doubt that the line lost money but that is only half the story. It also cost money to close the line. Unfortunately, the situation is complicated by inconsistencies in BR's figures. We could try to overcome the problem by adjusting all the figures to make them consistent but that would introduce too many opportunities for doubt and error. Instead, we need to take a different approach.

BR said that it saved nearly £9,000 by closing the branch, even after paying for replacement buses. The first step then is to look at the costs of the line's steam-worked services to see how much could have been saved without closing the line. That will tell us how much (or how little) BR really saved by closing the line. We will then ask how much more could have been saved by electrifying the line. If, as a result of this two-step process we can reduce the costs of running the line by £9,000 or more, we will have proved that it cost BR more to close the line than to keep it open and modernise it.

Withdraw freight and reduce signalling: BR's claim that the branch freight service cost virtually nothing to operate is untrue. To work the freight, the morning locomotive arrived at Dunton Green at 5.21am when the first passenger train did not leave Westerham until 6.14. Similarly, the last weekday passenger train arrived at Westerham at 8.1pm but the locomotive didn't leave the branch until 9.55. That meant over two hours a day of additional crew time. BR even ignored the costs of the freight train guard in most of its figures. The costs may have been small but they were significant when measured against the line's tiny freight earnings and BR lost nothing by diverting the freight elsewhere.

Two locomotive crews covered the Monday–Friday Westerham service. In 1961 BR agreed to allow crews a rest break between the third and fifth hours of duty. This would ordinarily have required a third set of crew but, by removing the branch freight service, both morning and afternoon steam shifts could have returned to Tonbridge depot before the fifth hour was up, with two hours a day spare for other duties.

With the freight service gone, the branch signalling could have been simplified for much less than the signalling engineer suggested. Under a simplified system of signalling:

*Movement on and off the branch could have been controlled by shunt signals as only empty trains or light engines were involved.
*One-engine-in-steam operation would apply on the branch, controlled by means of a staff kept in an instrument on the branch platform at Dunton Green.
*Access to the goods yard at Dunton Green, if it was to be retained, would be by a ground frame unlocked by the staff.
This is based on the signalling that was actually introduced at Dunton Green after the branch closed (see Figure 4.1). Ignoring the equipment shown on this diagram – it was needed after the branch closed anyway – the extra equipment needed to allow a branch passenger service would have cost less than £1,000 compared to the £4,145 originally quoted by BR. Interest at 6 per cent on the reduced expenditure would have been £60 a year, with repairs at £70 a year and renewals at £24. In return for that, the signal box at Westerham would have been abolished, saving £950 a year in staff costs. The investment would have paid for itself in just over a year.

There were other measures that BR could have taken to reduce costs:

*Remove station staff: BR argued that station staff were needed at Westerham because they dealt not only with passengers but also freight and parcels. The withdrawal of freight and parcels would have removed that justification. BR's own figures show that only a dozen or so Westerham passengers bought daily tickets and they could easily have been catered for by selling tickets on the train. Season ticket holders would have been able to renew their tickets at Dunton Green or at their destination stations. Removing the two leading porters would have saved £884 a year.
*Reduce track maintenance staff: The Westerham branch had five track maintenance staff – one ganger, one sub-ganger and three lengthmen. In 1956 BR told the Ministry of Transport that a 10-mile-long line in Herefordshire, twice as long as the Westerham branch, needed four men for track maintenance[79]. Failure to renew the Westerham branch track between 1952 and 1958 may have increased day-to-day maintenance but, with most of the track renewed by 1960, this should no longer have been necessary. The suspicion must be that the Westerham gang was either spending much of its time on the main line or was permanently under strength but was still being charged to the branch at full cost.

On the basis of the Herefordshire line quoted in Parliament, a ganger and two lengthmen should have sufficed for Westerham. One of the lengthmen would have been kept on after the line closed for the maintenance of bridges and fences and 'disinfestation', so closure would only have saved two men's wages, not the four claimed.
*Abolish the summer Sunday service: The branch share of fares from the summer Sunday service amounted to around £250 a year but the service cost over £900 for wages and a further £800 for train running – mostly fuel. Even if all the income were lost, BR would have saved £1,444 a year. Some main line revenue may have been lost too, but it is likely that ramblers, for instance, would simply have travelled to another destination that was still served by train.

The costs of the Sunday service were high because three sets of locomotive crew were needed and all staff worked at overtime rates on Sundays. After 1961 four sets of crew would have been needed because of the need to provide relief for rest breaks, pushing the costs even higher.

BR expected to lose income of £3,379 when the line closed, including 10 per cent of the revenue that branch passengers contributed to the main line. It later claimed that this was a worst-case estimate but by the summer of 1962, 10 months after closure, only 48 of the original 140 branch season ticket holders were still using the replacement buses. Some of the passengers moved away from the area but anecdotal evidence suggests that many started driving to Bromley or even London. With the car parking problems at Sevenoaks, and the extra distance involved, it is unlikely that many Westerham passengers drove there to catch the train.

Taking these factors into account, a more realistic estimate is that BR lost at least £4,250 in revenue by closing the line, based on 1961 fares.

* * *

Although the extra buses cost more in the first year when rail passengers did not have to pay bus fares, the cost of the subsidy subsequently fell to £6,000 a year, thanks to lower than expected LT costs. In addition, BR found that the Westerham parcels traffic could easily be handled by the existing Oxted lorry, so a new lorry based at Sevenoaks was no longer required. The reduced costs of replacement road transport are taken into account in the figures but the subsequent increase in the bus subsidy mentioned earlier in this chapter has been ignored.

If the line had remained open, passengers had said they would be willing to pay higher fares for the service. A figure of over £3,800 was suggested by the Passengers' Association but such a large increase might have driven away passengers. A net increase of £2,500 is more realistic.

In conclusion

Disregarding track renewals (as required by the TUCC formula), BR expected to save £8,943 a year by closing the Westerham branch but this review has shown that £6,520 could have been saved without closing the line – even with steam. Appendix 15 shows the details. That meant that the real savings achieved by closure were only £2,423 a year. BR was relying on making much greater savings by escaping from the bus subsidy but, as we have seen, that did not happen.

When BR first thought about modernising some or all of the railways on the Isle of Wight, the idea of using redundant tube stock was developed and became the chosen solution when the Ryde–Shanklin line was electrified in 1967. IOW 3-TIS unit No 035 brings up the rear of a train as it leaves Shanklin. Was it really necessary to order a brand new electric unit for the Westerham branch? Couldn't a redundant unit from elsewhere on the Southern's electric network, suitably refurbished, have sufficed? ***Author's collection***

Electrification

Having seen that BR's real savings from closing the branch were only £2,423 a year, the next step is to see if electrification would have improved the line's finances. It might not have made the branch profitable but if it could have reduced costs by £2,500 or more compared with steam, it would have been cheaper to keep the line open than to close it.

The second table in Appendix 15 shows the comparative costs of operating the steam service and of running an electric service on the line. These are based on BR's costs for modernised working (Appendices 7 and 7A) but take into account the savings proposed here. Train working costs had increased because they included the cost of guards, who would be responsible for selling day tickets, but the junior porters, who previously carried out that role, were no longer required. The costs also allowed for a third driver to provide relief for rest break. With skilful rostering, these three drivers would have had time available to work on other services, defraying part of their cost, but the figures ignore this.

The interest charges for electrification are high but fuel and repair costs are substantially reduced. Even with the most pessimistic train crew costs (based on the crews being totally dedicated to the branch) and the high interest charges, the electric service would have cost £4,316 less than the equivalent steam costs.

Summary

By closing the steam service and substituting buses, BR really only saved £2,423 a year. Electrification would have cut the costs of running the line by another £4,316, meaning that BR would have been better off by electrifying the line than by closing it and experience elsewhere suggests that a modernised service would almost certainly have attracted additional custom to the line. A new platform for an electrified single track could have been built on the allotments behind the platform at Westerham so that the existing station and yard could have been sold off for development to help pay for the electrification. There is no indication that BR ever considered this idea.

The capital cost of electrification was given as £39,850. This covered the cost of an additional two-car unit at £29,850 plus £6,200 for improved fencing, £1,100 for work at level crossings (presumably accommodation crossings), £1,450 for work at stations, £750 for reballasting, and £500 for other works. Second-hand conductor rail and jumper cables would have cost £26,800, clearance work and second-hand high-speed circuit breakers adding a further £600. This would have brought the total cost of electrification to £67,250. To offset this, the capital cost of new buses would have been avoided.

However, for the Isle of Wight electrification in 1966-67, old LT tube cars were bought at scrap prices and refurbished at a cost of £2,695 per car. This suggests that a redundant two-car suburban electric unit could have been refurbished for another 10 years' use on the Westerham branch at a cost of around £5,500, saving over £24,000 compared to a brand-new unit.

To calculate the much-disputed interest charges for the line, BR added the £10,000 for the new works to the existing £67,450 capital value of the line but the value of redundant sidings and station buildings should have been deducted.

Off-peak service

The electrification figures become even more compelling if the off-peak service is taken into account. The extra cost of running off-peak electric trains was just £665. A fourth driver would have been required but with efficient rostering each driver would only have been needed for two-thirds of a shift and this has been taken into account. Ironically, an all-day electric service could have made more efficient use of train crews than a peak-only service.

Reinstatement of the off-peak service would have been expected to earn additional revenue of around £7,000. This is based on the 1955 earnings and includes contributory revenue on the main line since an all-day service would have encouraged greater casual use of rail for journeys from Westerham through to London.

Could it have made a difference?

The figures show how the fortunes of the Westerham branch could have been turned round with imagination and determination. Unfortunately, these qualities were in short supply in the BR of the 1950s and 60s. Reviving the Westerham branch would have been an ideal opportunity for an aspiring young manager to make his or her mark but, in those days, BR was an organisation in which those on the lower rungs of the ladder were expected to obey instructions from above, not to exercise innovative skills.

Would it have made a difference? It is difficult to imagine the line being ignored by the Beeching Report but it is equally difficult to imagine a line that had only just been electrified being closed. On the other hand, patronage of the branch might have fallen to an unsustainable level during the 1960s, regardless of modernisation. The Green Belt meant that there was never likely to be the kind of development that would have given the line a viable future. As the *Sevenoaks Chronicle* said at the time of closure, unaware then of what was to take its place:

'The choice rested, in fact, between having a typical suburban area grow up along the line – or losing the line. Relatively few may, in the long run, come to regret the official choice.'

5

The Vexed Question

When Ernest Marples announced in the summer of 1961 that the branch was to close, thoughts began to turn to its future. In line with its normal policy, BR refused to discuss selling the line with anyone before it actually closed – anyone, that is, except Kent County Council. The council's roads department was in touch with the Southern Region estates surveyor on 9 August 1961, barely a week after Marples' announcement, and references in other letters tell us that these contacts had been going on for some months. On 6 October, again before the line closed, county surveyor Henry Bowdler asked for plans of the land that would become available, confirming that the Divisional Road Engineer (DRE) at the Ministry of Transport supported his approach[80]. He wanted a large part of the Westerham station site plus the trackbed between Chevening and Brasted but he admitted that not all Kent councillors supported his ideas. Three separate road schemes were involved. One was the Sevenoaks Bypass, which was to cross the trackbed at Chevening, the second the South Orbital Road, and the third a bypass for Westerham town centre. It is important to mention at this stage that the impetus behind all of

Preserved SECR 'P' class 0-6-0 tank No 323 ***Bluebell*** **at Sheffield Park station on the opening day of the Bluebell Railway, 7 August 1960.** *Bluebell Railway Museum – John J. Smith*

NORMAL SERVICE WILL BE RESUMED AS SOON AS POSSIBLE BY THE

WESTERHAM BRANCH RAILWAY PASSENGERS ASSOCIATION

We plan to restore the train service between Westerham and Dunton Green. A diesel railcar will run at times convenient for you.

THIS IS YOUR LINE – JOIN NOW

We are a voluntary organisation, acting on behalf of the community. We can only succeed in achieving our aims if we can rely on your support. Membership approaches 500, and many more members are needed to back the project. All who are interested in saving this line, both potential users and those who support us in principle, are urged to send their subscriptions(initially and nominally 2/6) or donations to the Hon. Treasurer:-
MR.D.E.WALTER, 9 MARLBOROUGH COURT, WESTERHAM, KENT.

Enquiries regarding investment or further details from the Chairman:-
MR.W.G.GRAY, FLAT 2, 'FARLEY WEST', WESTERHAM, KENT.

The first WBRPA leaflet appealing for support and funds. Note that the emphasis is purely on running a commuter service with diesel railcars. ***Author's collection***

these schemes was from the Kent roads department and not the Ministry of Transport. Given that such things are not planned overnight, the idea of using the trackbed had clearly been considered well before it was decided to close the line, at a time, of course, when the full Kent County Council still officially opposed the closure.

It is widely believed that it was the line's potential for road building that led to its closure. This is something we will consider later but the possibility of using the formation, if the line did close, was mentioned at the TUCC hearing in February 1961 and was confirmed in a letter of 18 July 1961 from Bowdler to Mr F. J. Howlett of Combe Bank, Brasted, part of whose garden was to be taken for the South Orbital Road, as originally planned:

'... the Ministry of Transport has not, as yet, included in the construction programme this section of the South Orbital Road planned to pass on the north side of Combe Bank Wood. In the event of the closure of the Westerham–Dunton Green branch railway line we would endeavour to use the line as part of the new road. I am sorry I cannot be definite but the indications are that construction is unlikely to start within 5 years.'

However, the use of the railway for a road flew in the face of BR's agreed policy that it should keep the trackbed in case there was significant development in Westerham[81]. This was reiterated in a memo from C. P. Hopkins, the Southern's general manager, dated 22 August 1961:

'. . . I have received an enquiry through the TUCC for London regarding the purchase of certain land in the Westerham area, and I was proposing to forward this to the Estates and Rating Surveyor for him to pursue, subject only to ensuring that our minimum possible future land requirements are safeguarded and that no negotiations are opened until the Branch has actually been closed.'

What was going on? Why was the Southern's estates surveyor negotiating to sell the line to the council, apparently behind his general manager's back, even before it had been agreed that the line should close? It wasn't until 18 October that he asked for permission to do what, in fact, he had been doing for months – negotiating with the county surveyor. On 3 November, after the line had closed, the general manager agreed, on the basis that:

'. . . there seems no prospect of the Westerham Branch Line being re-opened and you may proceed with your negotiations for the sale of large "parcels" of the land to the Kent County Council and other parties who might be interested.'

We will return to this question later.

Thoughts of preservation

Inspired by the successful takeover of a number of disused railways by enthusiasts, some people began to think about reopening the Westerham line.

Given the subsequent success of railway preservation, it can be hard to remember that the idea of enthusiasts running railways was in its infancy in 1961 and it was an anathema to many in BR and the Ministry of Transport. Fortunately, neither of the first two preserved lines – the narrow-gauge Talyllyn and Festiniog Railways in Wales – had been nationalised in 1948 and both were virtually derelict. Enthusiasts took them over by acquiring shares in the companies that had originally built them, meaning that they didn't have to buy the lines from BR and they had all the authority they needed to operate the lines. As a result, the question never came up as to whether it was desirable for enthusiastic amateurs to run railways.

Curiously, the idea of preserving an ex-BR line probably had its roots in the 1953 Ealing Studios film *The Titfield Thunderbolt* which was inspired by the story of the Talyllyn. It showed a group of villagers taking over their local line when BR wanted to close it and succeeding against the

On 7 August 1980, 20 years to the day after the *Bluebell* Railway re-opened as a preserved railway, SECR 'P' class 0-6-0 tank No 323 Bluebell helps to recreate the opening train at Horsted Keynes station. The only slight inaccuracy is that in 1960 Bluebell trains were not allowed into Horsted Keynes station. The crowds had grown massively by 1980 too. ***Author***

odds. The story appealed to the public in an age when reaction was setting in against bureaucratic monoliths.

The first non-fictional standard-gauge preserved line was the one-mile-long Middleton Railway in Leeds, which dated from 1758. Part of it was bought by a local company in June 1960 for use as a private siding; it was run for it by a preservation society started by staff and students of Leeds University. The emphasis was on the operation of freight and it was not until 1969 that passenger trains became a regular feature of the line so, once again, officialdom's involvement was limited.

Just weeks later, in August 1960, the Middleton was followed, by the Bluebell Railway in Sussex. This was the first ex-BR standard-gauge line to be preserved and the change of ownership was amazingly simple. BR granted the preservation society a lease of the line and the necessary Light Railway Orders were approved by the Ministry of Transport without a hitch. Indeed, the only real issues that concerned the Ministry were the correct legal procedures for granting a Light Railway Order. A process was devised whereby BR obtained an LRO to convert the line into a light railway and a second order (called an Amending or Transfer Order) transferred the right to operate the railway to a company set up by the enthusiasts[82].

In retrospect, the Bluebell was incredibly fortunate. Once it dropped its initial ideas of reopening the whole line from East Grinstead to Culver Junction as a commercial service, its ambitions aroused no concerns. The line that it finally leased – Sheffield Park to just short of Horsted Keynes – was in deep countryside with no road overbridges or level crossings and services were limited to summer weekends and bank holidays. The land was not particularly valuable and BR was able to dispose of five miles in one go instead of having to sell it piecemeal to neighbouring landowners.

To those in authority, the Bluebell raised none of the issues that were to arise at Westerham. It gave enthusiasts an opportunity to 'play trains' in an out of the way spot where they could do little harm[83]. It wasn't trying to run a public service and it wasn't even expected to bring in large numbers of visitors. In the words of one official, any passengers they did manage to attract would simply help to pay for the rent and coal.

BR blocks attempts to save the line

One of those interested in reopening the Westerham line was a Captain Mark Cross from Bedfordshire. In August 1961 he wrote to Dr Beeching asking to be put in touch

The branch side of Dunton Green station. The connection to the goods yard is at the far end of the platform, the branch line and its run-round loop curving to the right. ***Ian Nolan***

with someone with whom he could discuss buying or renting the line. His was a serious proposal, he stressed, and he had capital available. We do not know how true this was or why he had an interest in the Westerham branch but his intention was to run it to the existing timetable and at existing fares, possibly as a light railway or on a 'railway club basis' but using different locomotives and rolling stock. He claimed to be experienced in railway transport practice both in theatres of war and in peacetime and he thought he could offer a worthwhile service to the public while deriving pleasure in the line's operation. He did not expect to make a great profit but he felt he could make the line pay for its upkeep.

Cross's letter was passed to the Southern Region general manager who duly sent it on to Tim Bolland, the local Line Traffic Manager, and Graham Tunbridge, the Southern's estates surveyor – both of whom ignored it. Cross wrote again over the next couple of months. His letters were again passed on but not followed up. In the end, angry at the lack of response, he withdrew his offer – BR simply acknowledged his letter. If he really did have sufficient capital to buy the line, it might have changed the whole story, especially if he had made contact with others with similar interests.

Meanwhile, civil servant Denis Pope of Sidcup approached BR on behalf of a group of enthusiasts who felt that the branch was ideal for preservation. Ellison added a handwritten note to the letter: 'Treat in same way as previous enquiries'. Again, there is no record of a response from BR but, undeterred, Pope and his group went on to form the Westerham Valley Railway Society.

Just after closure, BR received a letter from the Railway Preservation Society, a body that planned to coordinate railway preservation on a national basis[84]. It felt that it had sufficient support to preserve the line and wanted to know what the rent would be for Westerham station. Ellison, in the general manager's office, wrote on it: 'Haven't we now made this impossible?' A pencilled reply stated: 'Yes, we've told the Estates Department to go ahead and negotiate with the County Surveyor for the sale of a large parcel of former line', which wasn't quite what the general manager had authorised.

The Passengers' Association bid

The main interest in re-opening the line came from the Westerham Branch Railway Passengers' Association which had led the fight against closure and which now wanted to buy the line and re-open it for commuter services. The new chairman of the Association, economist William Gray, wrote to Dr Beeching in late November 1961. His letter was passed to the Southern Region for reply.

Gray's early letters to BR have not survived but we can track them from BR's letters of acknowledgement. The first was headed 'Plea for reopening of Westerham branch', followed, a week later, by 'Refusal of S.R. to consider bid

Chevening Halt seen in August 1962 after closure. BR noted that there was no apparent value to the site. ***Ian Nolan***

for Westerham–Dunton Green line'. Another week later, the secretary of the Association, wrote to Beeching in 'Support of bid for Westerham–Dunton Green branch line by Westerham Valley Railway Society'.

* * *

Why were BR managers so opposed to enthusiasts taking over the Westerham line? For a start, those behind the Passengers' Association scheme were the very people who had fought BR to stop the line being closed – and had almost succeeded. On top of that, the Westerham scheme intended to run a year-round commuter service, not just to 'play trains'. We have seen how BR could have run the branch more efficiently than it did and a privately run line might have proved that point. This was no small matter of a few BR people being left with egg on their faces. If it succeeded, objectors to every subsequent closure would have been able to point to the Westerham example and cast doubt on BR's figures and its ability to run local lines. It would have made hard to push through the Beeching closures.

However, this didn't explain why BR opposed all preservation schemes for the line, and not just that put forward by the Passengers' Association.

* * *

Despite the obstacles that BR put in their way, the WBRPA persisted and in January 1962 it merged with the enthusiasts' Westerham Valley Railway Society. The new

Seen during 1961, the final year of operation of the branch, the traditional motive power of latter years, a Class 'H' 0-4-4T – in this instance No 31177 – waits at Westerham's attractive wooden terminus. Note the advertising hoarding graphically extolling the virtues of beer! *Wikipedia, licensed under the Creative Commons Attribution-Share Alike 4.0 International license. (Lamberhurst)*

organisation, using what seems to have been a degree of subterfuge, arranged a meeting with Mr J. W. Hawkins, the branch lines assistant in the Southern's estates department. He reported:

'On the 'phone Mr. Gray said that his Society was interested in purchasing the land forming the branch and that he would like to come and discuss it. At the meeting, however, it was clear that their intention is also to buy the track and other equipment and to attempt to continue to run the railway from Dunton Green to Westerham in a similar manner to British Railways service.

'I pointed out that the Kent County Council had expressed an interest in practically the whole of the branch line but Mr. Gray said he had contacted the Council who would be prepared to waive their scheme if the railway proposal was accepted. I added that several Development Companies were interested in Westerham Station and they, therefore, may be priced out of the market. Mr. Gray said that he hoped to get sufficient financial backing to make a competitive bid for the land.

'The difficulties of running a railway ... were pointed out to them but they were undeterred and wanted to know what their first move should be.

'I 'phoned Mr. Johnson of the [Line Traffic Manager's] Office who said that his Department was no longer concerned except to discourage Preservation Societies and could not, therefore, issue instructions for the track to be left in situ for the time being.

'I 'phoned Mr. A. Edwards, Assistant to the General Manager (Works Progress), who emphasized that it was purely a business matter and that if the price they were prepared to pay for the land and fixed assets exceeds the value of the land cleared for sale, together with the value of the recovered assets, then their offer may be considered. Mr. Edwards seemed to think that the Society would be easily discouraged but this was not the impression they gave me. I could not have a full conversation with Mr. Edwards with the Committee Members sitting in my room.

'He later 'phoned back to say that the assets were not due for recovery in the immediate future.

'The Society intend to obtain Sir Winston Churchill's support and they will hold public meetings, film shows, use advertising media etc. They consider that the 200 commuters per day and weekend traffic to see Chartwell and for walks in the country will make the line an economic proposition, they also pointed out that by their running into Dunton Green Station, British Railways receipts would benefit from through bookings.

'I suggested that they should write to the General Manager telling him of their plans as only he could give instructions for the track to be left down for a limited period of time and he would pass the matter to me for a valuation of the land and to the appropriate Department for a valuation of the recovered assets.

'In the meantime I would be making a survey and valuation of the branch so that any offer they may make can be compared with what it is considered that the land would fetch in separate sales.

'I had the feeling that a blunt refusal to treat with them may cause considerable adverse criticism of the Commission and it would be advisable to refuse them only on the grounds of their not being able to make a sufficiently attractive offer.'

This memo is revealing in several ways, not least the determination of Bolland and his colleagues to have nothing to do with railway preservation. Following the meeting, Gray wrote to the Southern Region general manager, setting out the proposal to lease or purchase the line in order to run a service for the commuters, community and railway enthusiast members of the Passengers' Association. It planned to operate a diesel railcar service for the commuters and the community from Monday to Friday, and for the railway enthusiasts to run a steam service for themselves and tourists mainly at summer week-ends and holidays. The scheme was to be presented to a public meeting in Westerham on Saturday 3 March 1962 at which it was hoped to enlist financial support with guarantees from members and to set up a Trust.

The Association wanted to acquire the line intact with all its fixtures so Gray asked BR to stop any action to remove the rails and fixtures. He also asked for a quotation for leasing or renting the line, taking into account the 200 commuters from the line who travelled on BR between Dunton Green and London, the casual passengers passing through Dunton Green for destinations anywhere on BR, and the tourists and visitors from London and elsewhere travelling to Chevening, Brasted and Westerham to attend such events as Chartwell and Chevening Place Open Days, Westerham and Brasted Galas etc. The letter suggested a sliding rental based on the traffic passing through Dunton Green to and from the branch – the higher the volume, the lower the rental.

* * *

The result of this letter was an invitation for the Association to meet the Southern Region's new Assistant General Manager, Mr R. L. P. (Robert) Cobb, and other BR managers. Cobb asked Ellison to list the points that should be raised at the meeting, based on the example of the Bluebell, but in the meantime Bolland fired a broadside against the Association in a memo to the general manager.

Westerham goods yard in 1962. The photograph shows the extensive site that was available here which resulted in a high valuation based on its redevelopment potential. ***Ian Nolan***

It is worth quoting this in full as it sets out the issues that were to dog the Association's relationship with BR for months and explains why many in BR were determined to sell to the council:

'I note, with some apprehension, from your letter of the 5th February, the further approach of the Westerham Branch Passengers' Association, to inveigle us into either leasing or selling to them the branch line.

There has, as you no doubt know, recently been a rash of Preservation Societies – indeed practically every closure now brings forth such Organisations – most of which are inevitably foredoomed to failure; and there are, in my opinion, very strong reasons, why the Westerham effort would similarly fail.

Firstly, such Societies depend almost entirely on voluntary labour, and receive considerable financial assistance from well wishers. Secondly, the successful Societies, such as the Talyllyn, Festiniog and Bluebell, operate primarily for the benefit of railway enthusiasts; and secondly for tourists: and their operations are confined to the Summer Season and Bank Holidays. Obviously, the more Societies there are the more limited the labour and money supply.

The mainstay of the Westerham branch was, of course,

the Commuter traffic, which would require a service every weekday, Winter and Summer alike; and I think it extremely unlikely voluntary labour will be available to work such a service, which would, of course, require starting up at 6.0am and not finishing until about 8.0pm. (Incidentally, the number of Commuters quoted is grossly inflated – there were about 140 Season Ticket Holders plus 14 Scholars with a total of about 170 all told travelling daily at the time of the T.U.C.C. Hearing.) Inevitably, therefore, the Society would have to have recourse to paid labour.

'Against the costs of this and the costs of running the Trains – even if one discounts any question of interest on capital, depreciation or rental charges, and, of course, maintenance – the Society could only be sure of getting some of the £2,700 per annum passenger receipts, applicable to the branch before closure.

'(Although there was a further £800 per annum from freight and miscellaneous receipts, this was mostly from Coal, and the 2 traders concerned have now moved away from the branch, the remaining traffic being dealt with by Road Zonal Motors.) The so-called "tourist" element was negligible – despite the provision of an hourly service on Saturdays and Sundays through much of the year; and Chartwell, etc., are much too far away from the line to influence passengers to rail. In any case, with the good rail/'bus connections at Sevenoaks with a half-hourly fast service to and from London this Summer, much of this would not, in any case, go back to a re-opened branch. The same remarks apply equally to the casual traffic which formerly passed from the branch via Dunton Green.

'It can be argued that the success or otherwise of such a society is of little interest to us: but it must be remembered that all the time we wait upon the Society to raise capital we cannot dispose of our redundant assets or rid ourselves of our statutory obligations – and the costs they entail. More important, however, we have of course, very substantially cut our savings, in order to subsidise the provision of additional 'bus services on route 403 – subvention is at present running at the rate of £8,700 per annum – in addition to which we sacrificed a further portion of the savings in the first year in an endeavour to secure the approval of the T.U.C.C. by continuing to issue Season Tickets at the branch rates, valid for travel without charge on the 403 'Bus Route.

'Therefore, if we permit the Society – and it is able to reopen the branch, we will be faced with the position

The goods shed and the entrance to the goods yard at Westerham. ***Ian Nolan***

of providing facilities elsewhere to replace the branch, which in theory would no longer be required, but which, in practice, we would find it extremely difficult to discontinue, bearing in mind that this is not a case of a new self-contained bus service, but of additional journeys on an existing route on which ordinary and ex rail passengers now mingle indiscriminately.

Accordingly, we would be faced with the position of incurring heavy costs for a replacement 'bus service, whilst at the same time losing the revenue formerly derived from the branch. To add to this by offering a sliding rental for traffic received from the Society via Dunton Green – 90% of which London Transport and/or ourselves would get anyway – would be foolish in the extreme.

'It was with the foregoing factors in mind that I declined the previous applications of the Society which you sent to me to deal with; and I remain firmly of the opinion that we should have no part of their proposals, particularly in view of our opportunity to dispose of most of the land to the County Council.'

It would be unfair, with the advantage of hindsight, to pick holes in Bolland's arguments about the prospects for railway preservation but his memo was misguided in other ways. Indeed, some of his arguments were contradictory: for example, the buses provided such a good service that he could not imagine why anyone would want to use a revived branch service but he worried that passengers might abandon the buses for a re-opened railway, leaving BR to pay for buses that ran empty.

Bolland clearly imagined that the Association intended to operate the branch exactly as BR had done. To be fair, it did set out to fulfil a transport function but, like the Bluebell and other preserved lines, it also intended to tap a new market that Bolland didn't understand. The idea of steam trains operated by volunteers appealed to the public. There is little excuse for Bolland's failure to notice this new market since the Bluebell had carried 15,000 passengers over three months in 1960, running at weekends only. The following year it carried 91,000 passengers in nine months. To put this in context, the Bluebell carried more passengers in a day than BR carried in a full week on the Westerham branch. Bolland claimed that the tourist potential of the Westerham line was negligible but the evidence was that steam railways drew in visitors in large numbers.

Bolland's concern that labour and money might be a problem as the number of societies grew is understandable. There were many in the emerging world of railway preservation who felt the same and wanted to limit the number of preserved railways for just that reason. However, if three railways in rural Wales could draw in sufficient support, one that was less than 20 miles from the heart of London must have stood an excellent chance of success.

Maybe more bitter reasons lay behind Bolland's opposition. His memo could almost be summarised as: 'I do not want these people to succeed where we failed'. It must have been a galling prospect and a sale to the council promised a quick and clean solution to the problem.

* * *

From the start there were three aspects of the Association's plans that were to cause problems. The first was that its revived commuter service would enable BR to dispense with its obligation to subsidise the replacement buses and it wanted BR to take this saving into account in setting the rent for the line. The idea of running a commuter trains is understandable, given that the scheme was promoted by those who opposed the line's closure, but it was never really a practical possibility. Furthermore, its commuter ambitions moved the scheme out of the arena of amateur operations. The second was the Association's insistence that it be allowed to lease the line, which stemmed from a lack of funds to buy the line outright. The last was its insistence that, because of the amount of traffic it could bring to the main line, BR should treat it as a partner and a fellow railway operator. All of these were to create stumbling blocks in the negotiations with BR.

* * *

Cobb was surprised to learn that Bolland had rebuffed the Association's first approach to BR when Ellison explained the background to him. Cobb let Bolland know that he understood his feelings and saw no difference between their intentions, only their approach. They should tease out more information about the Association's offer before turning it down.

What was for sale?

Hawkins produced an assessment of the branch assets ready for BR's meeting with the Association.

'The total area of the land, excluding station sites, is approximately 18 acres[86]. Very little of the track is level with and suitable for use in conjunction with the adjoining land. It is mainly in cutting or on embankments which vary in height but are generally about 15 feet in extremes.

'There are very many culverts involved despite which the adjoining land against embankments is usually waterlogged and the track drainage in cutting is not particularly efficient ... the track site is rather a liability and I cannot imagine that the adjoining owners will be keen on purchasing. There was no opportunity at the time of inspection to ascertain the extent of adjoining ownerships.

'Virtually all the adjoining land is agricultural, mainly pasture but small stretches are arable and woodland. There is no apparent development potentiality.

DUNTON GREEN (Branch platform and Goods Yard)
'It would be possible to split the Station buildings to give a Preservation Society the branch platform and the sidings and goods yard can be thrown in to give a total area of about 2¼ acres; there is, of course, a subway under the branch platform giving out on to a path leading to Dunton Green. Alternatively there is space to build a new platform on the curve leading in to the Station and it may be possible to do this without affecting the goods yard site or other railway property.

'In the triangle between the lines there is housing development but this is at a lower level. The goods yard may have other possible uses but there is none apparent.

CHEVENING HALT
'This consists merely of a short platform in a cutting with steps leading up to a public road. The surrounding area is agricultural on one side and extremely low density housing on the other. There is no apparent value to this site.

BRASTED
'The area of land available at Brasted totals some 5½ acres which includes the Station Masters house. A considerable part of the yard is at the moment occupied by a coal merchant and it must be found whether the Traffic Department have given any undertaking that he should be allowed to remain. The Station is an extremely isolated

Dr Richard Beeching, Chairman of the British Transport Commission, with the driver of 'P' class 0-6-0T No 323 at Sheffield Park on the Bluebell Railway on 1 April 1962, the day that the Bluebell started its second full season. Beeching lived at nearby East Grinstead. As far as we know, the Westerham association did not take advantage of the occasion to persuade him to agree to a lease of its line rather than an outright sale. *Trinity Mirror/Mirrorpix/Alamy Stock Photo*

position being over ½ mile from the village and ¼ mile from the commencement of the housing development in the area. In view of the nature of the site I can see little prospect of development save perhaps as agricultural industry, which is unlikely to need the full area, or perhaps dwellings for agricultural labourers.

WESTERHAM

'On the face of it the approximate 3½ acres of land here would lend itself to shops fronting on the main road with houses or light industry at the rear. The extreme south-western tip of the site would no doubt be of value to the County Council for road improvements. There is a timber yard and a builders merchant adjoining the site on the south-eastern side and housing on the northern side.

'In view of the Preservation Society's application, consideration was given to the practicability of splitting the site so as to give the Society the Station buildings and enough track and width for a runround and retaining the remainder for sale or lease for development purposes.

'If this is done it will completely prohibit economical development of the remainder on the south-east side for housing purposes as it would not be possible to have double frontages on the service road. It would not, however, prevent the expansion of the adjoining owners on to the site at this side if they are interested in expanding but, so far as I am aware, no application has been received from either of them. This would leave us with a frontage of 100 ft. on the northern side of the Station but a rather awkwardly shaped site to develop.

'The line from Westerham to just beyond Chevening Halt is in the Metropolitan green belt and in an area of high scenic value. There is no town map for this area and it will, therefore, be necessary to call and discuss with the Planning Officer what uses may be made of the land. An appointment has been made with the Divisional Planning Officer for Monday morning the 19th February (Mr. Munday at Chislehurst – Imperial 5561).

'Although it was understood from the Railway Preservation Society that they had seen the County Council who were prepared to waive their orbital road scheme in the event of the railway being re-opened it may be that we could split

Horsted Keynes station on 29 October 1961, the day after the Westerham branch closed; Bluebell Railway trains were allowed to enter the station for the first time rather than having to terminate at a makeshift platform a little to the south of the junction. On the left a 2-BIL electric unit waits to leave on a service to Seaford via Haywards Heath. On the right, the Bluebell train has SECR 'P' class 0-6-0Ts Nos 323 *Bluebell* and 27 *Primrose* at the front. LSWR '0415' class 4-4-2T No 488 and LBSCR 'A1X' 0-6-0T No 55 Stepney are at the rear. Joint BR/Bluebell use of the station was to last only two years. BR closed the link to Haywards Heath as from Monday 28 October 1963. ***Ian Nolan***

BR closed the electrified line from Haywards Heath to Horsted Keynes from Monday 28 October 1963, severing the Bluebell's link to the main line. On its final day the Bluebell ran the 'Brighton Blue Belle' railtour from Brighton to Horsted Keynes and back, hauled by two Bluebell locomotives, Class E4 No 473 Birch Grove and Class A1X No 55 *Stepney*. The train is seen here at Ardingly on the outward journey. It was to be the last through train to the Bluebell for nearly 50 years. ***Author's collection***

the Station sites more advantageously if the road proposal is adopted and I have, therefore, arranged an appointment on Monday the 19th February to call on Mr. Machonaci of the Roads Department, Kent County Council to ascertain their precise intentions.'[87] Meanwhile, the chief civil engineer came up with a figure of £41,500 for the permanent way, comprising:

Permanent Way:	9,570 yards at £3.10.0d per yard stock value	£33,495
Ballast:	12ft. width x 1ft deep = 12,760 cu.yds @ 10/-	£ 6,380
Other Assets:	Estimates prepared in 1951 indicated that recovery of the majority of assets would result in an expenditure of some £5,500 and these were therefore ignored. The remaining assets with a residual value of £2,200 were shown as recoverable at a cost of £1,045, a credit balance of £1,155 – giving a 1962 value of	£ 1,620

The BTC's chief solicitor thought it would be wise, before proceeding too far, to check the Ministry's attitude to the scheme. He was also concerned that plans to take over branch lines by preservation societies were on the increase and leasing lines, rather than selling them, could encourage too many Bluebell-type railways.

In a handwritten document, Mr J. H. C. Fulford of the estates team wrote that:

'If the Association are to be discouraged, it would seem that we must take a strong line and tell them that the Commission would only consider a straight sale. Some of the costs shown below might deter them . . .'

BR decides on tactics

On 22 February 1962, immediately before their meeting with the Association, Cobb and his team gathered to agree their tactics. The notes of the discussion make it clear that most of the team opposed the preservation scheme, wanting to 'discourage continued operation of the branch, with its attendant difficulties'. Cobb, though, possibly because he had not been involved in the closure saga, said that the Association should be treated the same as anyone who wanted to buy the line and were willing to pay the best price.

One obstacle, though, was the Association's idea of a sliding-scale lease, paying a reduced rent if more passengers were exchanged between branch and main line at Dunton Green. That created a problem for BR. If the reopened line took passengers off the buses, BR would have to increase the subsidy to make up the shortfall in fares. It would be doubly worse off – paying a larger subsidy and receiving a smaller lease payment. The Association's logic was understandable but it was not a sensible idea. (Perversely, it might have been better for the Association to have offered an increased rent if it carried more passengers, helping to compensate for any increased bus subsidy and encouraging BR to bring traffic to the line.)

Bolland did not think that the TUCC would release BR

A Westerham Branch Railway Passengers Association leaflet from the summer of 1962. It now includes the proposal to operate steam trains at weekends and bank holidays. Interestingly, it was printed by Ian Allan (Printing) Ltd. Author's collection

WESTERHAM RAILWAY

COMMUTERS • COMMUNITY • ENTHUSIASTS • TOURISTS

From Dunton Green (20 miles from London) to historic Westerham—through the beautiful upper Darenth Valley

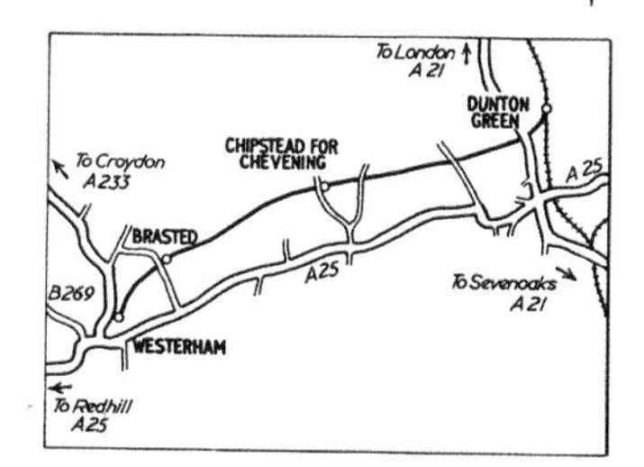

Steam Trains will operate at week—ends and Bank holidays

Diesel Railcars will provide a Commuter service from Monday to Friday

FOR FURTHER DETAILS OF
THE WESTERHAM BRANCH
Railway Passengers Association
WRITE TO THE MEMBERSHIP SECRETARY
R. Edwards
9 Marlborough Court
WESTERHAM
Kent

YOU CAN HELP US SAVE THIS BRANCH !

...OR CALL AT WESTERHAM STATION ANY WEEK—END

IAN ALLAN (PRINTING) LTD

from paying the bus subsidy because it would have no control over the Association's commuter services, which could be withdrawn at any time. The TUCC would also demand a similar level of service to that provided before closure and the Association might find it difficult to run trains from six in the morning until eight at night.

The problem with the bus subsidies might have been resolved with goodwill and determination if it had been dealt with quickly and BR might then have avoided the subsidy problems described in the previous chapter. Instead, it became an issue that was to undermine negotiations for the sale of the line.

Cobb was not prepared to give a firm price for the line but he was thinking of £60-70,000. The chief civil engineer had priced the track at £41,495 and the land had been valued at £22,000; £15,000 for the Westerham station site, £5,000 for Brasted and £2,000 for the rest of the trackbed. (BR had decided privately that, if it did consider a lease, the rent would be about £6,000 a year.)

To try to scare the Association, BR was to say that £13,700 needed to be spent on track maintenance and signalling by 1964. Cobb also intended to mention the council's interest in the line. BR, he said, had to weigh the importance of the road scheme from the national viewpoint against the Association's aspirations. This was nonsense as it was never BR's job to decide between national and local interests[88] – its duty was to obtain the best possible price when selling redundant assets so, in the absence of a compulsory purchase order, BR had to sell to whoever offered the highest price.

Meeting with the Association

Cobb opened the meeting with the Association by explaining that the discussion could only be exploratory. He listed the things that the Association would need to know and suggested that its members should ask questions as the meeting went on.

As the BR team had agreed, Cobb started by trying to deter the Association. He pointed out that the £700 cost of obtaining two Light Railway Orders would have to be paid by the Association and, before it would grant these, the Ministry of Transport would need to be satisfied that the line was safe and that it met the requirements laid down for the working of light railways. Fulford of the estates department then spoke about the liabilities that the Association would be taking on, including the maintenance of five overbridges and three underbridges, together with culverts, ditches, fencing and drainage, and cutting the banks to prevent fires spreading to adjoining property. There is an irony in the last point in that many pre-closure photographs show long lineside vegetation!

The Association said it hoped to use the branch platform at Dunton Green and to retain the connection with the main line to enable stock to be worked to and from the branch. In particular, it hoped to have coal delivered. Cobb said the connection could be kept if the Association was willing to bear the costs but it would not be possible to arrange the frequent transfers that coal deliveries would require. In addition, the branch side of the station would need to be segregated from the main station to allow proper ticket checks and security.

Figure 5.1: Breakdown of purchase price of Westerham branch (February 1962)

1	Value of Permanent Way, etc. (i) Permanent way – 9570 yards in main line and sidings (7907 yards serviceable @ £3-15-0 per yard stock value – total £29,651 – and 1663 yards @ scrap value of £2-6-0 per yard – total £3,825 – excluding labour). (ii) Ballast – (12 ft. width x 1 ft. depth) = 12,760 cubic yards @ 10/- per cubic yard (iii) Other assets – value of recoverable material	 £33,477 £6,380 £1,620
	Say	£41,477 **£41,000**
2	Value of Stations and Buildings No value as the platforms, buildings, etc. (apart from the Station House at Brasted – see item 3) would be demolished in connection with the development.	
3	Value of land with accent on development potential Westerham Station Site Approximately 4 acres; Housing discouraged – considered to be wrong position for shops. Local light industry which does not cause influx of labour acceptable.	£15,000
	Brasted Station Site Approximately 5½ acres; No form of housing, commercial or industrial development likely to be permitted. Allowing for road on track site, the decontrolled Station House could be used as small holding or residence with 3 acres.	£5,000
	Track site to be sold to Kent County Council for highway Approximately 32 acres @ £70 per acre	£2,200
	Track site to be sold to adjoining owners Approximately 15 acres @ £20	£300
	Dunton Green Platform	£1,000
	There are proposals for letting part of the Goods Yard at Dunton Green, but should the negotiations be abortive the above amount should be increased by a further sum of approximately £3,000. The uses considered for the above valuation are based on suggestions made by the Divisional Planning Officer, subject to approval by the appropriate Planning Committee.	**£23,500**
4	Estimated cost of recovery Bridges, Platforms, Buildings, etc Permanent Way Less	 £4,600 £5,400 £10,000
	Net total	**£54,500**

Notes
The sum of £2 6 0 per yard for scrap is at current market prices (Mr. Church – Supplies and Contracts Manager's Office). In view of this the amount of £3 10 0 average referred to in the Chief Civil Engineer's letter of [blank] 1962, has been increased to £3 15 0 per yard for stock value of serviceable track and the total amended to £33,477 accordingly. Mr. Mainprice (Chief Civil Engineer's Office) advises that £3 15 0 per yard for serviceable track is realistic. Messrs. Mainprice and Church advised that the figures were required at BTC and they confirm that the amounts would stand up to detailed investigation.
Information from Mr. Hawkins, Branch Line Surveyor.
See Estates and Rating Surveyor's letter of [blank]

The Association explained its suggestion of a sliding-scale rental but BR rejected this as likely to lead to reduced bus receipts and a further loss to BR. In any case, BR had to get the quickest possible return on its disused assets and therefore an outright sale was likely to be required.

The Association asked whether, if they operated the branch, their fares would be governed by those of the LT bus services as the branch was within the London Passenger Transport Area, but they were told that they would have to make their own enquiries on that point[89].

Cobb voiced his concern that the Association would have difficulty because of its reliance on voluntary subscriptions and labour. It might feel positive about the potential of the branch but BR had already found that, despite its efforts, it had not been possible to run economical services. There was no certainty that the Association would succeed in perpetuity. The Association challenged this, saying that combined visits to Chartwell, the Wolfe home, and other local places of historical interest would prove a great attraction to the public.

Cobb then explained how the council wanted parts of the formation. Mr Gray, the Association chairman, said that they had been told that it was likely to be 20-30 years before the road would be constructed, in which case it could run beside the railway as previously intended. Cobb said that this was not what they had been told by council officers and they would get in touch with the council again.

Cobb also said that if demolition was to be delayed, BR would expect the Association to start making some form of payment by June 1962 at the latest.

The meeting ended with agreement that the Association would tell BR of its intentions as soon as possible after its public meeting on 7 April. In the meantime BR would contact the council about its road plans and would think again about leasing the line and retaining the connection at Dunton Green[90]. Meanwhile, the Association would find out from the TUCC whether it would be allowed to take over BR's obligation to provide a commuter service.

The value of the line

Behind the scenes, BR carried out a more detailed valuation of the branch and its assets as shown in Figure 5.1.

The sum of £260 per yard for scrap is at current market prices (Mr. Church – Supplies and Contracts Manager's Office). In view of this the amount of £3100 average referred to in the Chief Civil Engineer's letter of [blank] 1962, has been increased to £3150 per yard for stock value of serviceable track and the total amended to £33,477 accordingly. Mr. Mainprice (Chief Civil Engineer's Office) advises that £3150 per yard for serviceable track is realistic. Messrs. Mainprice and Church advised that the figures were required at BTC and they confirm that the amounts would stand up to detailed investigation.

Following the meeting, the Association told Cobb that it was not only writing to the TUCC but was also contacting the council about its proposal to buy part of the railway. This seems to have startled BR; maybe the Association realised that there was a cosy relationship between some in BR and Kent's roads department and that it would be better if it sorted things out through its own contacts at County Hall. As if to confirm this, the Southern's estates department wrote to their counterparts in the Kent roads department. Far from being a simple enquiry as to the council's intentions, the letter was virtually an ultimatum. It was also more revealing than perhaps its author intended:

'With reference to your letter of the 14th December and the recent call by my representative, I enclose herewith a plan showing by green verge the extent of the Commission's property on the Westerham Branch.

'I shall be glad if you will return the plan to me marking on the area of land in which your Council is interested in connection with the South Orbital Road. As you are no doubt aware there is a Railway Society wishing to purchase the whole of the line and I shall, therefore, be glad to hear from you at the earliest possible date as to whether your Council is prepared to proceed with the purchase in the near future or whether the proposed acquisition will not be for some time.

'It is also understood that you are now interested in a greater area of Westerham Station than contemplated in our correspondence of June and July last and I shall be glad if you will indicate this on the plan and confirm that your Council wish to proceed forthwith in this case.'

This letter shows that BR's estates team and the council had been discussing the sale of the line since at least June 1961. In June 1961, we need to remember, it was still the council's policy to fight the closure; the CTCC had only just recommended the line should be kept open; and other parts of the Southern Region were working on plans to electrify and resignal the line. Contrast this with the reply BR sent to an enquiry that it received in August 1961, after closure had been agreed. Fenella Lampshades had told BR that, if the line did close, it wanted to buy part of the Westerham station site to expand its premises. BR's reply followed the official line approved by the Southern's general manager. The branch right of way was to be retained in case of a change of policy on building in the Green Belt and nothing regarding disposal could be arranged until the line had actually closed.

So, were the dealings between the Southern's estates department and the council's roads department a case of two maverick departments pursuing their own unofficial agenda or were they evidence of the conspiracy that so many have alleged over the years? We will probably never know for sure but relations between the two teams were close. It was as if the railway estates team was acting hand-in-hand with the council's roads department.

The Question of Leasing

Soon after the meeting with the Association, BR's Southern Area Board considered the question of leasing and Cobb was asked to write to Major-General Wansbrough-Jones, the Secretary-General at the BTC, seeking his views. However, far from simply sounding him out, Cobb pressed his own views on Wansbrough-Jones:

'This branch line, as you are aware, was closed on and from the 30th October last and an application has been received from the Westerham Branch Railway Passengers' Association to rent it with all its assets in order that they may re-introduce railway services.

'They are of course encouraged in their attempts to take over the branch, by the leasing of the "Bluebell" line and similar precedents on other regions and it is most probable that other Societies will be formed as further branch closures are effected. In fact, another Society has already applied to rent the Kent & East Sussex branch line which was closed on and from the 12th June, 1961.

'Each case has of course to be examined on its merits but there is no doubt that we shall run into difficulties if we lease branches to Societies whose viability is open to question, as, in the likely event of failure to maintain a lease arrangement, the reversion to the Commission of the branch and effects will leave us with a serious and costly liability with the deterioration of bridges, etc., whereas at present we have an opportunity in the case of the Westerham branch of obtaining a capital return on our assets of some £60,000[91].

'If more of these Societies are allowed to lease branch lines, their competition with each other and their reliance on voluntary subscriptions and labour will inevitably weaken their initial expectations.

'The Westerham line is quite different in character from the Bluebell line and we feel that we should insist on outright sale. Before informing the Society of our decision, I should be glad to know that I can take it that the Region will have the Commission's support to the stand they wish to take.'

Wansbrough-Jones spotted what was going on and was quick to reply:

'I should be glad if you would let me know precisely what you mean by saying that at present you have an opportunity in the case of the Westerham branch of obtaining a capital return on your assets of some £60,000. Does that

By August 1962 the WVRA had begun to rent the station building at Westerham as its headquarters. BR had removed all the poster boards after closure so a crudely painted 'Westerham Railway' on the front wall of the building was all that marked its new 'ownership'. The young onlooker, dressed in his school uniform, seems a bit puzzled by what was going on. ***Ian Nolan***

represent the sale value of the displaced assets or what precisely is covered by the sum? If it does represent the value of the assets to be acquired by the Westerham Branch Railway Passengers' Association, then the sort of rental we should require would be about £4,000 a year, plus perhaps some arrangement for safeguarding the continuance of central maintenance.

'We should also want adequate assurances that the rent would be paid.'

Cobb, in turn, responded:

'With reference to your letter of 2 March, I confirm that the figure of £60,000 represents the sale value of the displaced assets and land which comprise the Westerham branch line. The value of the permanent way material is estimated at some £40,000, and the balance is the land value, some of which has development potential. Our estimate of the rent is somewhat higher than yours, being of the order of £5/6,000 per annum.

'My point is that although the Bluebell railway has been financially successful so far, it is obvious that if more of these Societies are set up, they will be in competition with each other for the limited number of people who are interested in this sort of activity and there will consequently be a grave danger that they will be unable to meet their commitments which will involve us in difficulties and extra costs.

'I think it would be wise to take a firm line with this Society and insist on an outright sale. Nevertheless, we shall have to explore their financial position further before taking a final decision.'

A week or two later the matter assumed greater urgency when Dr Beeching accepted an invitation to open the Bluebell Railway's 1962 season. Fearing that the Westerham people might use the occasion to ambush him and get him to commit to a lease for the line, Hopkins urged Wansbrough-Jones to brief Beeching about the situation. (He also wanted Beeching to know that they were about to announce plans to close the electrified Haywards Heath to Horsted Keynes link, which would cut off rail access to the Bluebell line[92].) Wansbrough-Jones replied that a paper on the Westerham case and the subject of leasing lines to preservation societies would be submitted to the BTC.

One step forward, two steps back

In the meantime, the Association wrote to the TUCC about the bus subsidy. The letter argued that once the line had been reopened and the requirements of the commuters – who, it said, were all Association members – were adequately met, BR should be relieved of its obligation to subsidise the replacement buses. It asked the TUCC to give the necessary assurances to the Southern Region's general manager.

Activity at Westerham on 5 August 1962. The lady in the foreground, busy cutting back the weeds, is Mrs Vera Bryan from Halstead. *Photo by National Media Museum/Daily Herald Archive/SSPL/Getty Images*

The reply from the TUCC, when it came, was less than helpful – it could only consider matters referred to it by BR. However, the Association refused to take such a dismissal lying down. Gray telephoned the TUCC and was assured that permission to withdraw the additional bus services between Westerham and Dunton Green would not be unreasonably withheld provided that the Association was able to provide an adequate rail service.

There was bad news, though, from another direction in the form of a reply from the county surveyor to BR's letter. He revealed that the council was prepared to open negotiations for parts of the branch, including the whole of the Brasted site, and would proceed with the purchase as soon as terms were agreed. The council was also thinking of acquiring more of Westerham station than previously intended – half the site – for an improved junction with the proposed new town bypass although details of the scheme had yet to be prepared[93]. It is as if the council was trying to justify taking as much of the railway land as possible. An unknown BR officer noted: 'I think things are going our way.'

Public meeting

BR clearly hadn't learned much from its long drawn-out closure battle – the Association was not about to give up! The notice advising supporters of the public meeting was upbeat about its progress and stressed the line's potential as a preserved railway.

On 5 April, two days before the public meeting, Gray phoned BR asking about the likely cost of the line but Fulford was unable to go beyond the £60-70,000 assessment given at the Waterloo meeting. However, while it prevaricated with the Association, the estates department acted far more positively with the council. In a memo dated 6 April, Tunbridge reported that:

'Further to my letter of the 21st March, I enclose herewith a plan shewing by pink colour the area required by the Kent County Council and copies of my recent correspondence with the Council. I am asking the Chief Civil Engineer and the Line Manager for their comments on the sale of this branch in the usual way and, in particularly, relating to this sale. When these comments are received I intend writing [to] the County Council quoting terms making it clear that the arrangement is subject to confirmation by the Commission.'

A week later, Mr J. W. Cowell of the Line Traffic Manager's office reported on the Association's public meeting:

'In addition to Mr. Gray (Chairman) and other officers of the Association, the Chairmen of the Westerham and Chipstead Parish Councils were on the platform, together with certain other persons representing various Preservation Organisations such as the Bluebell Society.

'The local press were also represented, together with the "Sunday Express". The hall was well filled – about 150 people all told - mostly teenage railway enthusiasts, together with a smattering of older men and what were obviously housewives. So far as I could ascertain only one commuter was actually present.

'... Extracts from messages of goodwill from the following persons and organisations were then read out, although for various reasons none of them were, apparently, able to attend in person: Sir Charles Pym of the C.T.C.C.
Mr. J. C. Chambers of the C.T.C.C.
Mr. John Rodgers, M.P.
Mr. Fenner Brockway, M.P.
Jeremy Thorpe, M.P.
Mr. E. Lubbock, M.P.
Sevenoaks R.D.C.
Also the Bluebell and Kent and East Sussex Preservation Societies.

'Westerham, Chipstead, Brasted and Chevening Parish Councils also expressed more or less unqualified support for the Society, although the last two mentioned Councils were not actually represented at the Meeting.

'Mention was made of the fact that a deputation had visited the Kent County Council in connection with their proposal to make use of part of the branch for the South Orbital Road and according to the information given to the meeting, the Chairman of the General Purposes Committee and the Road Committee had said that the Council were prepared to stand aside if the Society were successful in restarting a service on the branch. An approach had also been made to the London Area T.U.C.C. who apparently had no objection provided the Society could run a service, although it was not clear if the Consultative Committee had actually agreed to withdrawal of the additional buses.

'Subsequently Mr. Gray outlined the basis of the service they hope to provide, consisting of (1) a steam service for approximately 9 months of the year on a volunteer basis by enthusiasts for enthusiasts, tourists, hikers and the like and (2) a diesel rail-car service for business travellers and the local community as a whole, 5 days a week throughout the year. Apparently it was envisaged that there would be 8 trips each way morning and evening.

'The following estimates of annual receipts from operation of the branch were given to the meeting:

	£
Commuter traffic (180 season ticket holders plus 20 casuals per day, i.e. 200 passengers at an average fare of 1/6d per person return on 5 days a week basis)	3,750
Tourists, Visitors, etc. (100,000 journeys in 9 months operation at an average fare of 2/-)	8,000
Subscriptions from Society members	1,500
Commission as BR agency (!)	500
Bookstall	250
Miscellaneous	250
	14,250

		£
Initial Outlay Rolling stock	-2 Diesel R/Cs at £600 2 H.Class 0-4-4 T. Locos 4 coaches at £200 2 Brakevans	1,200 3,000 800 100
First year operating costs Staff	2 guards 2 motormen 2 platelayers Manager and Asst. Manager (latter part time) Coal Fuel oil (£2 per day) Track maintenance Servicing of diesel railcars Administration, also Lt. Rly Order and insurance, etc Provision for depreciation on R/Cars Lease from B.Rlys (!) Total inc. other misc.items	 2,000 1,000 1,500 600 400 150 1,400 2,000 2,500 12,250

'In the questions from the floor that followed a certain amount of criticism was directed at some of the figures. For example, one person considered that if the Western Region were prepared to sell railcars at £600 each then these could be little better than scrap.

'Finally Mr. Gray made it eminently clear that the Association desired to lease and not purchase the line. As soon as a decision is received from British Railways it will invite financial support – probably at a further public meeting.

'At this point I left as the remainder of the time was to be devoted to a film show of the Bluebell Line. Before departing I promised Mr. Gray that a reply would be sent to the Society on the question of a lease or sale as soon as possible, At question time one person had also questioned the necessity for a Light Railway Order in view of the absence of any public road crossings and I promised that we would confirm whether in fact any such Order would be necessary.'

Council withdraws

Within a few days of the Association's meeting BR received a letter from Bowdler, the Kent county surveyor:

'With reference to our recent correspondence regarding the possible acquisition of parts of the disused Westerham Branch line by the County Council for highway purposes, I am informed that further endeavours are being made by the Westerham Branch Railway Passengers' Association to secure the re-opening of the line under private ownership.

'The County Council, although interested in the acquisition of parts of the line for highway purposes in the event of it being permanently closed as a railway, has given an assurance to the Association that it will not oppose the Association's proposal to re-open the line, and that the negotiations with the British Transport Commission will not be conducted so as to prejudice in any way the Association's endeavours.

'I have therefore been asked to make it clear that the present enquiries are exploratory only and that the County Council would not wish to enter into any definite negotiations until the outcome of the Westerham Railway Users' Association's representations is known.'

Pressure had obviously been brought to bear. However, this encouraging step was negated by news from the BTC, which had decided that disused lines were no longer to be leased to preservation societies. Wansbrough-Jones wrote to all the Regional general managers, telling them to implement the decision, largely repeating the arguments originally put forward by Cobb. Because of this decision, it was to be 1968 before another ex-BR line was re-opened as a preserved line[94]. Even the Bluebell faced difficulties when its five-year lease expired in 1965 and BR was reluctant to renew it.

The news must have come as a disappointment to the Association but it was still not put off. Indeed, the Association replied by asking if it could rent Westerham station for its headquarters. Cobb demurred from a decision on that until

Two WVRA volunteers – sadly their names weren't recorded – patching the corrugated iron roof of the station canopy at Westerham. ***Photo by National Media Museum/Daily Herald Archive/SSPL/Getty Images***

the Association's intentions were clearer.

The Association sent a newsletter headlined 'Growth and Not Decay' to members and supporters at the end of April 1962, telling them of its steady progress. Membership was approaching the 400 mark and was expected to reach 1,000 by the end of June. It included details of the Association's financial plans and said that progress would be reported to another public meeting on 17 May.

May 1962 – an eventful month

May 1962 was to be an eventful month for the Association. It opened with two high-level meetings on the 2nd, the first with Cobb at Waterloo and the second with Mr Hilton Gillender, an assistant secretary at the Ministry of Transport.

With BR, Gray voiced the Association's disappointment that it was insisting on an outright sale of the line but Cobb pointed out that the ruling did not apply only to the Westerham scheme but to all future disposals of disused lines.

Gray admitted that the Association would have difficulty raising the capital and, in any case, BR would derive considerable income from its activities – he estimated £25,000 a year – so that BR would recover the equivalent of the purchase price in three years. Cobb was surprised by the figures but agreed to have a look at them. Even so, he thought it unlikely that BR would change its mind about a lease and, if the profits forecast by the Association were so great, it should have no difficulty in raising a loan.

Gray said that if the Association did not lease the line or couldn't raise the money to buy it, BR would find itself paying an increased bus subsidy. Cobb retorted that the subsidy was fixed at £8,700 and added the threat that BR planned to invite tenders for the demolition of the line. It sounds to have been an ill-tempered meeting with little progress being made.

Later that day, Gray and his colleagues explained to Gillender that BR had changed its policy on leasing but, if they hoped that the Ministry might bring pressure to bear on BR, they were to be disappointed. Gillender made it clear that this was a matter between the Association and BR and told them that the Ministry's only involvement would be in giving legal effect to the transfer of the line – by a Light Railway Order if the Bluebell precedent was followed. The Railway Inspectorate would also be involved as far as safety requirements were concerned.

The Association also raised questions about the South Orbital Road and the bridge that would be needed to take the Sevenoaks Bypass over the line. They told Gillender that they had discussed the matter with the county council, describing it as being sympathetic and willing to step aside in favour of the railway proposal. Once again, if the Association was hoping for support in keeping the road interests at bay, it does not seem to have been forthcoming, although the Association afterwards claimed that the Ministry appeared to be impressed with its scheme.

Meanwhile, the Southern's estates department had not given up hope of selling at least part of the branch to the council. Tunbridge wrote asking if the council wanted to continue with the purchase of part of the Westerham station area for road improvements, whether or not the Association's scheme proceeded. The council replied that the land was still required and asked BR for a price.

Having failed to persuade it to offer a lease, the Association asked BR for a firm and realistic price for purchase, saying that the original valuation was excessive and that for the track particularly so. The branch ran within the Green Belt so it was unlikely that the planners would allow the land to be used for development. The Association also wanted to know if it would be possible to defer payment, perhaps on a hire purchase basis. BR agreed to look at its valuation in more detail but in a memo to the general manager, Tunbridge simply reiterated the previous figures. Now, though, Dunton Green yard was excluded from the deal as the Line Traffic Manager had plans for it – according to a handwritten note, it was to be let to Cerebos, the salt manufacturer.

In the meantime, the civil engineer had revised the cost of recovering the redundant assets to £6,900 for the permanent way and £5,940 for bridges, buildings, and platforms but he could not see why he should deduct the cost of recovery from the price asked – the Association wanted the branch as a going concern and should pay for the assets as they stood. This was silly: whatever its book value, the redundant track was worth nothing to BR where it was, nor had BR asked the Association to pay the value of the land as it stood – it insisted that its development potential be taken into account.

When Cobb replied to the Association he was not encouraging. Although BR had privately revalued the line at £54,000, he insisted that the original estimate of between £60,000 and £70,000 was realistic, taking into account the condition of the permanent way and the value of the land. He also made it plain that BR would not allow deferred payments.

* * *

The Association revised its financial plans in time for its public meeting on 17 May. BR went over the figures with a fine toothcomb to try to discredit them. It queried the wages figures, comparing them with its own rates of pay, and it noted that the Association allowed only £2,500 a year for rent, compared with BR's expectation of £5-6,000. It felt that the £150 a year estimate for railcar servicing was 'optimistic' and there was no provision for major overhauls. The £400 a year allowed for track maintenance was little more than BR claimed to spend each year on slips, while £1,000 income from membership subscriptions would require 8,000 members at 2/6 a year.

Mr A. Andrews attended the meeting on behalf of BR and reported back afterwards:

'I attended the further meeting of the Association held at Westerham on Thursday evening the 17th May. As previously, the Hall was well filled with about 200 people present – mostly locals.

'Those present were informed that they had been advised that the purchase price would be between £60,000 and £70,000 but it was clear that this was quite unacceptable and their own valuation was in the region of £20,000/£30,000 inclusive. It was suggested that the Minister of Transport should be asked to intervene, if the Commission's figure was not lowered to something more in keeping with their own valuations.

'One lady in the audience queried the right of the Commission to sell the land, as this had originally been given by people such as Lord Stanhope.

'However, it was quite clear that the Association still desired to lease the line and not purchase – it being felt that, the Association's financial considerations apart, such an arrangement would mean that the Commission would still have a vested interest in the success of the Society.

'Three possible ways of approach were mentioned

(a) Lease at a price of £2,250 per annum for a limited number of years.

(b) Lease with subsequent purchase at £20,000 after 5 years,

(c) Purchase with similar guarantees to those given in the case of the Bluebell Line.

'At the conclusion of the meeting it was left that the Association should make a further approach to the Commission on the foregoing lines, as soon as possible.'

As a result, the Association sought a meeting with Wansbrough-Jones at BTC headquarters to discuss the economics of the scheme and BR's policy on the disposal of closed lines. Before meeting Gray, Wansbrough-Jones asked Cobb to brief him on the situation but reassured him that any sale would be dealt with by the Southern Region. However, he suggested to Cobb that it would be a good idea to deduct the cost of track lifting, which BR would incur in any case. It was the first glimmer of hope in the negotiations and the suggestion came none too

The branch side of Dunton Green station in January 1965. Fresh ballast seems to have been applied to the track, perhaps in connect with the use of the goods yard for delivering stone for the Sevenoaks bypass. Iain Whitlam

soon. The Association's public meeting had been widely publicised and newspaper headlines were critical of BR's unyielding stand on the price[95].

Wansbrough-Jones also asked Cobb for a more detailed breakdown of the purchase price, bearing in mind the far lower price that BR had charged the Bluebell. The figures would be challenged and he wanted the estimate to be as sound as possible, broken down into:
*the permanent way less the cost of its recovery;
*the value of the stations and their fittings;
*and the actual value of the property.

When Cobb asked the estates department how the Bluebell price had been worked out, it turned out that the £34,000 comprised the value of the land plus a percentage (based on mileage) of the highest tender received for the scrap material on the whole line from Horsted Keynes to Culver Junction, with annual rent calculated at 6.6 per cent of the total purchase price:

Permanent way (Sheffield Park to Horsted Keynes = 39% of whole) £23,460
Five underline bridges £2,000
The pumping plant and tank house at Sheffield Park £120
Material not included in tender such as ballast, fencing, etc. £1,920
Land Horsted Keynes to Sheffield Park plus station house £3,400
Four cottages (occupied) at Sheffield Park £1,600
Sheffield Park station buildings, platforms, etc. £1,500

Even when Horsted Keynes station was later added to the deal, the total only came to £43,500, and that included two station houses and 10 cottages! In contrast, BR continued to demand £60,000 or more for the Westerham branch. Excluding the Westerham station site, BR wanted £8,500 for the land, most of it in the Green Belt. For the Bluebell BR had only asked £6,500 for all the land including a house and four cottages.

Meeting at the BTC

The meeting between the Association and Wansbrough-Jones at the BTC took place on 4 June 1962. Gray opened the proceedings by saying that they continued to seek a lease of the branch – they appreciated that the BTC's policy was to sell but the Westerham case justified an exception. They intended to operate a regular daily service which would complement the service run by BR. They could

Dunton Green goods yard in January 1965. The yard was being used for the delivery and storage of roadstone for use on the construction of the Sevenoaks bypass. The third siding in the yard (nearest to camera) has been lifted, which implies that these are the original sidings and that they were not removed after closure and then reinstated as some have suggested. ***Iain Whitlam***

Approaching the London Road bridge at Dunton Green from the junction in January 1965. The pedestrian footbridge is still in place beside the road bridge and there are allotments on the cutting side behind the houses in Lennard Road. The descent at 1 in 73 to the road bridge is clear and so too is the straight run of the line that continues all the way to Chevening. ***Iain Whitlam***

operate the service more cheaply by employing retired staff and volunteers but they wanted BR to have a financial interest in the branch to ensure that it would maintain the service to Dunton Green. The Association stressed how its venture would be of financial benefit to BR.

Gray argued that BR's valuation of the line was unrealistic. Wansbrough-Jones agreed that the Association's surveyor and engineer should discuss this with the Southern but he insisted that the track was realistically valued. However, he was prepared to deduct the cost of demolition and he accepted that the station platforms and buildings were only of value to an operational railway. As far as the land was concerned, the valuable part consisted of about 4 acres at Westerham and 5½ acres at Brasted. The value of this was arguable – the planners had given different information to the Association and BR – so he suggested that BR and the Association should approach the authorities together.

Wansbrough-Jones emphasised that BR's policy was now to sell disused branch lines. If the Association thought it could operate the service profitably, there was no reason why it could not raise the capital to buy the branch but Mr. Curran, the Association's secretary, suggested that a three-year lease would enable it to prove its ability to operate the service and make it easier to raise capital[96]8. It was agreed that the Association would submit its estimates of costs and receipts to Cobb, who would arrange meetings with appropriate BR officers. They would comment on the figures before sending them on to the BTC. He offered to meet the Association's representatives again when the figures had been reviewed. BR would leave track in place until 1 August but demolition would start during the summer unless agreement was reached.

Finances

On 17 June Gray sent Cobb the Association's revised estimates of its initial outlay and income and expenditure for the first four years. Once again, Gray argued the substantial benefits to BR of the scheme and asked BR to value the line on that basis. The Association intended to use the line as a railway and it was wrong for BR to put an industrial value on the land. His suggested lease cost of

Chevening Halt in January 1965. The track has been lifted through the halt but remains in place beyond. The initial infilling was supposedly to allow heavy construction plant to cross the line without having to use the nearby bridge which could not have taken the weight.

£2,250 was based on the amount paid by the Bluebell line for a similar length of railway.

With 160 regular commuters and 10 casual passengers a day the Association estimated its annual weekday income as £3,750. Cobb was doubtful. Only 105 people were still taking advantage of the season ticket concession, so many former branch passengers had made other arrangements. Once passengers had found another means of travel, they rarely came back, he added. In any case, the commuter traffic would bring BR nothing beyond what it already earned.

Gray had calculated that BR must have carried 44,000 weekend passengers a year on the Westerham line before it closed and he reckoned that the Association could increase this to 66,000, bringing in revenue of £8,000 a year. Cobb disputed this. He said that BR carried no more than 8,000 weekend passengers a year and, even if the Association doubled this, the total would be only 16,000 as against the Association's estimate of 66,000. At the proposed fare of 2/6 a head, the revenue would be only £2,000.

Cobb also disputed the Association's £500 estimate of the commission it would earn from a British Railways ticket agency[97]9. This not only assumed that BR would grant such an agency but also that it would give commission on selling season tickets, which was not its practice. The Association would have had to sell nearly £7,000 of ordinary BR tickets a year to reach its target. Similarly, the £250 which it expected to earn from handling parcels was unrealistic. BR had earned only £180 a year from parcels before closure and that traffic was now handled by the road-based collection and delivery service.

Benefits for BR

Gray explained how BR would gain almost £35,000 a year from selling the line to the Association, thanks to rent of £2,250, savings of £8,700 from ending the bus subsidy, and income of £24,000 a year from weekend passengers travelling to the line. BR had a choice, according to Gray. It could sell the line to someone else for a one-off £60,000 or it could lease or sell the line to the Association at lower cost with on-going benefits of £35,000 a year. Gray's claims about these benefits were to be at the heart of the Association's negotiations with BR over the following months and were to bring them to the point of breakdown, so it is important to understand how he worked out his figures – and got them so badly wrong. It was an unhelpful episode that only served to undermine confidence in the Association's professionalism and its financial competence. Gray's 44,000 weekend passengers a year represented an average of over 500 passengers a day (including winter Saturdays). Such a high figure would surely have been mentioned during the closure proceedings as it was completely at variance with BR's traffic census results. These showed that the passenger total for a good weekend (Saturday and Sunday together) was some 200 passengers. Even if that figure was taken as an average and applied to all weekends for nine months, it gave a total of less than 8,000 passengers a year.

Gray later tried to justify his figure in a letter to BR dated 8 August 1962. It was based on his muddled belief (his source for this figure is unclear) that BR's total earnings from the branch amounted to £9,000 a year. Of this, £3,500 came from weekday commuters, so the remaining £5,500 must have come from weekend traffic. At a return fare of 2/6 each, this gave 44,000 passengers.

Gray suggested that BR had failed to take account of weekend passengers travelling to special events, such as Chartwell open days (which were actually held on weekdays). Using figures which he said were obtained from former station staff at Westerham and Dunton Green and event organisers, Gray claimed that 3,000 passengers travelled on the branch to attend the Whit Monday Westerham Gala Day – that would have been an average of 200 passengers on every train, from first to last. His claims for other special events were similarly optimistic but, even so, he could only account for 18,000 of the huge gap between his and BR's figures. Gray then compounded matters by insisting that every one of these 44,000 visitors would travel to Dunton Green by train, the vast majority from central London, and their fares on the main line would earn BR £24,000.

The whole thing was a mess. BR dismissed his claim – 'All rubbish, most will come by car!' said a handwritten note added to the foot of the letter. Looking at the busy car parks at most heritage railways today, even those that have rail connections, it is hard to disagree.

One in ten weekend visitors might have arrived by train but they would have brought BR revenue of no more than £3,000 a year. It undermined the whole basis on which Gray sought to have the line valued and, in particular, his justification for a lease.

On the other hand, Gray did underestimate the number of weekend passengers that a preserved Westerham line would attract and he did the Association no favours by basing its likely traffic on BR's numbers. It would have been better if he had used the experience of the Bluebell Railway to forecast Westerham's weekend traffic.

Cobb accepted that the appeal of a steam service was hard to estimate but he argued that the Westerham line would have to compete with the Bluebell – and the K&ESR scheme if that came about – all within 25 miles of each other[98]0.

His assertion was based, of course, on BR's lacklustre efforts at running and promoting the weekend service on the branch. Although the Westerham line would have been in competition with the Bluebell, both would have had their own catchment areas. In its first year, the Bluebell achieved an average 5,000 weekend passengers a month during the peak of the season. During its second year it doubled this number during a longer season. There is no reason why Westerham should not have matched these traffic levels after a year or so, even allowing for some competition between the two lines.

Unhelpful stance

Gray's negotiating stance did not help at all. BR was totally opposed to his concept of a 'partnership' between itself and the Association while his insistence that the Association should be sold the line cheaply as a railway operator flew in the face of BR's need to get the best possible price for its assets. His pressure for a lease was

Track in the Combe Bank area between Chevening and Brasted. Despite the fact that the track was only relaid in 1958, by 1965 much of the ballast had already vanished into the Gault Clay beneath the formation and the cutting is waterlogged. *Iain Whitlam*

based partly on his unrealistic estimates of the benefits that BR would gain from the re-opened line and partly on the fact, which he admitted, that the Association would have difficulty raising funds to buy the line.

We do not know how much of this was personal to Gray. It is clear that he was wedded to the idea of the line being run as a public transport operation and comparisons that he was to make between the nationalised BR and private enterprise (see page 113) suggest that there may have been a political aspect to his approach2[99]. He could also be belligerent when he did not get his way. Neither of these things can have endeared him to those with whom he was trying to negotiate. Over the following months there were signs that more rational views were brought to bear but by then the damage had been done.

On 4 July 1962 Association representatives met the Southern's estates department to discuss the valuation of the line. Gray once again insisted that the Association had to be regarded as a potential railway operator. Cobb had told the estates department to reject this argument, insisting that BR must take account of the development value of the land. When Gray said that the land should be valued as it would be by the District Valuer, BR had to explain to him that even the District Valuer had to take account of open market property values. It also turned out that the Association was unaware that the purchase included Brasted station house and grounds, which it did not want. BR insisted that the sale must be for the whole of the land, buildings and materials. Not surprisingly, the meeting made no progress.

As far as BR was concerned, there was little likelihood of bridging the gap while the Association refused to accept the basis of BR's valuations. Meanwhile, Gray placed the blame for the deadlock squarely on the failure of the Southern Region to accept his viewpoint. In a letter to BR dated 10 July he stressed, yet again, his four 'wishes' – though they read more like demands:

'(a) to be treated as potential railway operators and partners and NOT as land developers, speculators or land agents.

(b) valuation to be made or calculated as a whole and not piecemeal, since we sought to lease or purchase the line, buildings and land of a railway system as a railway system.

(c) account to be taken of the business proposition which would yield extra traffic revenue to Southern Region of about £35,000 per annum, and

(d) regard to be given to the realistic and planning position at the WESTERHAM end of the Line (set in the centre of the "Green Belt") rather than the hypothetical, possible or probable potential which might be enforced by Parliamentary Statute through the Ministry of Transport.

Brasted hardly looks its best on a bleak day in January 1965 but it is surprisingly intact more than three years after closure. The platelayers' hut, the lamp hut, the old LBSCR van body, and the loading gauge survive. The station master's house is in the distance. The signal box was removed in the 1920s but the timber crossing that led to it across the track remained some 40 years later.

Vandals get everywhere, even to a remote location like Brasted. The station stands empty in January 1965 after the WVRA had abandoned its attempt to reopen the line. *Iain Whitlam*

'If, therefore, the Region will stretch to their lowest or minimum point (lease or purchase) we, on our part, will stretch to our maximum or highest offer in the hope that we shall meet to mutual advantage – recognising that we also seek the maximum public interest – in providing revenue to the Region as well as a public transport service for which there is a very strong demand.'

Gray was intransigent and over the following few weeks he repeatedly demanded that BR respond to the points raised in this letter while BR insisted that they had all been answered. It was impasse.

Battling on

As the end of July approached, Gray continued to battle with BR. He demanded that the price be reduced by £5,000 on the grounds that BR would no longer be responsible for the line's overbridges once the Association took over. BR pointed out that, if the council bought the line for a road, the bridges would be rebuilt anyway. Gray insisted that the refusal of planning permission for a development adjacent to Westerham station reduced the value of the land; BR pointed out that permission was refused because the land was wanted for a road.

The Southern's estates department doubted whether much would be achieved by joint talks with the planners. In a memo to Cobb, Fulford pointed out that:

'I have twelve applications for the purchase of the station site, seven of which would be for development of an industrial or commercial nature. In these circumstances, there is every possibility of [us] receiving an offer based on the "hope" value of the site, that is something between say, agricultural value and full industrial or residential value and it is this figure that I have had in mind so far.'

Cobb told him that, in view of the promises made by Wansbrough-Jones, they had no option but to take part in a joint approach to the planners, despite their reservations, but he thought that the Association should be made aware of the interest in Westerham station site.

Progress report

Despite everything, the Association's newsletter of July 1962 – written by Gray – was upbeat. It reported progress on what he described as three-pronged negotiations:

*with the Southern Region over the exchange of traffic at Dunton Green;
*with the estates and civil engineer's departments in reducing the price for the line from £70,000 to £53,000;
*and an appeal to the BTC on the question of leasing the line.

With a hint of his political beliefs intruding, Gray was scathing about Cobb's view that the majority of visitors to the line would travel by car:

'While the Assistant General Manager (Mr. Cobb) has examined the proposition from the overcautious stand point of a nationalised undertaking, dwelling on the past and looking to the future pessimistically, the Committee of the Association has tended to look at the proposition from a bolder business and private enterprise angle with optimism and faith as well as realism.'

The one bright note in the midst of stalemate was the renting of the station building at Westerham, giving the Association a focus for its efforts for just 10 shillings a month. The newsletter said that the premises needed to be made habitable and services of water and lighting renewed and a plea was made for volunteers to help with tidying and renovation work. A slightly odd condition of the agreement was that no photographs were to be taken, not that any notice was taken of that. (In August an article about the scheme to save the line appeared, with photograph, in the *London Evening Standard*. It was reprinted in the November issue of the Meccano Magazine.)

The newsletter also reported that the TUCC had been asked to continue the season ticket concession beyond its one-year limit, pending the resumption of the rail service. In what may have been a hint at a falling off in interest by local people, it was suggested that any extended concession might only be available to Association members, so commuters were urged to renew their membership. There is no evidence that the TUCC ever considered the idea.

Stalemate

With negotiations deadlocked, Gray phoned the estates department. BR's notes of the call say that he sounded bellicose. He insisted on being given answers to his letter of 10 July and threatened that he would go to the BTC

The sign's exhortation is somewhat too late in January 1965 as the station was by then deserted. Enough flints remained to allow visitors to recreate the station name opposite the platform. Today this grassy bank lies beneath the tarmac of the west-bound M25.

or the Minister if he could get no satisfaction from the Southern Region. When told that none of his points in his letter remained unanswered, he simply repeated his demand that the Association be treated as a railway operator and the land and assets valued on that basis. This, he said, had been brushed aside.

An exchange of letters followed, in which the estates department stated that:

'. . . I will be pleased to meet you or your representatives to discuss any details of the valuation but I must reiterate that the basis has been fully considered and must remain unchanged.'

while the Association replied:

'I refer to your letters . . . which deal with certain details of difference in your valuation but do not reply to our letter of 10th July which seeks an entirely different basis of valuation. It would appear from your letter of 3rd August that you are not permitted to negotiate, and accordingly we are raising this whole question with the Secretary General to the British Transport Commission.'

The Association followed this uncompromising response with a letter to Cobb, rebutting his criticisms of its scheme and telling him that they intended to submit an offer for the line direct to the BTC within a few days.

The Association's offer

On 13 August 1962 the Association wrote to Wansbrough-Jones offering £30,000 for the line – track, land and buildings, including the branch platform at Dunton Green – subject to arrangements being made regarding connections at Dunton Green. In addition to the purchase price, BR would benefit from an additional £5,500 a year in income from tourists and visitors (still an optimistic sum but a huge reduction from Gray's original £35,000) and a saving of £8,700 on bus subsidies.

Wansbrough-Jones discussed the situation with Dr Beeching and Philip Shirley, a recent top-level recruit to the BTC1002. The effect was electric; their decision was that BR should dispose of the line as quickly as possible provided that a reasonable price could be obtained for it. Wansbrough-Jones met Hopkins and Cobb on 21 August and told them to accept the Association's offer of £30,000 but on the understanding that the sale had to free BR from the bus subsidy. Hopkins and Cobb were unhappy but Beeching and Shirley were pragmatic. They presumably realised that a sale of the whole line would be cash in hand whereas piecemeal sales might leave BR with awkward, unwanted bits of line. Apart from that, the whole affair was distracting to BR managers who had better things to do.

Hopkins and Cobb doubted whether the TUCC would accept the idea of the Association running a commuter service. They also told Wansbrough-Jones that they did not accept the Association's estimates of the revenue which the line would earn for BR and they would not alter main line services to connect with branch trains. These conditions would have to be included in the contract if a sale took place. They also wanted it clearly understood that the decision to reduce the price was a BTC one.

The matter was considered by the BTC Railways Committee, which recognised that there might be problems with the bus subsidy. It agreed, though, that the situation would have to be dealt with on its merits if that happened. In any case, the committee doubted whether the Association could relieve BR of its subsidy obligation in perpetuity but accepting the Association's offer would at least break the deadlock.

Offer accepted

On 31 August 1962, after 10 months of fruitless negotiation, Wansbrough-Jones wrote to the Association saying that the BTC had authorised the Southern Region to negotiate for the sale of the line, including the branch platform at Dunton Green, for £30,000. Facilities would be provided for the transfer of passenger and goods traffic at Dunton Green, albeit at the cost of the Westerham company.

Gray telephoned Cobb a day or two after receiving the BTC's formal letter to tell him that the Association would form a company to take over the line. It was agreed that, once the Association had made definite plans for the line's operation, it and BR would jointly approach the TUCC for its reactions. In the meantime, an announcement should be issued to the press.

Things were now moving quickly. On 9 September, Gray replied to Wansbrough-Jones accepting the BTC's conditions and telling him that a scheme to set up a company to raise the finance would be put to the Association's AGM on Saturday 6 October. Following that, BR would draw up proposals to be put to the TUCC in late October or November. If all went well, the Association or its operating company would apply for a Light Railway Order in November 1962 and agree a date for payment to be made to BR to complete the sale.

At last – and less than a year after closure – there was optimism in the air but, in reality, Beeching and Shirley had made an astute move. No longer could BR be accused of sabotaging negotiations by holding out for an unrealistic price. The onus was now on the Association to show that it could raise the purchase price – £30,000 was still a lot of money at a time when average annual wage was only £650 (today's equivalent would be around £1.2 million). Assuming it could do this, it still had to persuade the TUCC to release BR from the bus subsidy and get its Light Railway Order.

6

THE MEN FROM THE MINISTRY

Despite these optimistic events, problems were emerging behind the scenes – the sale of the branch had interested senior people within the Ministry of Transport after they were tipped off by Wansbrough-Jones. On 24 July 1962, David Serpell, the deputy secretary in charge of the Ministry's rail division, wrote to his opposite number for roads and traffic:

'1. Some time ago, we closed a branch railway line from Westerham to Dunton Green. There was considerable local agitation before the closure was finally agreed and announced; and at one time the suggestion was made that the Ministry had its own axe to grind because of its desire to use part of the railway line for (I think) the Southern Ring Road.
2. In fact, this motive had not been in our minds because, rightly or wrongly, this side of the Ministry had not even known that there was a line on a plan somewhere indicating that this development might one day take place.
3. I revert to the incident, however, since General Wansbrough-Jones tells me there is quite considerable local pressure from a sort of "Bluebell Line Society" to be allowed to take the line over and run trains on it which will connect up with the main line. As I understand it, the local Society originally hoped to buy the line but, finding difficulty in obtaining the necessary capital, they are now suggesting that they be allowed to lease the line or, perhaps, just borrow it.
4. If there is, in fact, a serious possibility of the Ministry wishing to use part of the line, we ought perhaps to let the B.T.C. know. What happens thereafter will no doubt need further discussion.'

The 14-year-old author waits on the platform at Brasted as if in expectation of a train that will never come. ***Iain Whitlam***

The following day, prompted by receiving a copy of this minute, Hilton Gillender belatedly told Serpell about his meeting with the WVRA the previous May (see page 105). Serpell wrote on the bottom of his note:
'. . . the next question for us, I suppose, is whether we as a Ministry are content with it or, if not, whether we could do anything about it. Perhaps you would let me know if there is anything I ought to say to General Wansbrough-Jones?'

Astoundingly, given Kent's interest in the line, the highways side of the Ministry dismissed Serpell's worries about selling the Westerham line to enthusiasts[101]. It was far from clear, it said, whether the South Orbital would be located in the area at all and, even if it were, it was impossible to say whether the railway line should be used – the road was originally planned when closure of the railway was not in prospect. It added that the Kent county surveyor now favoured routeing the new road via Croydon and the questions of the South Orbital and of relieving the A25 had become two entirely separate issues. If the Ministry objected to a sale to the Association there was a risk that it might once more be exposed to the groundless charge that it encouraged the railway closure because of the road proposals.

There is no sign that Serpell passed this message on to BR – it might have made quite a difference if he had – but he did maintain a close interest in the scheme. In the middle of August he wrote to Gillender, having heard about the WVRA offer for the line. If the Association bought the line, it would become responsible for bridge maintenance and, as this involved safety, Serpell assumed that the Ministry's

The bridge over Hogtrough Hill in January 1965, with Brasted station in the background. *Iain Whitlam*

Railway Inspectorate would have to be satisfied about the arrangements. He thought, too, that the Ministry should consider the hypothetical question of what would happen if the Association went bankrupt. It was as if Serpell was hunting for reasons to block the scheme.

Gillender sought advice on Serpell's question, asking whether it had been considered in connection with the Bluebell and other light railways. In fact, the question was far from hypothetical and, if the Ministry had checked its files, it would have found that plenty of light railways had gone bankrupt over the years. The simple answer was that the receiver or liquidator of a bankrupt railway became responsible for its bridges but it took Gillender over a month to reply to Serpell's question. In a lengthy minute to C. P. Scott-Malden, a fellow assistant secretary in the Ministry he set out a fine statement of the legal and administrative position regarding abandonment orders and the position of local highway authorities but he didn't answer the practical question: what would happen if a railway went bankrupt with one of its bridges collapsing?[102] In a further minute, dated 3 October, Scott-Malden asked: 'What about the safety of rail passenger traffic? How would this be assured?' This was a curious question. Railways had been operating under the Light Railways Acts for over 60 years. How had safety been assured in those cases and why should Westerham have been any different? Once again, it seemed that senior civil servants were looking for reasons to block the scheme? Subsequent events were to support that possibility.

Faltering start to negotiations

While these issues were being aired within the Ministry, negotiations between BR and the Association were moving along at a faltering pace. Wansbrough-Jones rejected several of its negotiating points. There could be no obligation on BR to provide services to Dunton Green nor could it be involved legally or financially in any scheme to operate the line. In addition, it was for the Association to prepare proposals for the TUCC about the bus subsidy though BR would be happy to submit them.

Wansbrough-Jones was also unhappy that the Association wanted to continue negotiations through the BTC. Having made more progress than it had in months of negotiations with the Southern Region, it is hardly surprising that the Association wanted to keep that channel of communication open but the BTC did not

Westerham's down fixed distance signal with the bridge over Beggars Lane immediately beyond. ***Iain Whitlam***

want to get involved in the details. Nor, it seems, did Cobb. He suggested that the Association should meet Bolland to settle operating and commercial questions, saying that:

'As far as the closure of Dunton Green station is concerned, this is certainly not contemplated at present but you will appreciate that the future of many of our stations and indeed lines is dependent upon Government transport policy which is not only outside the control of the Region but also the Commission. In these circumstances we are not competent to give you any definite undertaking and indeed I cannot see that anyone other than the Minister of Transport himself can do so.

'As regards the service here again I think you will see on reflection, that we cannot possibly bind ourselves to maintain the present timings in perpetuity. In considering the service which we provide to any particular place, we have to take into account the competing needs of all the other places served by the line and this applies particularly with peak hour services for commuters, Clearly we must retain the freedom to make adjustments to accord with such traffic developments as take place, We would undertake, however, to apply precisely the same considerations to Dunton Green as to any other station; in other words if you purchase the line and run a service on it we would treat it as if it was one of our own branch lines from the point of view of determining the need for connecting services.

'On the point you raise about the subvention I suggest that we should arrange for a clause to be written into the agreement which would relieve you of the liability in the event of our failing to maintain a certain minimum connecting service. I think, however, that this would best be considered a little later and after your meeting with the Line Manager.'

The Association replied to Wansbrough-Jones, stressing its concerns that, through its control of the train service at Dunton Green, BR could make it impossible for the Association to provide a commuter service. It was not asking for extra fast trains but it wanted an assurance that the number of trains stopping at Dunton Green, especially the existing fast trains, would not be reduced and that the station would not be closed.

Undaunted, the Association organised two public meetings, one for residents of Westerham and the surrounding villages and another for supporters from a wider area. These were followed by a general meeting of the Association's members, which heard that a new constitution was being drawn up, but in the meantime the Association was to change its name to the Westerham Valley Railway Association (WVRA) and the subscription, which had been reduced from 10/- to 2/6 the previous year, was to be increased.

Ian Allan comes on the scene

The newly-renamed WVRA's plans for raising capital were revealed at the general meeting. A private limited company was to be set up by the railway publisher Ian Allan and his associates, as part of the Ian Allan group of companies. It was proposed to operate the line through a management committee on which the WVRA would have two members. The WVRA would represent the supporters, invest in the company – it hoped to be able to take up a £5,000 block of shares, give advice, assist with the operation and management of the line and, most importantly, organise voluntary help for the operation of the steam service and the maintenance of the railway. It would be free to spend its own income as it wished, such as for buying rolling stock.

Gray told the meeting that the venture would be a unique experiment in organisation, management and co-partnership which sought to combine the profit motive with the voluntary spirit. It would reconcile the interests of commuters, community and railway enthusiasts, integrate local with national transport interests, and bring about co-operation between a private company, a nationalised industry and a voluntary association. It would be watched with interest.

Some members questioned this. Wasn't the WVRA giving away too much of what it had won? What about local investors? The committee explained that it had tried to raise money for six months without success and there would still be an opportunity to invest in the scheme. When asked if Allan was prepared to take only a 50 per cent holding, Gray replied that they had never been in a position to raise the other 50 per cent.

We know now that this was much the same kind of structure that Ian Allan set up, also in 1962, to buy the Dart Valley line from Totnes to Buckfastleigh in Devon. That scheme succeeded – the line reopened in 1969 – but the mix of commercial company and supporters' association never worked well and there is no reason to suppose that it would have worked any better at Westerham[103].

Gray also revealed that membership, which had fallen to around two dozen in late 1961, had since risen to nearly 1,000.

While most members of the new committee were elected without a vote, both Gray and Denis Pope were nominated for the post of chairman, which suggests a split between commuters and enthusiasts. It has been said to the author that Gray's attitude towards the enthusiast element of the WVRA tended towards the hostile. His main concern was restoration of year-round commuter services and he became impatient when matters such as motive power, rolling stock, permanent way and ticketing were discussed. In the end, though, Gray was elected by a large majority with Mr Sid Beacon as vice-chairman, Mr F. C. Bryan as secretary and Mr F. J. Howland as treasurer. The other committee members were P. Cope, S. F. Curran, A. Snowdon, R. Edwards, D. Pope, K. Carr, J. Cameron, D. Kitton, D. Pocock and D. Walter.

Approaching Westerham station, with the connection to the goods yard diverging to the left. *Iain Whitlam*

Negotiations unfold

With a mandate from its members, the WVRA met Bolland and his colleagues on 11 October. Gray opened the meeting by explaining the company structure that had been announced the previous weekend. Bolland then dealt with the question of services to Dunton Green. Although there were no immediate proposals to close the station, he could not give any long-term guarantees about its future but on the basis of the current traffic it seemed unlikely that it would close in the foreseeable future. Nor were there any immediate plans to alter the service at Dunton Green. It might be necessary to adjust timings but BR would naturally bear in mind the value of the traffic to and from the branch in planning any changes.

The two sides agreed that the approach to the TUCC over the subsidised buses would have to come from BR but the WVRA would present the case to the TUCC. The WVRA representatives thought that an approach should be made to the TUCC the following month but Bolland said it would be better if the Light Railway Orders were obtained first. This would reassure the TUCC that the WVRA could operate the line on a permanent basis before it approved the withdrawal of the replacement buses.

Turning to questions of detail, the WVRA asked if through bookings could be introduced – cheap day and ordinary returns as well as season tickets (including scholars) to principal destinations. Bolland said that this could be considered but BR would want the full fare to or from Dunton Green in any apportionment. Arrangements for ticket checks at Dunton Green would be dealt with at a site meeting. BR said that the WVRA would have to bear the cost of work at Dunton Green and it would not provide any extra staff.

Westerham's water tower and water crane stand by the site of the one-time engine shed, the only remains of which are the low brick foundation walls, subsequently surmounted, for some curious reason, by iron railings. ***Iain Whitlam***

The WVRA was anxious that a physical connection be maintained at Dunton Green, not least because Ian Allan might want to run through specials to the branch. It was suggested that the trailing connection with the up main line could be retained but clipped and padlocked, the keys being kept at Sevenoaks signal box. If the existing crossover was removed, access to the branch would be from the up line only and down trains would have to continue to Sevenoaks and reverse there. It was agreed that BR would investigate the cheapest and most suitable method of providing and working the connection, and come up with an estimate of the annual cost, including provision for eventual renewal. There would also be a charge whenever the facilities were used.

The WVRA asked if it could carry out day-to-day maintenance on the branch, to which Bolland saw no objection. It also asked for the redundant siding in Dunton Green yard to be included in the sale, which BR agreed to consider, though part of the roadway was being used for car parking and BR wanted to keep space for this in future.

Trouble on the buses

While progress was being made between the WVRA and BR, things were not going so well as far as the replacement buses were concerned. On 16 October, Scott-Malden at the Ministry of Transport finally replied to a letter from Wansbrough-Jones. It did not help that the law regarding BR-subsidised buses had changed.

'In the light of your letter of 11th September, filling out the details of our discussion on this subject, I have been thinking over the way in which it would be possible to achieve our object of transferring the liability for providing the alternative service from the Commission to the Westerham Passengers' Association. At this stage you will not expect me to commit the Minister formally, but it may be useful if I indicate how the thing looks to us at the moment.

'I do not see how the Minister can become directly concerned with the Westerham Passengers' Association as such any more than he will be directly concerned with any bus company which may be providing an alternative service.

The Minister is bound to look to the Commission or its successor Board for the fulfilment of his assurance given in the House of Commons, which now has the statutory backing, as you mention, of paragraph 11(3) of the Seventh Schedule of the 1962 Act. If the Minister considered, or the T.U.C.C. reported to him, that an adequate alternative service was not being provided, the action which he would have to take would be to direct the Commission or the Board to secure the provision of necessary service. Accordingly, if the transfer of the branch line as a light railway to the Passengers' Association is completed, it will be up to the Commission to ensure that they have a sufficient hold over the Association under the terms of the transfer to enable them to require the Association to provide an appropriate service.

The details of the service required would no doubt have to be worked out with the T.U.C.C. Here, however, I might perhaps mention that on my own reading of the Act (I have not taken legal advice) any formal reference of the case to the T.U.C.C. would have to be initiated by the Minister under paragraph 11(4) of the Seventh Schedule and not by the Commission or the Board; this is because, apart from that sub-paragraph, the Committee are precluded from considering any matter relating to discontinuance or reduction of railway services except as provided in Sub-Section (7) onwards of Section 56 of the Act. I would not envisage any difficulty, however, in the Minister making a formal reference to the Committee under paragraph 11(4) and then leaving it to the Commission (or Board) and the Association to work out details with the Committee.

'If you think it would be useful to have a talk about this, I shall of course be glad to do so. In any case I hope that these thoughts may be of some use in your own consideration of the subject.'

The situation did not look good. BR could no longer raise the matter of the replacement buses with the TUCC; under the 1962 Transport Act, only the Minister could do so. At the same time, it would be up to BR to ensure that the WVRA provided an adequate service and, if it didn't, the Minister could order BR to provide an alternative. Wansbrough-Jones passed this unwelcome news to Hopkins at the Southern Region. He found it hard to see how BR could have a sufficient hold over the WVRA to make it provide an adequate service.

A Catch-22 situation was developing but this time both BR and the WVRA were keen to find a solution that would allow the WVRA to operate its commuter service so that BR no longer needed to subsidise the bus service. It was the Ministry of Transport that seemed disinclined to find a practical answer. Wansbrough-Jones decided to sidestep the problem. He wrote to Scott-Malden, thanking him for his ideas on the way in which BR might solve the intractable question:

'We are very anxious not to tie ourselves up with the Westerham Branch Railway Passengers' Association in any way which might be construed as a partnership.

'It is most important that we should be completely free agents as to the use we make of Dunton Green Station and as to the rail services which [we] decide to stop there. For this reason, I do not think that we should attempt to obtain a hold over the Association sufficient to enable us to require them to provide an appropriate service. On the other hand, the negotiations are actively in hand between the Region and the Association and they are being pursued on a very sensible and objective basis.

It seems clear that the first step is for the Association to obtain the necessary Light Railway Orders because whoever makes the approach to the T.U.C.C., the latter body will certainly wish to be satisfied that the Association are capable of operating the line on a permanent basis before they can contemplate the withdrawal of the additional buses.

'I think it best to leave the matter to be negotiated as it is now between the Region and the Association and, as soon as we reach the stage at which some active consideration can be given to the cessation of the subvention we now pay to London Transport, we will bring the matter up to you.'

The curious case of the shrinking bridges

A few days short of the first anniversary of the line's closure saw the start of a curious chain of developments that was finally to undermine the preservation scheme. With success for the WVRA seemingly close, was the timing really a coincidence or was it part of a renewed attempt to block the scheme?

On 26 October 1962, the Highways Engineering Division of the Ministry of Transport wrote to Col J. R. H. Robertson of HM Railway Inspectorate (HMRI) concerning the proposed A21 Sevenoaks Bypass. It pointed out that the original intention was to fill in the cutting for the new road but, because of the plans to reopen the line, arrangements were being made to build a bridge instead. The problem was that the bypass would have to cross over the railway and, in turn, the local Chevening to Chipstead road had to cross over the bypass and it would have to be raised to do this. To avoid very steep gradients on this minor road, the council were keen that the bypass should cross the railway at as low a height as possible above rail level. In theory, the bypass bridge needed to give the railway no more headroom than that of any other bridge on the line so, to find out what that was, the council had surveyed them all. The lowest headroom – 13' 3½" – was at Bridge 1426 at Chevening Road.

We have to ask why Robertson had been brought into the matter as the survey had answered the question. Was he was simply being asked whether such a clearance was technically feasible or was there more to it? And were BR involved? One cannot imagine the council carrying out a survey on the line without asking permission from its owner.

Robertson wrote to the WVRA a few days later:

'I understand that you are Chairman of an Organisation or Society that is at present in progress of negotiating with the Southern Region of British Railways for the lease or purchase of the Westerham Branch with a view to running passenger trains over it under the authority of a Light Railway Order. I understand also that you have been in communication with other Branches of this Ministry in connection with this project, and you will appreciate that anything in this letter is without prejudice to anything that those Branches may decide.

'At this stage the Railway Inspectorate is not yet directly concerned with your project and will not be so until it is somewhat more advanced, although at any stage we shall be happy to advise you from the technical safety aspect. In the meantime however a technical point has arisen in connection with a proposed road overbridge to carry the Sevenoaks By Pass (A.21) over the Westerham Branch near Chevening Halt. My present concern is with the vertical clearance that might he needed under this bridge and I shall be grateful if you will tell me to what load gauge you would work should your project mature, i.e. what would be the maximum height of your highest vehicle above rail level.'

This was an obtuse way of raising the matter. Why didn't Robertson simply say that the headroom at Bridge 1426 was restricted and explain the repercussions? It is almost

A group of young WVRA volunteers take a break from work in 1963 or 1964. It is already obvious how the grass is trying to take over. *Richard Ferris*

as if he was setting a trap. The question must have come as a surprise to the WVRA, which cannot have been aware that the branch had any problems with headroom. After all, large locomotives and standard BR Mark I coaching stock had operated over the line in the previous five years, including on the last day, and there had been no complaints about trains arriving back at Dunton Green with dented roofs. The WVRA replied that its clearances would conform to those of the South Eastern Division of BR Southern Region.

A second letter from Robertson then revealed the results of the council's survey, which showed that four of the line's five overbridges had clearances less than the South Eastern Division standard of 13ft 7in. The bad news was that, not only would passenger vehicles be limited to less than normal for the South Eastern Division, but also the MOT could hardly insist on the new bypass bridge having a greater clearance than 13ft 3½in.

What had happened? The most likely explanation is that when much of the track was relaid in 1958 the depth of ballast was increased in cuttings as an easy way of improving drainage. The last day trains must have been a bit of a squeeze beneath the bridges and possibly the Maunsell pull-push sets too, but no-one seems to have noticed or worried. Had Robertson been more open and had the WVRA been a bit more quick-witted, they could have replied that they intended to improve drainage in other ways so that the depth of the ballast could be reduced.

Robertson finally replied to his highways engineering colleagues at the end of November 1962:

'As there is already one vertical clearance as short as 13' 3½" at an existing bridge, I do not think that we can ask the Kent County Council to give a greater clearance than this at the new bridge, and so I have told the Association. On the other hand, the Association are likely to have trouble in keeping the maximum height of their vehicles down to this kind of headroom and I do not think that we should increase their difficulties by allowing the County Council to give a vertical clearance at the new bridge of less than 13' 3½".'

This episode raises another question. For how long had it been planned to fill in the cutting? If, by October 1962, the design was being altered to include a bridge, the original design to infill the cutting must have been drawn up long before, probably before the line closed. The phrase – 'It was originally intended to fill in the cutting as the line is recommended for closure' – is a strange one which suggests that the plan dated from when the TUCC originally recommended closure and no account had been taken of subsequent developments.

At about the same time, Robertson was also being drawn into the Ministry's discussion about the WVRA taking on responsibility for the line's existing bridges. Early in November 1962, Scott-Malden finally got a reply to his query about assuring the safety of the Westerham line – a reply which revealed a further looming problem:

'It seems to me more than likely that, if a company had reached the bankrupt or near bankrupt state in which they had ceased to fulfil their obligations in respect of the maintenance of bridges, they would also have ceased railway operations including any carriage of passengers.

'If a company continued, to operate their railway but, for whatever reason, neglected their maintenance duties, this could endanger passenger traffic. As explained in Minute 20, the Highway Authorities concerned would have a strong interest in seeking to enforce fulfilment of the company's obligations in respect of road overbridges (and also of rail overbridges to the extent that neglect of these might endanger the highway below e.g. by falling masonry). Apart from this, however, the direct safeguard for railway passengers lies in the powers of the Railway Inspectorate. The current form of the safeguarding provision inserted in Light Railway Orders is as follows:"... except that no part of the railway shall be used for the public conveyance of passengers without the permission in writing of the Minister first being had and obtained, which permission shall not be withheld if the Minister is satisfied that such use will not be attended with danger to the public, and the Company shall comply with the conditions (if any) which the Minister may from time to time prescribe for the safety of the public using the railway."

'If I may take this opportunity to mention an unrelated point, Mr. Scott-Malden may like to know, in connection with his letter to General Wansbrough-Jones [. . .], that there is a possibility that the speed limit on trains which would be imposed by the Light Railway Order would conflict with the aim to provide an adequate alternative rail service. R.I. are not disposed to relax the speed limit of 25 m.p.h. normally applied to light railways. The Association say this would prevent them providing a service comparable to the one run by the B.T.C. before the closure.

'I am passing this minute through R.I. in case they wish to comment.'

This was a devastating prospect. The commuter service

WVRA volunteers, including a young Gordon Lamming, at work at Westerham. The purpose of the contraption in the foreground is unclear but, given that it seems to involve pouring inflammable liquid onto a fire, it is doubtful whether today's health and safety procedures would encompass its use. Richard Ferris

would not work if the line's speed limit was cut to 25mph. The journey time would have been extended from 11 minutes to something like 20 minutes, limiting trains to every 45 minutes or so. It threatened to bring the whole scheme to an end[104].

In a minute to Scott-Malden, dated 7 November, Brigadier C. A. Langley, the chief inspecting officer at the Railway Inspectorate, elaborated but also introduced wider concerns:

'. . . this case raises an important point of principle. It is all very well for railway amateurs to "play at trains" at the week-end or to run railways of local or historical interest as holiday attractions. Such railways as the Festiniog, the Talyllyn and the Bluebell clearly fill a holiday need as well as giving an outlet for railway enthusiasm; they can be kept safe with little supervision, and if they do break down occasionally it is all part of the fun. It is, however in my opinion, a very different matter when railway amateurs seek to provide a regular passenger transport service for commuters,

'No matter how good their initial financial backing and their intentions may be it is likely that they will have to run the service on a shoe string . . . and with amateur assistance (when, say the paid motorman is sick or on leave). Although they may start off well it is doubtful whether they will be able to maintain their engines, stock and track to the high standard needed for fairly fast regular and safe passenger running. A narrow gauge derailment at 8 m.p.h., as happened recently on the Festiniog railway, is one thing but a 40 m.p.h. derailment of a commuter train on the Westerham line would be quite another.

'I consider that the real question here is not whether the Association would be able to keep their road bridges in repair, of which I am doubtful, but whether they should be enabled to try to provide a commuter service.

'In my view such an attempt should be discouraged. In this particular case a speed limit of 25 m.p.h., which

This rather truncated photograph of 'H' class No 31533 propelling its train between Brasted and Chevening on 15 April 1961 provides evidence of the extent of the reballasting, intended to solve the problems of the line's poor drainage, which was later to cause such problems for the preservation scheme. ***Author's collection***

I regard as essential for safety, will probably provide sufficient discouragement.'

The whole question of enthusiasts or local businessmen running serious transport services was being dealt a fatal blow.

Dunton Green site meeting

Despite the obstacles that were building up behind the scenes, the WVRA, together with representatives of Ian Allan, met BR on site at Dunton Green on 15 November 1962 to settle outstanding issues and to define the area of land to be included in the transaction. Somewhat ironically, BR had decided that the land at Dunton Green should be leased for either a nominal £1 a year or a peppercorn, rather than sold, and it would ask for a higher price if the WVRA wanted the sidings as well.

The WVRA asked for the passage between the branch platform and the up platform to be included in the lease. It planned to block it up at the main line end and use it as a ticket office, with a new entrance in the forecourt side. BR had no objection to this. The WVRA was to pay for a fence from the existing concrete paling, in line with the back of the platform buildings, along the platform to the bottom of the ramp. The dividing line was to be three feet on the western side of the lamp posts so that the platform flower beds remained in BR's ownership!

When it came to the question of the yard and sidings, there was a difference of opinion between the WVRA, which doubted whether the yard would be of great use, and the Ian Allan representatives who, with an eye on its development possibilities, wanted the yard to be included in the sale. This was the first that the Ian Allan team had heard of a lease. The WVRA were only thinking about railway uses and were willing to accept a covenant to that effect but, even so, its representatives were divided among themselves. Gray thought the sidings could be used for storing carriages bought by members while Alan Snowdon, chairman of the technical committee, wanted the carriages to be kept at Brasted and, in any case, they might need to extend the platform over the yard connection. Bolland pointed out the area of the yard that was available and said that, like the platform, BR would only be prepared to lease it. Furthermore, since it was valuable land, an economic rent would be charged. This inclined the WVRA to decide against using the yard but the Ian Allan team wanted time to consider the situation.

Westerham Flyer

November 1962 saw the publication of the preliminary issue of the WVRA's *Westerham Flyer* newsletter, heralding the launch of a quarterly printed newsletter that was to follow in the New Year. It explained that, although BR had accepted the WVRA's offer for the line, there were still many formalities to go through before the actual takeover and until then the WVRA's activities were limited to the station buildings at Westerham. The newsletter also sought contributions towards the 'substantial stake' that the WVRA hoped to acquire in the new operating company, the formation of which was under way.

Coming to terms

At the end of November 1962 BR drew up draft terms for the sale agreement. It covered 52 acres of land for £30,000 plus 2,803 square yards at Dunton Green that was to be leased for 99 years at £1 a year. The document listed the tenancies and easements that would be affected by the sale. They included an agreement with B. Horton & Sons for 'openings', for which BR received 5 shillings a year. At Westerham there were nine tenancies for 'garden grounds' – presumably the allotments behind the platform – ranging in cost from 3s 2d to 17s 6d a year. At Brasted the coal merchant Mr L. Bowser paid £77 a year for the use of the yard while Mr E. Asselberghs paid £84 14s 4d a year rent for the station house. An advertisement hoarding at Dunton Green brought in £130 a year, while that at Westerham, which featured in many photographs of the station, was let to a contractor at £16 10s a year. Hopkins had a draft clause about the bus subsidies removed because the matter was a complicated and delicate one which was still being discussed between the Ministry, Wansbrough-Jones and himself.

On 7 December Cobb chased the WVRA for its response, not realising that the estates department hadn't posted the document. Gray replied that Ian Allan wasn't prepared to form a company without it but he reported that they had met with Bolland and had drawn up two versions of its timetable, one for 40mph and one for 25mph running.

New Year 1963 – glimmers of hope

By New Year's Day 1963 the draft terms had been agreed within BR and were sent out, only for the package to burst open in the post. A meeting to discuss the terms had to be delayed until 30 January as a result.

When the meeting finally took place Cobb urged haste in reaching a decision, fearing that the plan that Beeching was about to unveil would contain so many closure proposals that re-opening the Westerham line might be delayed if the TUCCs became overwhelmed. The WVRA explained that it hoped to be able to accept BR's offer during February, after which it would be in a position to work with BR on the submission to the TUCC.

Turning to the draft terms, BR made it clear that it had no plans to reduce train services at Dunton Green but a clause that it was under no obligation to provide connecting services had been included in case it had to cut services in the future. Another clause required the station buildings to be painted in the Southern Region colour scheme but this only applied to the leased property at Dunton Green. BR agreed that a site on the south east side of the leased area, which the WVRA wanted for the construction of a berthing siding, could be included at no additional rent but if the WVRA wanted a larger area it would have to pay the full economic rent or make an offer to purchase it.

The notes of the meeting show a curious difference between BR's original draft and the final agreed version. The first version said:

'If it should transpire that the T.U.C.C. are not empowered to approve or are unable to agree to the Association assuming the Railway Board's obligations for the subvention by the provision of a satisfactory rail service for business passengers, the Chairman of the Association stated that they might still like to purchase the branch line and operate as a Preservation Society.

'The Association were informed that in this event they would be expected to pay for the assets, including the land, based on a straight valuation, and taking into account any industrial development potential in the Westerham Station area (already the subject of planning applications) having regard to the fact that the present offer made allowance for the Railway Board to be relieved of the subvention.'

Gray asked for this to be changed. Mention of paying the full price for the land had only arisen, he said, because it turned out that Ian Allan had applied to develop the station sites at Westerham and Brasted – it had nothing to do with the bus subsidies. The revised version of the note read:

'On the attention of the Association's representatives being drawn to the recent application made by one of their financial sponsors to seek planning permission to develop sites at Westerham and Brasted stations, they strongly dissociated themselves with this action which had been taken without the Association's support or concurrence. Mr. Gray reaffirmed that the Association had consistently maintained that they were potential railway operators and not land developers in their negotiations with the former British Transport Commission and the Southern Region of British Railways, and sought always to be regarded and treated as such.'

This sign of tension between the WVRA and Ian Allan was followed by a report in the *Westerham Courier* newspaper under the headline of 'Branch line users not consulted on development'. Sevenoaks Rural District Council had received planning applications from the Westerham Valley Light Railway Company for the development of about 2.3 acres of land at Westerham station for industry and a petrol station and 1.8 acres at Brasted for housing. The report continued:

'Mr. W. Gray, chairman of the Westerham Valley Railway Users' Association, said: "We disassociate ourselves from this application, which was made without pre-consultation with us.

"Our approach to the problem and our negotiations with the British Transport Commission and with the Southern Region of British Railways has always been as potential railway operators and not as land developers. So far as we know, no company has yet been formed, although there have been proposals for one.

"Both the B.T.C. and the Southern Region regard our Association as the negotiating authority for the acquisition of the Westerham-Dunton Green line."'

Since the Westerham station site totalled about 4 acres, Allan proposed to develop over half the land – presumably the goods yard. This would have left the railway with the platform and run-round loop plus, presumably, the allotment area behind the platform on which sidings could have been laid. Even so, it would have made operations very cramped.

The final part of the tale came at the end of February. Gould reveals that negotiations with Ian Allan were conducted by Gray alone and it is said that he unilaterally broke off negotiations when he discovered that Allan was thinking about converting the line to either 15-inch or 3-feet gauge. The WVRA committee were furious. They felt that Gray should have consulted them before taking such a drastic step, and forced him out of office. To be fair to Gray, it must have become clear that a relationship between the WVRA and Ian Allan was not going to work and that the WRVA was always going to be a minor partner. In any case, the refusal of Allan's bid for planning permission in early May 1963 would have led to his withdrawal anyway – he was later to claim that he did not think the project viable.[105] However, we have already seen how Gray took a dominating and often uncompromising role in negotiations and maybe this was the final straw for the committee. Cobb noted that Gray's departure was 'an interesting development'.

Business as usual

Despite the mounting problems, not least the fact that it no longer had any financial backing to buy the line, the WVRA adopted a surreal attitude of 'business as usual' when it sent out a newsletter in February 1963. It announced a special meeting on 6 April, at which the new constitution was to be considered, and a public meeting on 19 March at which plans for work on the line were to be outlined. It also revealed that the first item of rolling stock had been bought for the line – the last surviving South Eastern & Chatham designed 'Matchboard' boat train carriage, No S3554S.

Negotiations were also under way to buy steam locomotives. BR had offered the best two remaining 'H' class tank engines, Nos 31518 and 31263. They had been inspected at Three Bridges by Percy Cope and Sid Beacon (members of the Technical Committee) both in and out of steam, and were reported as being in very good condition. The price quoted was £1,000 each. BR had also offered the last 'O1' class, No 31065, which was in store at Ashford, and Beattie well tank No 30585. A member, Mr R. F. Stephens, had also started a fund to buy one of the last Wainwright 'C' class engines, which it was hoped would run at Westerham.

It was not just the WVRA that adopted a 'business as usual' approach. Cobb had spoken to Cameron at what had become the headquarters of the new British Railways Board (BRB) to see what could be done about the impasse on the bus subsidies. Cameron investigated and replied:

'. . . the Consultative Committee comes into this purely on the question of whether or not the rail service which the Westerham Valley Light Railway Company Limited propose to give is sufficient to release us from our obligation to operate a bus service, which is currently costing us some £6,000 per annum.

'The position today is governed by Section 11 of the 7th Schedule of the Transport Act, 1962, Subsections 3 and 4. The Westerham case is clearly one where we were providing, or assisting in the provision, of an alternative service at the time Section 56 of the Act came into force; and the Minister may, therefore, give us directions about the alternative service. He can also refer any matter relating to these alternative services to an Area

The driver of 'H' class No 31308 leans out of his cab as if to take a closer look at the black smoke coming out of the chimney. The train is heading towards bridge 1428 at Combe Bank on its way to Brasted and Westerham on 27 August 1961. None of the trains before closure had any problems with the headroom under the line's bridges. *Author's collection*

Committee, when the Committee has to consider and report to the Minister on the matter.

'In view of this, our next step would seem to be to write to the Minister giving him the details of the rail service which the Westerham Valley Company proposes to operate, and seeking his agreement to the withdrawal of the bus service when this rail service begins. It is possible that he might give us a direct answer; but quite probable that he would refer the matter to the London Committee.

'If, after receiving this letter, you would still like me to come over and talk at 2.30 p.m. on Monday I shall be happy to do so. On the other hand you may want us to write to the Minister forthwith, and if so perhaps we can be given details of the train service proposed.

'It is still conceivable that the Minister might like the London Committee's opinion on the reliability of the service proposed and the extent to which the Company can be depended on to continue to operate it and not to withdraw it without due notice.'

The WVRA secretary, Mr F. C. Bryan, sent details of the proposed timetable to Cobb at the end of February, as shown in Appendix 16. Original documents say that timings for both 40mph and 25mph running were worked out, but it is not clear if the latter were intended for commuter services – they may have been for weekend steam trains. Bryan explained that the schedule for summer Saturdays, Sundays, bank holidays and other special occasions had still to be finalised but the branch service would connect with alternate BR trains from about 10am until about 8pm, with gaps of 90 minutes at the start, at midday, and towards the close of the service.

Cobb asked Bolland to comment on any shortcomings in the timetable compared with the previous rail service or the replacement buses. He also asked the Southern Region's commercial manager to start work on the case for withdrawing the replacement buses to be put to the Minister.

Bolland reported that the major omission was an equivalent for BR's 06.10 train from Westerham, which had been replaced by a subsidised bus at 05.58. (BR had just started to use the 24-hour clock, internally at least.) The former 06.59 train from Westerham was not replicated but, as trains were now to run at 06.47 and 07.15, this would hardly cause any great inconvenience. However, Bolland felt that the omission of the early service would damage the proposal to withdraw the replacement buses, which was cheeky, given that BR had claimed that only six passengers used the first train and was soon to insist that the first bus was unnecessary.

In the evening, the new timetable differed from the BR service to fit in with altered main line timings. Of the remaining services, Bolland noted that the principal connections from London (the 17.30 from Cannon Street and the 18.28 from Charing Cross) remained and he thought that new connections off the 16.44 from Charing Cross and the 18.04 from Cannon Street would be welcomed by many. He did note, though, that in some cases the bus/rail service via Sevenoaks would still be quicker than the proposed branch timings.

When BR asked the WVRA to reconsider the omission of the early train it explained that the weekday services were expected to run at a loss and would be subsidised by the summer weekend trains. It intended to ask potential daily travellers which train they would use and, although the 06.10 would not be listed, anyone could indicate if they wanted to travel at other times. The WVRA said it would run an early service if more than 10 people wanted it but if usage dropped it would have to be withdrawn. It recalled that in BR days only two passengers regularly used the 06.10 train, one of whom had retired and the other left the district.[106] However, with worsening street congestion, together with an earlier Cannon Street arrival now possible by changing at Orpington, there might be potential for the train.

There is an impression that Bolland was warming towards the enthusiasts and was doing his best to help. Perhaps he secretly admired their resilience or maybe he was aware of his impending move to the Eastern Region, where he would leave the problems of Westerham far behind him.

Fervent hopes

The WVRA's public meeting in March 1963 heard that it was hoped to re-open the line by October that year. Committee member Roy Edwards told the audience that the adventure had begun and appealed to everyone to come to Westerham station at weekends armed with old clothing, rainwear, wellington boots and a spade. However, the WVRA also needed to raise £40,000 and would be going cap-in-hand to industry and local traders and setting up a share scheme for members. It still planned to buy three ex-GWR railcars built in 1941 for £600 each to operate the commuter service.

The *Westerham Flyer* finally arrived in May 1963, with a picture of the newly acquired SE&CR matchboard carriage on the cover. Inside was a report on the special general meeting, which had heard that the WVRA was investigating ways of raising the £40,000 needed to buy the line. It was hoped that most could be obtained initially by a low-interest loan, which members would repay over a short period by progressive investment. Even though subscription charges had increased from 2s 6d to £1 a year, it was hoped that membership would soon reach 2,000 and at that rate £40,000 would only be £20 per member, or £5 a year over four years. Members were reminded that this would be an investment, not a loan or gift, and would earn a dividend. It was also intended to set up a locomotive and carriage fund, and the stock that it bought would be owned by the WVRA as distinct from the operating company that was to be set up.

Out on the line, ditch clearing had started at Westerham and had reached beyond Brasted, once the undergrowth had been removed to find the ditches. Work on oiling fish-plates was also under way. BR had agreed to rent Brasted station on the same terms as Westerham and this was to become the base for working parties.

'O1' class No 31065 had been inspected at Ashford Works and seemed to be in sound condition, having done little work since having a major overhaul in 1960. The purchase price of £1,000 was to include a general service and delivery in working order. The Wainwright 'C' Class Preservation Society had also inspected its intended locomotive, No 31592. The Western Region had offered five ex-GWR railcars – numbers 20, 23, 24, 26 and 32 – from which to choose the best three. They had been inspected at Worcester earlier in the year and were in reasonable condition.

At the beginning of May 1963 the WVRA began to think about the requirements it would have to meet to be granted a Light Railway Order. Alan Snowdon, chairman of the technical committee, asked the Railway Inspectorate to clarify various details. In particular, he asked whether, with one-engine-in-steam working and the connections to sidings locked by a key on the train staff, it would be possible to dispense with main running signals.

Bus subsidies

At the end of May 1963 the Southern Region sent the proposal to withdraw the replacement buses to the BRB for onward transmission to the Ministry. It is worth reproducing the Southern's letter in full so that we can compare it with the rather different letter that was finally sent to the Ministry by the BRB.

'Following the closure of the Dunton Green–Westerham Branch Line at the end of October 1961, the Westerham Valley Railway Association was formed with a view to taking over and re-introducing a rail service on the now disused line.

'Negotiations with the Association for the sale of the branch have continued for some time and have now reached the stage where firm proposals have been made. In order, however, that they may be satisfactorily concluded, it is necessary to ascertain whether upon the re-introduction of a rail service by the Association we can be relieved of the requirement to subsidise certain of the bus services publicised as "alternatives" when the line was closed.

'Attached is a copy of the Association's proposed time table, together with details of the present bus and previous rail services and whilst at this stage no provision is made in the Association's proposed time table to cater for the few passengers who at present travel by the 5.58 a.m. subsidised bus from Westerham, the Association have said that it is their intention to circularise local residents to ascertain the requirement for early services, and if more than about 10 residents indicated that a service at 6.10 a.m. (the original B.R. train time for which the 5.58 bus was introduced) was needed, they would be prepared to introduce it, with the proviso that should patronage drop to a too low level it would have to be withdrawn.

'Whilst originally a subsidy of £8,700 was agreed with the L.T.B in respect of the additional buses, this figure was subsequently reduced to £8,200, following a review of the operating costs, and was further reduced in October 1962 to its present level of £6,000 when the season ticket concession expired 12 months after the closure of the line and ordinary bus fares were paid to the L.T.B. by the season ticket holders.

'In order, therefore, that the negotiations for the sale of the Westerham Branch may be concluded, will you please advise me whether the Minister of Transport would agree to the termination of the subvention upon the re-introduction of a rail service on the branch.'

This was a fair summary of the WVRA's proposals for operating a commuter service and the lack of an early train in its timetable was admirably dealt with. Wansbrough-Jones took the matter up with the Ministry, starting with a discussion with Scott-Malden which identified two complications.

The first was that the Ministry wanted the view of the Chief Inspecting Officer of Railways as to the WVRA's fitness to operate the line. As we have already seen, the Railway Inspectorate was against the idea of amateurs providing a regular passenger transport service for commuters and Scott-Malden was fully aware of this. The second was that the newly formed London Transport Board had a duty to provide an adequate and properly co-ordinated system of passenger transport in its area. Could services in the Westerham area really be said to be adequate without the replacement buses? If not, LT might have to provide them without any subsidy from BR. The Ministry wanted BR to raise the matter in the new BR/LT Co-ordinating Committee. Of course, if it turned out that BR no longer had to subsidise the buses, there was no reason why it should sell the line cheaply to the WVRA.

Wansbrough-Jones warned the Southern Region that the case might take some time to resolve. He suggested that a time limit should be put on the negotiations with the WVRA, asking if it was practicable to set 1 October 1963 (less than four months away) as the date by which all the formalities should have been completed, failing which BR would remove the track. This was harsh – it would hardly have been the WVRA's fault if the deadline was missed as the pace was now being set by BR and the Ministry.

Wansbrough-Jones wrote a formal letter to Scott-Malden at the Ministry on 6 June 1963. Far from simply passing on the Southern Region's case for supporting the WVRA proposals to replace the subsidised buses, his letter seemed to invite the Ministry to reject the idea:

'The Westerham Valley Railway Association with whom we have been negotiating for the sale of this disused line have now put forward firm proposals.

These include the timetable attached (Statement A) based on the same journey times as the former Southern Region service, i.e. with a maximum speed of 40 mph average of 30 mph and on many trips a 3-minute turn round.

'The price which we have agreed to accept for the line was based on the assumption that the rail service to be operated by the Association would be such as to enable the Minister to agree to our discontinuing the subsidy of £6,000 a year we are paying to London Transport for the additional bus services introduced when the train service was withdrawn.

'We shall therefore, need to know that the Minister accepts the train service now proposed as an adequate substitute for the subsidised bus trips, which are indicated on Statement B enclosed together with the former rail service.

'But the prior consideration would seem to be safety and reliability. Is the Minister prepared to permit a private Association to operate a commuter service in the same times and under the same conditions as the Southern Region?

'A Bluebell Line type of service operating for tourists and sightseers on summer weekends is one thing; a regular commuter service spread over some four hours each morning and five hours each evening, with scheduled main line connections, is quite different.

'So far as we are concerned we should naturally like to sell the line and terminate our subsidy as soon as possible; but if the sale is not going to take place, then we want to lift the track and recover the usable material quickly; and we should value your help in achieving one aim or the other without delay.

'There is a conflict of priorities here which could well be the precursor of others, so that this could be regarded as a test case.

'We should like to apply for a Light Railway Order in the very near future and it seems as well that the Chief Inspecting Officer should know what is in the wind. This is a matter which may drag on unless we keep the pressure on and I hope you will agree that it should be dealt with expeditiously.'

Wansbrough-Jones was doing no more than repeat back the Ministry's own concerns about the scheme; political scheming was at work. With an application for a Light Railway Order in the offing, the Ministry could not be seen to be pre-judging the issue but it was fine if BR raised problems. Clearly there must have been undocumented discussions between the BRB and the Ministry leading up to this. We must remember, too, that the Beeching

Westerham Valley Railway Association handbill c1963. *Kent & East Sussex Railway archives*

Plan had been published two months previously and the successful re-opening of a closed line as a commercial service might be unhelpful.

Scott-Malden replied to Wansbrough-Jones just a few days later:

'Thank you for your letter of 6th June. This is clearly a difficult question which we shall have to consider with some care, but I note your request for a speedy answer and we shall certainly do our best.'

He then wrote to a colleague, Mr P. R. Sheaf. Other senior people, including Col McMullen of the Railway Inspectorate and Serpell, were copied in, indicating the seriousness with which the question was being considered:

'You will see from the attached letter of 6th June from General Wansbrough-Jones that the Westerham Valley Railway Association have now put forward firm proposals for the purchase of the branch line from the Railways Board, including a timetable proposing a commuter service with the same journey times as the former Southern Region service. General Wansbrough-Jones expresses some doubts about the ability of the Association to operate under these requirements, and raises the question, which you and Colonel McMullen are already (I think) considering, whether the Minister is prepared to permit operation on these lines by a private Association.

'General Wansbrough-Jones concludes by asking for early action from the Ministry either to enable the sale to go ahead or to facilitate the final closure of the line and the recovery of the track. I should be grateful if you would pursue this urgently with the Chief Inspecting Officer and advise me, if possible by 26th June.'

Assumptions were being made, without any supporting evidence, that the WVRA could not operate the line safely. This was ironic considering that BR ran the branch in the 1950s – at 40 mph – with the track in desperate need of renewal. At least the WVRA was starting out with track that had been largely renewed.

Yes to playing trains, no to commercial services

Wansbrough-Jones's concern that the scheme might be '. . . the precursor of others, so that this could be regarded as a test case' supports the idea that there were fears of a host of private companies seeking to re-open lines as fast as BR was closing them. The whole question of railway revival schemes was uppermost in official minds, as McMullen made clear:

'. . . while we have no objection in principle to the local operation of lines closed by British Railways, we must necessarily be cautious about the ability and resources of some of these local bodies to carry on such an undertaking safely after the first flush of enthusiasm has passed and essential maintenance problems arise which turn out to be costly. It seems likely that prospective runners will be of three general types. Firstly there are societies of railway enthusiasts who want to run a little railway primarily for their own satisfaction. Most of the existing cases are of this type and they are not likely to present a problem since that would probably not be seriously incommoded by the quite severe restrictions on their operations that we might have to impose. Secondly, and at the other end of the scale, are local authorities and other big undertakings who already have the administrative and financial backing for and, in the case of a local authority, existing and up-to-date experience in, the running of a public service. Such bodies should be able to run a light railway in such a way that we should probably not have to impose severe safety restrictions on their operations. Thirdly however are the smaller local bodies, of enthusiasts and optimistic businessmen, who would seek to run a railway as a commercial enterprise or public service or both, but with only the backing and experience suitable for a little railway of the first type. Such bodies would be quite a different matter from the first two: safety considerations must be paramount and we should have to look at any scheme put forward by a body of this kind very carefully from this point of view, and consider seriously whether we should authorise it at all. I say all this rather for your own background information than for passing on verbatim. I do not want to seem to throw cold water on some praiseworthy local enterprise, but on the other hand I do not want to raise false hopes'.[107]

The situation was made far worse when an item headlined 'Railway society seeks backer' appeared in the *Sevenoaks Chronicle* on 21 June 1963. In a spectacular own goal – the report was based on the latest issue of the *Westerham Flyer* – the headline continued '£40,000 is needed for purchase of line – no-one has yet come forward'. As soon as he read the article, Cobb wrote to the WVRA, copying his letter to Wansbrough-Jones:

'I have had my notice drawn to a cutting from the *Sevenoaks Chronicle* for 21st June and whilst it is appreciated that newspaper articles are not always entirely correct, the statements in regard to the Society's financial position are, on the face of it, somewhat disturbing. Having regard to the prolonged negotiations and the Board's approach to the Ministry for your Association to take over the Westerham/Dunton Green branch line, we would be placed in an extremely embarrassing position if the Association were unable at this late stage, to raise the necessary capital.

'I think you will agree that the Board require to have the position clarified and perhaps you will therefore be good enough to let me have your comments as quickly as possible.

'May I take the opportunity of reminding you that if the Association are not granted permission to assume responsibility for the subvention the Board would only agree to the sale of the assets and land on the basis of a straight valuation, which, as you already know, is in the region of £50,000.'

In the meantime, Wansbrough-Jones kept Cobb in touch with how things were developing:

'The Ministry are finding themselves in a certain amount of difficulty because they naturally find it somewhat hard to arrive at any basis on which they can say that certain persons are fit to run a railway on their own account and others are not. A natural division would be those lines which are operated by local authorities and those by private concerns but, as you can appreciate, it is not quite as easy as all that.

'However, I have spoken to the Ministry and told them that the prospects of the Association finding the money

The Westerham Valley Railway Association issued souvenir platform tickets for visitors to Westerham station. The charge of 1d probably didn't raise a vast amount towards the re-opening funds and the ticket number may have slightly exaggerated the number of visitors. ***Author's collection***

to purchase the line are not as bright as they were and the Ministry are perfectly happy to see the whole business fold up if the money is not forthcoming, even though the matter is under consideration by them in the light of my letter to Scott-Malden dated 6th June.

'I have also told the Ministry that I feel we must put a time limit on this matter and that, without prejudice to any representations we made to the Ministry, we might wish to call all negotiations off if nothing has been finalised by 1st October. I hope this will help you to carry the matter a little bit further.

'Meanwhile, I am doing my best to arrange a talk over lunch with you and McMullen. This is, naturally, an extremely informal letter just to let you know how matters stand.'

At the Ministry progress was slow. Sheaf sent a long minute to Scott-Malden, part of which noted that:

'4. Col. McMullen is not keen on keeping the amateurs out by keeping them to a speed limit of 25 m.p.h. It is quite likely that in one or two "enthusiast" type cases we shall be prepared to allow a higher speed limit (say 40 m.p.h.) and we might want to for the local authority services, if any. It would be very difficult to defend discrimination against amateurs who happened to want to run a commuter service – provided they could demonstrate that their service was as safe as any other. If a group of amateurs can operate safely, we should be on poor ground in trying to put special restrictions upon them.
5. This makes it all the more important to make sure that they can operate safely. But it is difficult to lay down the right rules. Col. McMullen has made the point to me that we can impose conditions about speed limits, weights of rail, types of rolling stock, methods of block working etc; but it is far more difficult to lay down standards of maintenance either of the track or equipment. It seems to us, therefore, that the Minister is entitled to pretty comprehensive information to show that:
(a) the promoters of the proposals have the right ideas – particularly about maintenance standards;
(b) that the promoters are financially sound enough to carry out their obligations.
6. On maintenance standards, we can no doubt rely on some British Railways help. In theory, I suppose we could even suggest that the promoters should pay British Railways to do their maintenance for them – though that might be economically pretty difficult for them, and unattractive to British Railways. I understand that something of the kind is done in Germany, however. The financial conditions are particularly important, however. Westerham/Dunton Green will probably be a test case for other proposals of the same kind. We must therefore try to make sure that, in this case, we ask for all the information we are likely to need. We will probably not get to 100% on the first occasion, but we must do the best we can. A kind of pro forma has been devised, after our discussion, by Col. McMullen. There is no objection from the Treasury Solicitor to our asking for information of this kind …'
This cries out for comment. The view that enthusiasts, many of whom were professional railwaymen, could not be trusted to run 'serious' services safely was insupportable. It was also nonsense to say that it would have been difficult to lay down standards of maintenance. Maybe the worry was that a lot of BR track would have been found to be inadequate if standards had been published.

Apart from the fact that it was illegal for BR to carry out work for external organisations, Sheaf's suggestion that the WVRA might pay BR to maintain its track and bridges to ensure a proper standard of work showed complacency as to the quality of the Southern Region's maintenance. It was soon belied by events such as the collapse of a signal box above the tracks at Clapham Junction in 1965 and, just 12 miles from Dunton Green, the 1967 Hither Green crash in which a Hastings to London train was derailed by a broken rail causing the deaths of 49 passengers. The Southern's maintenance was condemned in both cases. Ironically, it fell to Col McMullen to carry out both inquiries.

Questionnaire to frighten them off

Having received Sheaf's report, Scott-Malden wrote back to Wansbrough-Jones. He had obviously decided that the weak financial position of the WVRA might provide the best answer to the problem:

'We have been giving a good deal of thought to this subject, since the proposals constitute in effect a test case for other "serious" proposals which may come forward from other bodies as a result of the Reshaping plans. The nature and scale of the railway operations proposed put cases of this kind on a different footing from earlier ones such as the Bluebell line.

'We must of course be particularly concerned with the high standard of physical and operational safeguards that the running of a commuter service would require.

'But it seems to us that the implications of the basic question of safety run wider than this. For example, the Minister must, before he can consider granting an application for a Light Railway Order, be satisfied about the financial position and prospects of the body who would eventually be responsible for operations: in particular, he must be concerned about their ability to meet properly the maintenance and other obligations which would come to them with the sale of the line. Under section 1 of the Railway Companies (Accounts and Returns), Act, 1911 as amended by section 10 of the Transport Charges &c. (Miscellaneous Provisions) Act, 1954, independent railway undertakings are required to render annual accounts and returns in such forms and containing such particulars as the Minister may direct. In view of this background, I think that responsible bodies proposing to take on the running of a railway will not object to providing the Minister with evidence of their financial stability.

'I do not of course know what details the Westerham Valley Railway Association have given you with the firm proposals I understand you have now had from them. But now that they have produced their proposals, it is clear that the sooner we can get down to detail on them the better. I am enclosing a list which indicates the sort of points we should like to go into with the Association. This may well not be exhaustive, but I think it contains most of the main topics on which we feel we need information to enable us to decide whether we could recommend to the Minister a proposal for a regular service of the kind the Association have in mind.

'I would therefore suggest that you should inform the Association that the Minister, in view of his responsibilities in relation to a Light Railway Order and under Section 41 of the Road and Rail Traffic Act, 1933, will wish to have full details of the Association's proposed operations. They should therefore, if they wish to proceed with their proposals, submit such details with as much of the information listed as they can at this stage make available. We envisage, for your information, that the next step might then be detailed discussions with the Association, and perhaps you.'

Attached to this letter was a questionnaire that was to be put to the WVRA. It is reproduced in Appendix 17 with the WVRA's responses, which explain in detail how the WVRA intended to operate the line. As Scott-Malden's letter makes clear, this was the first time that the promoters of a preserved railway had been asked to complete such a document. Many of the questions were reasonable ones but, given that the Ministry had never felt the need to issue such questionnaires for earlier schemes, it is hard to ignore the suspicion that its real purpose was to stop the Westerham scheme in its tracks. Later documents confirm that this was indeed the case.

Nowadays, such information would be a routine part of a business case, but few 1960s preservation schemes would have succeeded if they had been required to produce detailed business cases. Nor, indeed, would BR have found it easy to answer some of the questions; at the Westerham TUCC hearing it couldn't even say how much, if any, of the branch track had been renewed yet the WVRA was expected to know the weight of the rails used on the line!

Cobb wrote to the WVRA on 18 July 1963, insisting that it reply to the questionnaire within two weeks. However, he realised that it was hardly reasonable to put a time limit on negotiations until it was known whether or not the Minister would agree to BR being relieved of the need to subsidise the replacement buses. The WVRA replied, carefully avoiding Cobb's earlier query about its financial resources, saying that the questionnaire would be considered by the committee but a number of its members were on holiday. Cobb noted on the reply 'See my note of my meeting today – we must press them hard'.

The meeting to which Cobb referred was his lunch with Wansbrough-Jones and McMullen to discuss general problems associated with the takeover of closed lines by enthusiasts. During the lunch McMullen had once again made it clear that the Ministry had no objection to societies 'playing trains', provided there were reasonable safety precautions. Nor was it worried about level

Westerham Flyer **issue No 1 February 1963**

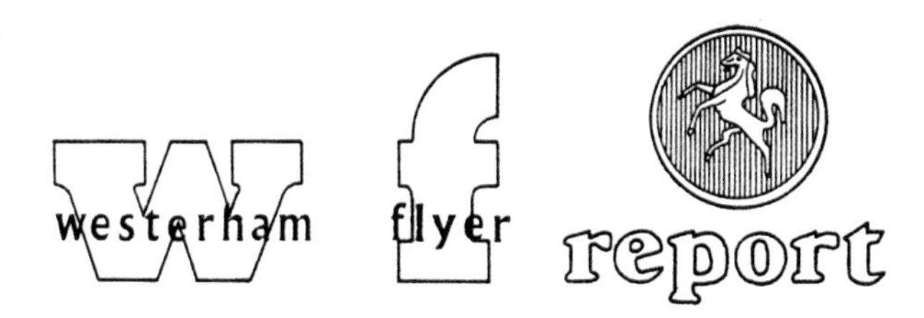

THE PUBLICITY COMMITTEE, W.V.R.A. NUMBER 1 FEBRUARY 1963.

161, RAVENSBOURNE AVENUE, SHORTLANDS, KENT.

EDITORIAL

First an apology. We stated in our news sheet in December that it was hoped to start publication of a fully fledged magazine in the New Year. This proved easier said than done, and a change of policy has been necessary. Owing to our present acute financial position, and the amount or organisation necessary before embarking on a printed periodical, it has been decided to issue a series of 'Reports' until we are able to rise to greater things.

This means that those of you who have sent in articles for publication will have to wait until the 'Westerham Flyer' itself appears before your works are published. It does NOT mean that we do not want any further articles, for once we start the 'Flyer' we shall be hard put to it to keep the pages filled. So please keep on sending in your contributions. Many thanks to those who have already answered the call.

We mentioned our dire financial position. In this Association we have been getting 'something for nothing' for far too long now, and at the Special Meeting, announced elsewhere in this issue, the subscription will be raised to a more realistic level, in line with other similar organisations. We feel sure that no one will begrudge this, in fact on reflection you will surely wonder how we can have survived so long on so little. So do we! For instance with the membership fee so low the last order of brochures exhausted the subscriptions of over 150 members! At that rate we could never hope to say or do much.

POINTS FROM THE AGM. **by the Secretary.**

For the benefit of those who were unable to attend we amplify the minutes which you will receive with this issue. During the meeting many questions were asked. Among them were these:-

1.Q. Was the complete line worth more than £30,000? This was the figure British Railways were asking.

A. Yes. British Railways had originally asked £80,000, then £53,000. The present figure had been reached after long negotiations.

2.Q. What would happen if the venture were to fail?

A. The operating company would have to bear the loss.

crossings, for which suitable safeguards could be provided, but the Ministry was completely opposed to societies running commuter services and McMullen said that the questionnaire he had produced for the Westerham people to complete was intended to frighten off any would-be providers of such services.

The discussion then turned to the Westerham branch itself. It was agreed that a meeting would be arranged between the WVRA and a Ministry inspecting officer once the WVRA had replied to the questionnaire. The Ministry would use this meeting to make it clear that they would only allow societies to run commuter services under the most stringent conditions which would, in fact, be virtually impossible to fulfil.

While all this was going on, the civil engineer had reduced the value of the track to £11,000 from the previous £31,000, after deducting the cost of track recovery. Needless to say, the Southern's new general manager, David McKenna, demanded an explanation. It turned out that the original value was based on notional prices for second-hand material but tenders received for the demolition of the Rye Harbour branch were much lower and the value of the Westerham track had been re-assessed on that basis.

August 1963 saw the publication of another *Westerham Flyer*. The only real news was that the WVRA was to form a company – the Westerham Valley Light Railway Company Ltd, a company with no share capital but limited by guarantee. The *Flyer* also reported that an unusual vehicle known as the Railmobile had taken to the rails at Westerham. This was a flat truck which was powered by a car's wheels through sets of rollers and a drive train. It was built by Mr C. J. Prescott of Bromley, who thought that the Westerham line would be a good place to try it out and obtained permission from BR to do so. Pathé News filmed the contraption in use, powered by a Ford Zephyr convertible. Another film exists of it using a Hillman Imp and a Landrover was also used. The first trip nearly ended in disaster when Prescott set off before the points at the end of the run-round loop had been changed and was only just stopped before a derailment occurred. Even the short trip to Brasted and back apparently did little for the health of the powering vehicle's gearbox.

Despite BR's request for a reply to the questionnaire within two weeks, it was eventually sent by the WVRA's solicitors at the end of August, with the comment that the document was extremely comprehensive and had taken a considerable time to complete. It was received by BR with less than outright enthusiasm and the decision was taken not to forward the answers to the Ministry until the WVRA had given assurances that it would be able to pay £30,000 immediately on completion of the sale. BR was worried that it would have to wait until the WVRA had sold surplus land before the money was available and it was adamant that there could be no question of deferring payment.

When October dawned, the WVRA was still unable to give BR the assurances it required though its solicitor promised an answer within a few days. Several offers had been made for land not required for the railway and it was intended to link these sales as simultaneous transactions when the purchase was completed. The rest of the price was to be raised by debentures to be issued by the company, which was in the process of being formed. In reply BR set a deadline of 16 October 1963.

Re-enter the council

However, before this deadline expired the Kent county surveyor wrote to BR, saying that the council's improvements sub-committee had decided at its meeting on 3 October to buy the whole of the branch. As the nature of the preservation society had changed, the sub-committee no longer felt bound to honour its undertaking not to prejudice the attempt to re-open the line, particularly as the original deadline set by BR was June 1962.

This was bizarre. What made the sub-committee think that the nature of the preservation society had changed? It must have been tipped off about the Ministry's reluctance to allow the WVRA to run commuter trains. Further mystery is added by the plans for the Sevenoaks Bypass – now held in the National Archives at Kew.108 One of the first drawings for the Chevening crossing, dated May 1963, shows nothing; the bypass stops at the edge of railway property. Clearly no decision had been taken as to how the road was to cross the railway. An associated drawing, though, shows that the bypass could have crossed the railway with greater clearance than the existing road bridge, which makes us wonder what the earlier fuss about bridges was about. However, by August 1963, the drawings had been updated and appear to show the bypass crossing the railway on an embankment – not a bridge. Regardless of the plans for the railway, the council intended to fill in the cutting at Chevening.

Commuter service abandoned

As it turned out, it was an academic point. On 15 October 1963, the WVRA's solicitors wrote to BR saying that, after lengthy discussion, its committee had decided to abandon the idea of running a commuter service. The letter described the reasoning behind the decision:

'The present proposal is that our Clients should relieve the Board of the subvention of £8,700, paid to London Transport, together with payment of a cash sum to the Board of £30,000.

'Because of the high cost of running the proposed commuter service and the possibility of still having to meet the cost of the subvention our Clients have come to the conclusion that it would be impracticable to continue with their scheme for the commuter service. The amount of capital required by the Company to purchase the line cannot be realised without the sale of the greater part of Westerham Station and sidings. Without these facilities it would not appear possible to run an effective scheduled weekday service.

'Further, even if such a service could be run it is thought that it will be difficult to persuade the Minister and the Transport Users Consultative Committee to agree to the release of liability for the subvention and our Clients would prefer to anticipate this decision rather than have their hopes dashed at a later stage.

'As it is known that the Commuter service cannot pay for itself the subsidy for it must come from the Weekend enthusiast service of steam trains and the burden on this source of revenue would be excessive.

'Our Clients, having faced these problems are therefore, of the opinion, as previously stated, that they must reluctantly give up ideas of operating the scheduled weekday service.

'In these circumstances our Clients are prepared to purchase the freehold of the line from the Board, at an agreed valuation. This follows a suggestion already made by you that, in the event of the Minister refusing permission to run the commuter service, as now anticipated, the opportunity would be given to our Clients to purchase the freehold at a straight valuation. Our Clients propose then to operate the weekend steam service as already outlined.

'We shall be pleased to hear from you agreeing to this suggestion and that our Clients' Surveyors may immediately approach your estates department for this purpose. We understand that figures have previously been mentioned but since then certain alterations to the proposals have been made which necessitate adjustment, e.g. the lease of part of Dunton Green as opposed to purchase.

'As to the prompt payment of the purchase price, the Association's Bankers have been approached as to the making of a bridging loan to the Association pending completion of the sale of unwanted parts of the land, subject to satisfactory contracts being exchanged. We have not yet, of course, received a draft Contract from you.

'In regard to the sales by the Association, we are informed that firm offers, subject to Contract, have been made and that there will be funds available, on completion and for payment of the deposit on exchange of Contracts.

'For your further information the proposed Company, Westerham Valley Light Railway Company Limited will probably be incorporated about the first week of November, after which a prospectus will be issued in regard to debentures for the working capital of the Company.'

What had happened to change the situation so quickly? The WVRA had presumably picked up on the Ministry's negative attitude and its prevarication over the replacement bus subsidy. Being singled out by having to answer the Ministry's questionnaire may have been another factor, even if the WVRA knew nothing about the objections to 40mph running.

The questionnaire was, without doubt, a demanding document to answer and it must have forced the WVRA to take a hard look at its proposals. The commuter service would have been expensive and difficult to run. Finding reliable staff willing to work part-time at 'unsocial' hours would have been a problem. Nor were the GWR railcars in the best of condition, a disadvantage for vehicles on which the service would totally depend. When the Kent & East Sussex Railway (K&ESR) bought car No 20 in 1966, it took six years and much effort to get it back into proper working order, only for it to be withdrawn again in 1980 for a complete rebuild due to corrosion. The budget allowed £1,000 for repair work on the railcars but time was the greater problem. Once BR had sold the line it would have expected the service to be started without delay but to restore even two railcars to operation would have taken a long while. After more than two years of disuse, the track would also have needed attention to make it acceptable for 40mph running. BR may well have expected the WVRA to pay all or part of the bus subsidy if, for any reason, it could not withdraw the replacement buses.

The finances of the commuter service were dubious. The WVRA was optimistic in expecting to carry 200 passengers a day. BR had carried an average of 167 and, two years on, many of those would have been happy with the new arrangements they had made. Some had moved away or retired, others had taken to the car. If, after any early flush of enthusiasm, the WVRA won only 150 back to the trains, the economics of the service would have been fragile. Income would have been outweighed by substantially higher costs, especially when the costs of replacing or rebuilding the railcars were factored in. The risk was that the commuter service would have sucked the lifeblood out of the weekend steam service.

'Very satisfactory'

Cobb and some of his BR colleagues were furious at this turn of events, even though it was exactly the outcome for which they and the Ministry had strived for so long. A note by an unknown hand was stridently headed 'THE LOST 13½ MONTHS'. BR clearly felt that its approach had been justified but that was unfair. Its obstructionism, its refusal to budge from the unrealistic price it had demanded and the problems of the bus subsidy had all contributed to the wasted months.

The road building plans also gave BR an alternative buyer for the line. The estates department quickly pointed out that it just happened to have a renewed offer from the council on the table. Cobb arranged an internal meeting to reconsider the valuation of the line and, in the meantime, wrote to the WVRA's solicitors:

'You have probably been informed by now that the undertaking given in early 1962 by the Kent County Council to the Westerham Valley Railway Association, to the effect that the Council would not prejudice the Association's endeavours to a acquire the line, has been withdrawn, in the light of the changed nature of the services to be operated and the Council have asked me to re-open negotiations. The Board must of course give serious consideration to this new development having regard to the delay in completing negotiations with the Association and the decision not to operate a commuter service at this very late stage.'

The solicitor replied, saying that the WVRA would hardly want to go to the expense of setting up a company if BR was not prepared to negotiate with it. He did, though, reaffirm that they wanted to pursue the scheme and there would be no problem in raising the 10 per cent deposit as soon as BR could provide a draft contract. BR pointed out to him that, in the changed circumstances, a new price would have to be agreed but Cobb did offer a meeting, which the WVRA accepted. It asked whether that meant that the council did not want to buy so much of the line as to prevent its use as a railway.

Cobb also wrote to Wansbrough-Jones, breaking the news and telling him about the council's renewed interest. He did not mention that he had been holding back the WVRA's response to the Ministry's questionnaire, instead saying that certain details in it were suspect and it was necessary to seek further information. He continued that:

'As the question of the Board being relieved of the subvention is no longer relative, I am having an up-to-date valuation prepared immediately and as soon as a price has been agreed with either the Association or the Council, I propose to place a limit on the time for completion of the transaction.

'In the above circumstances, I presume that the Ministry of Transport will not require to see the answers to the questionnaire.'

Wansbrough-Jones passed the news to Scott-Malden at the Ministry. This triggered a search for any information in the rail division's own files and those of the highways division about the council's interest in the line. It was, Sheaf said:

'... at least possible that they will be interested in using it, or some of it, as a road, and the Ministry may have some concern here.'

Sheaf also wrote to Col Robertson of the Railway Inspectorate:

'I enclose a copy of a letter we have just had from General Wansbrough-Jones. I am sure you will agree that this is very satisfactory. I had in fact heard in discussion on something else with Mr. Cobb, Assistant General Manager of the Southern Region, a few days ago that we were likely to get something of this kind shortly.

'We are now asked whether we still need the Association's answers to the questionnaire British Railways sent them at our request. I am sure that we do not need it, and indeed could not justify asking for this information now.[109] But I understand – this is confirmed by General Wansbrough-Jones's letter – that the Association still want to buy the line in order to "play trains". If this is so, ought we to ask for any information at all at this stage. Or, in view of the possibility that the line will in fact be sold to the Council rather than the Association, can we save trouble by waiting for a bit?

'I should, of course, be grateful for any other comments you may have: you may have heard the rumours of what the Association are up to from your own sources.'

At the end of October 1963 the Kent roads committee confirmed that negotiations should be re-opened for the acquisition of the line. The county surveyor told the committee that the situation had to be resolved quickly because the council could save £14,000 on the Sevenoaks Bypass and £82,000 on the South Orbital Road by using the line. According to the *Sevenoaks Chronicle*, the committee was told that the council had suspended negotiations with BR while the Passengers' Association tried to buy the line. BR had agreed to the Association's offer in September of the previous year but since then there appeared to be no further development. In a curious twist, which must have misled its members, the committee was also told that the original Association (to which the council had given its undertaking) no longer existed and had been replaced by another. This was untrue – the Association had simply changed its name.

Disappointing meeting

When the WVRA met on Saturday 2 November 1963 for what the press described as a 'disappointing' annual general meeting, the members were told about a last-ditch plan to save the line. The WVRA would take out a loan of £35,000 to pay BR for the freehold of the land. The railway would then vacate the station site at Westerham and it, together with the station house and spare land at Brasted, would be sold to raise £25,000 to repay much of the loan. A new platform would be built outside the existing station area at Westerham. Admittedly, this would be inconvenient for a commuter service but, given that BR's revised price was only £35,000, the original price of £30,000, which carried with it the liability to run a commuter service, no longer seemed attractive.

The meeting revealed a split. The new chairman, Mr Sid Beacon, discouraged optimism, saying that the WVRA had only a fortnight to raise the money. However, another committee member, Mr K. G. Carr, rejected such fatalism. He moved a resolution reaffirming faith in the project and demanding that the scheme should go ahead on the basis of a full service, which was carried by an overwhelming majority. There were a lot of enthusiasts who wanted preserved railways to do more than just run from one field to another; they wanted to run railways that had purpose.

Another committee member, Mr K. C. Tozer – who was soon to take over as chairman – said that it was a question of running a commuter service or nothing. While the commuter service would not cover its cost, the WVRA had to be prepared to subsidise it to get the line. He believed that the council would have no option but to stand aside if they did so.

The meeting supported a proposal that the WVRA should spend up to £150 of its dwindling funds to advertise for financial backers but, while those present were determined to pursue the dream, the fact was that support was fading. Only 294 members and 73 juniors had renewed their subscriptions.

A couple of weeks later, Fulford wrote to the general manager to tell him that the council wanted to buy the line whether or not the WVRA wanted to run a public service. It had not been possible to agree a sale price but the council had not been unduly concerned when a figure of about £22,500 was suggested as the land value. The council was also interested in the ballast but not the sleepers or rails. It had been put to the council

'H' class No 31263 takes on water at Tunbridge Wells West in 1963 in the last of her 58 years of service. She was withdrawn in January 1964 and, after almost a year in store, she was bought by the Westerham Valley Railway Association for preservation. ***Author's collection***

in confidence that a package deal of £34,000 could be recommended but the council representatives were doubtful about having to dispose of the rails and sleepers. BR promised to contact them again after its meeting with the WVRA.

In the meantime, Wansbrough-Jones informed the Southern Region of the Ministry's decision that there was no point in the submitting the WVRA's questionnaire answers. If it were to go ahead with the idea of buying the line, but not operating a commuter service, the Ministry would need information about level crossings and arrangements for the maintenance of bridges and other structures but this could wait until it was clear if there was any serious likelihood of it taking over the line.

On 20 November the WVRA went to Waterloo to meet a BR team. Cobb opened the meeting by saying that a new situation existed since the WVRA had given up its idea of operating a scheduled weekday service but Tozer interrupted to say that that decision had been reversed. Cobb continued that, in view of the time that BR's assets had lain idle, matters could not drag on while the WVRA dealt with the Ministry questionnaire and satisfied the Minister as to its ability to operate an adequate service – conveniently ignoring the fact that BR had been sitting on the WVRA's answers for two months. He therefore offered to sell the line to the WVRA at a price of £40,000, providing it could provide evidence of its ability to pay and subject to contracts being exchanged by the end of 1963. The WVRA representatives accepted this price as reasonable.

Cobb agreed that, if the WVRA later succeeded in

'O1' class 0-6-0 No 31065 was originally built by the South Eastern Railway in 1896 to the design of James Stirling but was rebuilt in 1908 with the same design of boiler as was used on the 'H' class. However, the tender with its outside frames and springs was a throwback to an earlier age. She was withdrawn in June 1961 but managed to survive in store for some years until she was bought by Mr Esmond Lewis-Evans. She is seen here at Shepherdswell in July 1960. *Dave Cobbe Collection/Rail Photoprints*

starting a weekday service some financial adjustment could be negotiated. He did, however, emphasise that BR had no obligation to provide connecting services at Dunton Green, mentioning a recently announced plan for changes to timetables. A hint as to what this might mean was the announcement that, as from January, the 5.30pm train from Cannon Street – formerly one of the most popular branch connections – was to call at Chelsfield instead of Dunton Green. The train could not make both stops and it had been estimated that three times as many people would use the Chelsfield stop as used Dunton Green, now that it was no longer a junction. This would have disrupted the proposed branch timetable and demonstrated the fragility of the WVRA's position.

Cobb said that the council was anxious to buy the line because of the savings it would make by using it for its new roads and it could resort to a compulsory purchase order which BR might find difficult to resist. The council also proposed road works at Westerham which might seriously reduce the value of the land which the WVRA had been planning to sell to raise capital. It was agreed that the next step would be for the WVRA to contact the council to check its intentions and its attitude towards the re-opening of the line.

A couple of days later, BR received a phone call asking for details of the bus subsidy from a firm of surveyors acting for a Mr Birch, who was described as a possible backer of the WVRA.

A week after its meeting with BR, the WVRA met the deputy county surveyor. It reported back to BR that the council wanted to buy part of the line for road projects but the WVRA understood that no compulsory purchase order was then being contemplated although the council wanted to settle the matter as soon as possible. In the circumstances the WVRA accepted BR's offer to sell the line for £40,000 and asked for an urgent meeting to discuss the exchange of contracts. BR took its time replying to this request, presumably because it was waiting to hear back from the council. Fulford, who had become estates and rating surveyor for the Southern Region in succession to the newly-retired Tunbridge, wrote to the council on 6 December, almost encouraging the council to issue a compulsory purchase order:

'I have also received a letter from the Westerham Valley Railway Association to the effect that they wish to proceed with the purchase of the Branch.

'You will appreciate that since terms have been agreed with the Railway Association the Board may be considered to be under an obligation to sell to them. If, on the other hand, your Council's interest is such that you would consider making a Compulsory Purchase Order in the event of the Board not being willing to treat with you, then I would be undertaking a considerable amount of abortive work in continuing with the Railway Association.'

It had the desired effect; the county surveyor replied a few days later:

'Thank you for your letter of the 6th instant and in the circumstances I am recommending to my Committee at its meeting on January 2nd next, that a C.P.O. should be made in connection with this acquisition.'

Fulford's reply revealed that, while these letters were being exchanged, a representative from the estates department had met with the council, leaving a plan on which the council was asked to mark the land it wanted to buy at Dunton Green. Fulford was playing a two-faced game, keeping the WVRA dangling while moving things along with the council. In the absence of any reply from BR, the WVRA's solicitors wrote again on 13 December:

'Further to your letter of the 5th December, and to our Clients offer for the purchase of the line, we have now heard from Kent County Council that the Council has approved of its purchase of the line for road purposes and that negotiations have been opened with the British Railways Board to this end.

As, at present, there does not appear to be a compulsory purchase order affecting the property our Clients are anxious to know in which direction the Board intends to go for a purchaser of the line.

'Will you please confirm that our Client's offer to you has been made in compliance with the conditions laid down at the joint meeting held recently under Mr. Cobb's chairmanship, i.e. an offer prior to 31st December 1963?'

A few days later the county surveyor wrote to Fulford clarifying the situation, saying that, while he was sure that the council was willing to buy the whole line by negotiation, if it had to use compulsory purchase it could only be for the parts of the line that would be needed immediately for approved roads purposes. Although the county surveyor didn't say so at this stage – the admission came later – this covered only the narrow strip needed for the Sevenoaks Bypass as the other schemes had yet to be approved.

Cobb wrote back to the WVRA just before Christmas:

'With reference to your letter of 15th December, it is confirmed that the British Railways Board are willing to proceed with the sale of the above line to the Westerham Valley Railway Association and you have my assurance that we are not proposing to open negotiations with the Kent County Council.

'Unfortunately, we understand that the Council wish to acquire the whole of the land by negotiation and if necessary they will seek Compulsory Purchase powers for those parts of the line which would be required for their road scheme. It therefore seems pointless for the Board to sell the line to the Association, if the Council intend to obtain powers to acquire large proportions of

Beattie Well Tank No 30585 at Havenstreet on the Isle of Wight Steam Railway in May 2011. This locomotive, which was built in 1874, survived in BR service until December 1962. The following spring it was offered to the WVRA for use on the Westerham line but was turned down. It was eventually bought by the London Railway Preservation Society – now the Buckinghamshire Railway Centre at Quainton Road – for £750. *Author*

the track site from the Association.

'I would suggest that this matter can only be resolved by you asking the Council to state whether they would definitely resort to Compulsory Purchaser powers if the line is acquired by the Association. The Board are naturally anxious to realise on the valuable assets involved, and I shall be obliged if you will ask the Council for their early decision.'

Cobb was obviously under the erroneous impression that the compulsory purchase order would cover most of the trackbed. The WVRA's solicitors replied straightaway:

'Thank you for your letter of the 20th December. We are very pleased to note that the Board are willing to proceed with the sale to our Clients.

'We appreciate the observations contained in the remainder of your letter and whilst we received, in reply to the usual enquiries of the local Authority accompanying the Official Search of the local Land Charges Register, an indication that no compulsory purchase order or resolution has been made or proposed by the County Council, we are writing to them with a formal application under the Town and Country Planning Act 1954 for the appropriate certificate under Section 33. We will, of course, advise you of the result as soon as possible.

'We should be interested to learn whether the Board would agree to a conditional Contract of Sale pending the outcome of the Council's decision and if it will, whether or not the Board would, at our clients' expense, join in opposing any such resolution or order.'

This seems to have unsettled Cobb; he noted on the letter 'I would like Estate's advice on where we are getting to.' Meanwhile, the council replied to the WVRA's formal enquiry by saying that it would, if necessary, make a compulsory purchase order for the part of the line which was required at Chevening for the construction of the Sevenoaks Bypass.

Fulford recommended that the answer to the WVRA be that BR:

'... could not offer any useful support to an objection to a Compulsory Purchase Order. In view of the fact that this matter will soon be resolved there seems little point in completing a contract with the Railway Society at this stage.'

BR was about to reply to the WVRA on those lines when the council proposed a high-level meeting between itself, BR, the WVRA and the Ministry of Transport. The Ministry declined to take part but the meeting went ahead anyway and a date was set for 30 January 1964.

The council must have realised that it was on shaky ground. It could only use compulsory purchase for the narrow strip of land needed for the Sevenoaks Bypass, probably worth no more than about £100, leaving BR with the rest of the severed trackbed with no guarantee that the council would buy it. BR could have opposed compulsory purchase[110] on the grounds that it would be left with two severed lengths of trackbed but it preferred to leave the matter to be settled between the council and the WVRA rather than take sides, though in practice it was taking the council's side1. It was also aware that the council was going to try to persuade the WVRA that it would be pointless for it to acquire the line in view of the impending South Orbital road scheme.

Fulford chaired the meeting with the council and the WVRA. Tozer, the WVRA's chairman, repeated the offer to buy the line for £40,000 and asked that a draft contract be sent to them as soon as possible and immediate steps be taken to obtain the Light Railway Order.

Bowdler, the county surveyor said that the use of the railway land by the council would save public money. Avoiding the need to build a bridge for the Sevenoaks bypass would save about £14,000 and, as the council wanted to start construction in the near future, the matter

WVRA volunteers Dick Glover (left) and Richard Ferris demonstrate the procedure for reconstructing a platelayer's trolley using the goods yard crane at Westerham. The base of the crane survives in the industrial estate that occupies the site of the station. *Richard Ferris*

The WVRA's first piece of rolling stock complete and in working order once more to assist in work out on the line. In the background the station building looks better for a new coat of paint. In order to get the colours right, paint samples were taken from the very dilapidated wooden platform shelters at BR's Catford station which had not been repainted since the 1920s. *Richard Ferris*

was urgent. Use of the railway earthworks for the South Orbital Road would save between £80,000 and £100,000. The council also intended to build a new road that would take half the Westerham station site. Finally, the bridge over the railway near Dunton Green was to be widened and the railway trackbed would provide a subway under the road.

Bowdler said that the acquisition of the line was of the greatest importance and a compulsory purchase order would be made for the land needed for the Sevenoaks bypass if BR was unwilling to sell by agreement. Other parts were also needed but less urgently. Two short lengths were not required but the council was still willing to buy the whole line from Dunton Green bridge to Westerham. The council's stance was clearly intended to bully BR into selling to it. As we shall see in the next chapter, parts of the Ministry were undecided as to the future of the South Orbital Road and there was no certainty that it would be built. Did the council hope that if it owned part of the necessary land there was a much greater chance of it happening? In the meantime, though, there was a real risk that it was buying a white elephant.

After this discussion, the WVRA representatives decided that they still wanted to buy the line. However, Fulford said that he had no alternative but to recommend that BR sell the land to the council, bearing in mind the financial aspects from both a local and national viewpoint. He thanked both parties for the courteous nature of the discussion and extended his sympathy to the WVRA in its disappointment at the result of the discussion.

Even so, the WVRA's solicitor wrote to Cobb the following day, formally repeating its offer to buy the line. He reminded Cobb of BR's previous statement that it was willing to sell to the WVRA and the assurance it had given that it was not proposing to open negotiations with the council.

Fulford wrote to the general manager, asking for permission to break off negotiations with the WVRA. This was presumably given because Fulford drafted a press release to announce the sale of the line to the council. In his original version he included the sentence:

'But as a public undertaking we must look to public expenditure and a saving to the tax payer of over £100,000 is a powerful argument.'

Yet again, this should have been of no concern to BR. However, Fulford, like Tunbridge before him, seems to have been too closely tied in with the county roads department.

Cobb replied to the WVRA a few days later:

'With reference to your letter of 31st January, circumstances have altered since I wrote to you on 20th December, in that we have now been told quite definitely that the Kent County Council will, if necessary, serve a Compulsory Purchase Order, which would in all probability become effective before the line could be conveyed to the Association. It is quite clear to us, that there are no grounds on which we could resist such an Order, and it would therefore be a waste of time for the Board to continue with the sale to the Association, as this could only involve both parties in abortive expenditure.

'We are very sorry things have turned out this way and I trust you will agree that in all the circumstances, there is no point in the Board proceeding with the sale to the Association. Attached, for your information, is a copy of the Draft Press Release which is at present being considered by Mr. Tozer, the Chairman of the Westerham Valley Railway Association.'

The WVRA solicitor replied immediately to Cobb:

'Thank you for your letter of yesterday with its enclosure. We note, with considerably regret the decision that has been made by the Board and are advising our Clients accordingly. There will be a meeting of our Clients' Committee at the weekend and we shall be obliged if the press release may be held over until next week, when Mr. Locke, the Secretary, will get in touch with you.

'It has come to our notice that the statements made by the Kent County Council regarding the South Orbital Road and the proposed use of part of the line for road purposes are inconsistent with information provided by the Ministry of Transport, Highways Division. It is understood that there is no question at all of the South Orbital Road going anywhere near the line and that in any event no work on this project is anticipated for at least ten years.

'In these circumstances the alleged savings by the County Council to be made in the purchase of the whole line would not appear to be justified. The only part of the track site to be affected is, therefore, that to be crossed by the Sevenoaks By-pass.

'We hope to be able to adduce detailed confirmation of these facts from the Ministry of Transport within the next few days, and must ask again that in the light of this evidence the Board reconsider its decision.'

Cobb wrote an emphatic 'No!' against the final paragraph. He added a note: 'This is a matter between him and the KCC who are the responsible authority as far as we are concerned. We should write and make this clear.'

On 6 February 1964 Hawkins of the estates department took a phone call from Tozer. Tozer had been to the Ministry where he had been told that a railway route for the South Orbital Road was wrong. The gradient to reach the level of the railway was greater than the recommended 1 in 22 maximum for motorways, the 14 feet width of the railway formation was negligible compared to the 120 feet required for the new road, and in any event the road would be better sited to the north along the Pilgrims Way. The Ministry also suggested that, provided the WVRA were willing to bear the extra £14,000 cost for the Sevenoaks Bypass to bridge the railway, they saw no reason why the county council should not agree to this. In view of this, and since the WVRA was prepared to allow the council they land they needed at Westerham station, there appeared to be no reason why the Society's plans could not proceed.

Tozer suggested a fresh meeting with the council, but Hawkins said that, although he would need to consult colleagues, he felt that nothing would be gained by such a meeting unless the Ministry was prepared to be there too. Tozer felt that, if BR was to proceed with the proposed press release, it might be embarrassing if the Ministry subsequently pointed out errors in the council's plan and suggested that it should not be released without further investigation. Hawkins agreed that there was no reason why Tozer should not contact the council and the Ministry to see what could be done, but BR wanted the matter settled quickly. Tozer did arrange a meeting with Bowdler, the county surveyor, and the press release was held back.

Informed of these developments, Cobb noted: 'This won't do. We must decide a date on which we bring in a contractor to take the track up.'

The meeting between the council and the WVRA took place on 11 February. Bowdler admitted that the South Orbital Road scheme might change as a result of signs that traffic flows were changing. He therefore proposed

GWR railcar No W19W seen at Gloucester Central station, still in her early BR crimson and cream livery, probably in 1959. Five such railcars were inspected by the WVRA for possible use on the Westerham line. It was intended to buy three of them for the proposed commuter service. ***Author's collection***

that the council should buy the branch line, carry out the required work at Westerham, and lease the rest of the line to the WVRA. The council would build a bridge for the Sevenoaks Bypass and recover the cost in the rent charged.

Meanwhile, BR was pressing for a decision about the purchase of the three locomotives – 31263, 31518 and 31065 – reserved by the WVRA. The WVRA replied that negotiations were still on-going and asked for time. Fortunately, BR accepted that and allowed some breathing space.

The optimism was not to last. On 20 February the clerk to the council wrote to BR saying that the WVRA's offer for a lease of the line was unacceptable[111] and confirmed that, as work was to start on the Sevenoaks Bypass that year, the delay in buying the line had made the situation very serious. He asked BR to proceed at once with a sale of the line to the council, leaving the council to negotiate with the WVRA. If BR was unwilling to do so, the council would issue the necessary notices for a compulsory purchase order. He gave BR a week to agree. He added that the county surveyor had agreed with the Ministry's divisional road engineer that, if the council bought the line, the South Orbital Road would be routed along the greater part of it.

On 24 February, BR wrote to the council setting out its terms for the sale at a price of £40,000, including the track[123]. A few days later Cobb told the WVRA that, once the council had bought the line and agreed to grant the WVRA a lease, a single Light Railway Order was all that would be needed to give it powers to run the line.

'This vexed question is out of the way at last'

Cobb finally reported to Wansbrough-Jones that BR had virtually discontinued negotiations with the WVRA and that a sale to the council was being arranged. On 5 March 1964 Wansbrough-Jones, in turn, wrote to Scott-Malden at the Ministry:

'I have been informed by the Southern Region that the

Clapham Junction 'A' signal box which partially collapsed on 10 May 1965 when, as a result of very heavy corrosion, a component in a girder failed. After the collapse similar bridges were checked and that carrying the West London Junction signal box was also found to be in a precarious condition. The failure was blamed on lax examination, errors of judgment by the examiners and steelwork inspector, and a lack of proper organisation in the District Engineer's office. ***Author's collection.***

Ex-GWR railcar No W21W awaiting scrapping at Swindon on 1st December 1963 with an unknown Castle class locomotive behind it. W21W was not one of the railcars offered to the WVRA but it is unlikely that they were in much better condition. *Author's collection*

proposals for the sale to the Westerham Valley Railway Association are virtually at an end. The Association have clearly been temporizing for some time and meanwhile the Kent County Council have decided to purchase some of the land over which the line runs for highway purposes. This sale is now being arranged and the Railway Association have been told that there is no point in continuing negotiations with them for the sale of the line.

'I enclose another copy of this letter which I should be glad if you would pass on to Denis McMullen. I am glad that this vexed question is out of the way at last.'

There is no doubt that, while Kent's county surveyor had always wanted to buy the line for road building, the Ministry's overriding concern was to stop private companies from running commuter and commercial services. We know from Cobb's report of his lunch with McMullen that the Railway Inspectorate's questionnaire sent to the WVRA was intended to frighten off schemes that planned to run a proper service[134]. Kent's purchase of the line put an end to the preservation scheme but road building was not the reason why the Ministry wanted to block it. With senior Ministry figures such as Serpell involved, Marples himself cannot have been unaware of the situation. We may guess that the decisions being taken had his tacit agreement at the very least.

One last effort

The WVRA, in the guise of the Westerham Valley Light Railway Company, made one last effort to resolve the situation by writing a long and detailed letter to Mr R. C. Henbest, the BRB's chief estates officer, with a copy to Dr Beeching. The letter described the negotiations with the Southern Region and, in particular, the assurances given by Cobb in his letter of 20 December and the outcome of the meeting of 30 January between the council, the WVRA and BR:

'During the progress of the meeting the [Association's] Representatives were of the impression that prior discussion had been held by British Railways with the County Council with a view to reaching agreement in the Council's favour notwithstanding the previous assurance given by Mr. Cobb in his letter of the 20th December.'

It is hard to see what the WVRA hoped to achieve by this approach. Henbest simply passed the letter to McKenna, the Southern Region's general manager. Cobb replied to Henbest on McKenna's behalf, saying that the letter's basic facts were right, except that the decision had been made not because of the money the council would save but because of the threatened compulsory purchase order[145]. He pointed out that the Secretary of the BRB had taken a personal interest in the matter throughout the negotiations and was fully aware of the position.

'H' class 0-4-4T No 31263 undergoes restoration work at Robertsbridge on 23 April 1966. She was later transferred to the South Eastern Steam Centre at Ashford and, when that closed, to the Bluebell Railway. ***Author's collection***

A reply was finally sent to the WVRA by Wansbrough-Jones. It very curtly said that:

'I have to inform you that this is primarily a matter for the Southern Region. The British Railways Board see no grounds for any opposition by the Southern Region to the compulsory purchase of the Westerham-Dunton Green branch line by the Kent County Council. The negotiations for the future of this line have been extremely protracted since their initiation in 1962 and the Board are anxious to dispose of it with the minimum of delay.'

The WVRA's solicitor wrote back, asking BR to confirm that it was not prepared to re-open negotiations for the purchase of the line to enable the WVRA to oppose the compulsory purchase order. Wansbrough-Jones once more replied in curt fashion, saying that the BRB was not prepared to re-open negotiations for the purchase of the Westerham to Dunton Green branch line.

Ballast confusion

Meanwhile, Shirley, the financial member of the BR Board, wrote to McKenna, expressing disquiet that the purchase price quoted to the council included the track. He thought BR could get a better price. McKenna replied, outlining the history of the sale. The price of £40,000 was based on £23,000 for the land and buildings and £17,000 for the track (including £6,000 for the ballast). The track worked out at 36s a yard, which compared favourably with the quotations received for the recovery of track elsewhere. It was extremely unlikely that, allowing for the costs of recovery, a sum of £17,000 could be realised from contractors for the Westerham line. He added that he had kept Wansbrough-Jones fully informed about the negotiations because of his considerable interest in the Westerham case.

If McKenna thought that this would satisfy the terrier-like Shirley, he was mistaken. Shirley immediately noticed that, if the ballast was worth £6,000, BR was getting only £11,000 for the rails and sleepers, not the £17,000 claimed by McKenna. The embarrassment was confounded when the scrap sales controller pointed out that the current value of track taken up by contractors was actually 75s a yard, meaning that the track on the Westerham line was worth over £30,000. However, he followed this up with an explanation that the ballast on closed lines was rarely bought by demolition contractors.

Appeal to the Prime Minister

The WVRA invited a BR representative to attend its planned public meeting on 21 April but Cobb's view was that, in view of the position with the council, he did not think that a BR presence would be helpful. The WVRA persisted but to no avail.

While this was going on, Tozer, the WVRA's chairman, wrote to the Prime Minister, Sir Alec Douglas-Home. The WVRA suggested that the revival of the line should be a means of honouring Sir Winston Churchill, whose home was at nearby Chartwell. The WVRA proposed to set up an appeal fund and hoped that the Prime Minister would sit on its committee. Needless to say, the Ministry of Transport adamantly opposed this idea when Downing Street asked for its views. The reply sent on behalf of the Prime Minister was courteous but dismissive.

Storing the stock

As spring 1964 turned into summer, a problem began to arise. Various members of the WVRA were asked to take

1924-built Metropolitan Railway First Class 7-compartment coach No 509 at Ingrow on the Worth Valley Railway in October 2015. This and two sister third class coaches were bought by David Kitton for the Westerham preservation scheme and were sent north when they found themselves homeless.
Inset: the inside of a first class compartment. ***Author***

The Ashford Steam Centre, probably in the mid-1970s, with SER 'O1' class 0-6-0 No 65 and SECR 'H' class 0-4-4T No 263, both of which were originally destined for the preserved Westerham branch. They are seen pulling a train comprising a single SECR 'Birdcage' Brake Third vehicle. ***Author's collection***

delivery of the rolling stock they had bought for use on the line. One of those was David Kitton, the WVRA's publicity officer, who was buying three ex-Metropolitan Railway 'Dreadnought' carriages from LT, which wanted them moved as soon as possible. Kitton had agreed with BR that the carriages could be stored in Dunton Green yard at a rent of £1 per week per vehicle and the carriages were due to be delivered on Sunday 23 August. They were to be worked by an LT pannier tank from Neasden to Hither Green, where a BR diesel would take over for the final leg to Dunton Green. It was hoped to allow members to travel in the train for £2 to help defray the movement cost. Roy Edwards' SECR Matchboard carriage was to be moved from Hassocks at the same time.

Before this could happen, the WVRA issued a duplicated update dated July 1964 to its members, setting out the latest position. The council's terms for the lease were £3,000 a year if the WVRA took all the land. If the council were able to sell part of the land, the WVRA would pay a reduced rent. The WVRA was to pay the cost of the Sevenoaks bypass bridge, which had been estimated at £14,000, but the tenders the council had received were for £26,215. Furthermore, the council insisted that the money be paid before the council would accept the tender, and this had to be done by 24 August. It has never been explained why there was such a leap in the cost of the bridge.

Mr Pastry's heritage park

A late development was an approach by Richard Hearne, the comic film and TV star best known for his role as 'Mr Pastry'. Hearne wanted to create a heritage park in the Westerham valley, in which examples of British achievements, past and present, would be displayed in a parkland setting. The railway was to form a vital part of the scheme. (Hearne lived at St Mary Platt, near Wrotham.)

The WVRA still believed that the line's unrivalled position offered unique potential and that the threat of the line being used for the South Orbital Road would be much reduced after five years if, by then, they were seen to be operating a worthwhile service.

A lengthy article in the *Kentish Messenger* newspaper of 14 August under the heading of 'Peculiar problems of Westerham rail enthusiasts' set out the history of the affair and posed a number of questions, none of which were ever answered. Unfortunately, this splendid bit of publicity backfired when it came to the attention of BR, which was pondering the question of allowing the WVRA's stock to be stored at Dunton Green. Mr G. F. Huskisson, Bolland's successor as line manager, expressed his concern as to whether the WVRA would be able to raise the finance to lease the branch before the council's deadline. Without a clear sign that the vehicles would have a permanent home, he refused to allow the carriages to be stabled at Dunton Green.

A special general meeting of the WVRA was held on 19 August, only days before the council's deadline, at which it admitted that it was unable to raise the £26,215 to pay for the bridge at Chevening. However, it had informed the council that it still wanted to lease the line but no reply had been received. Despite this, it was agreed to go ahead with the purchase of 'H' class locomotive No 31263. £700 had been raised towards the cost and another £150 was needed.

Construction of the Sevenoaks bypass started on Monday 14 September. At this point, the Labour MP for Faversham, Terence Boston, became involved in the campaign. The WVRA suggested to him that an appeal to Dr Beeching might be in order and asked for his thoughts on this, particularly in terms of the stock storage problem. He took the hint and wrote to Beeching, seeking help but his letter ended up back with Fulford at the Southern Region estates department, who told the general manager, David McKenna, that:

'In the Line Manager's letters to Mr. Kitton stating the conditions upon which vehicles may be stored at Dunton Green, it was made clear that this should be regarded as a temporary arrangement only and that the Board wished to be assured that in the event of the Association being unsuccessful in acquiring the branch line then the Association could remove the vehicles to alternative accommodation without delay. I understand this assurance was not given and from Mr. Kitton's letter to Mr. Boston on the 15th September, it would appear that the Railway Association in fact have no alternative accommodation.

'Contracts have been exchanged for the sale of the branch line to Kent County Council. As the work on the Sevenoaks By-pass has already commenced and the council has asked permission to enter on the Board's land to prepare the point where the By-pass crosses the disused branch line, it could be assumed that there is now no chance whatsoever of the Association re-opening the line. I would like to commence negotiations for an alternative use of Dunton Green as soon as possible and feel, therefore, that any suggestion that the Westerham Valley Railway Association should be permitted to stable coaches in the sidings should be resisted.'

The WVRA instead arranged with the War Office to make use of disused sidings on its land at Sharnal Street,

'H' class 0-4-4T No 263, formerly BR No 31263, at the Ashford Steam Centre in around 1970. She had been restored into SECR green livery but that company's elaborate lining had yet to be applied. *Author's collection*

C Class 0-6-0 No 31592 at Sheffield Park on the Bluebell Railway. It survived in BR use at Ashford until July 1963 before being transferred to departmental use at Ashford Works as DS239. It was finally withdrawn in 1966 and was then bought by the Wainwright C Class Preservation Society, the original intention being for it to work on the re-opened Westerham branch. Like No 31263 it was used at the South Eastern Steam Centre at Ashford and, when that closed, it was transferred to the Bluebell Railway. ***Author***

on the Hundred of Hoo branch. The site was an ideal one but BR, maintaining its uncooperative attitude to the last, refused to work the stock to the sidings, claiming that the branch was closed. When challenged, it said that the line was virtually closed but was due to reopen the following year with a frequent train service! For both reasons, the WVRA could not be given access to the sidings. Once again, Boston stepped in to try to resolve the situation but without success.

The 'H' class locomotive finally made its way to Robertsbridge on the K&ESR and ownership of it was later transferred to an 'H' class trust. When it became clear that the locomotive was too heavy for the K&ESR line, it moved to the South Eastern Steam Centre at Ashford. However, in 1975 the Trustees decided that the locomotive would have more scope for running if it was based on the Bluebell Railway. It is now owned by the Bluebell Railway Trust.

Restricted clearances in the tunnels on the Hastings line prevented the WVRA's four carriages joining the locomotive at Robertsbridge so the three 'Dreadnoughts' were placed on a four-year loan to the Keighley & Worth Valley Railway (K&WVR) in Yorkshire and were subsequently bought by the Vintage Carriages Trust for use on that line. The Chatham Matchboard carriage also went to the K&WVR.

Of the other locomotives intended for the Westerham line, the WVRA could not afford the other 'H' class that had been reserved, No 31518, and it went for scrap. The last 'O1' class locomotive, No 31065, was bought by Mr Esmond Lewis-Evans, who set up the South Eastern Steam Centre at Ashford. When this closed, the locomotive moved to a private site in Kent but in 1996 it moved to the Bluebell Railway for restoration and operation. 'C' class No 31592 was bought by the Wainwright 'C' Class Preservation Society in December 1966. It, too, stayed at the South Eastern Steam Centre until 1970, when it moved to the Bluebell, entering service in 1975. In 2014 it was gifted to the Bluebell Railway Trust.

'Rowdy meeting'

The WVRA 1964 annual general meeting took place on 6 October. Among the options for discussion were:

*To form a joint company with the K&ESR.
*To endeavour to lease part of the Westerham line not scheduled for road works, i.e. from Westerham to Chevening or from Dunton Green to Chevening for either standard or narrow gauge railway operations.
*To transfer stock and assets to the London Railway Preservation Society or a similar organisation with the hope of running when they obtained a suitable line.

The meeting was described in the *Kentish Times* as 'rowdy'. Representatives of the K&ESR spoke in favour of the amalgamation but the meeting became noisy with speakers trying to shout each other down. The meeting concluded that, in view of continuing negotiations, thoughts of amalgamation were premature but, as those present knew little about the situation of the K&ESR, Mr George Pickin and Mr Robin Doust were asked to say a few words. The story the members heard was a confused one.

Pickin explained that two organisations existed, the K&ESR Company, which he controlled, and the Society, represented by Doust. The Society did not have the funds to buy the line but had the support of the enthusiasts, while the Company had a large part of the money but no support. The Society had told BR to negotiate with him but the Society had now 'declared war' on him, as he put it.

Doust agreed that Pickin now controlled the company and had offered to put up the greater part of the money needed. They had accepted him as a last resort, but differences of opinion had emerged regarding basic operation1156 and the enthusiasts had decided not to go on with him. They did not believe that Pickin intended to pay the full price asked, and BR had said that, if he failed to pay, the Society would have 24 hours' notice to find the money. It had raised £16,000 in cash and bank guarantees but could only raise the full amount of £36,000 by removing and selling the track from Northiam to Tenterden and replacing it later.

Angry exchanges took place between Picken and Doust and, not surprisingly, the meeting approved a proposal to defer discussion on any amalgamation.

'P' class 0-6-0T No 172 pilots 'H' class 0-4-4T No 263 on a train from Sheffield Park to East Grinstead on 1 April 2013, a week after the Bluebell Railway completed its Northern Extension. *Author*

The general election of 15 October 1964 saw the election of a Labour government. The WVRA reported that the future of the line was to be considered by Tom Fraser, the new Minister of Transport, and Fred Willey, Minister of Lands and Natural Resources. Meanwhile, the council had been active at Chevening, removing a section of the track and announcing its intention to fill in the cutting. The engineer in charge explained that it was essential for the contractor to be able to cross the line in order that heavy equipment could be moved along the whole length of the route as the existing bridge was not strong enough to carry the loads. Whether the line was to remain blocked or be bridged would depend on the outcome of discussions.

As we know, nothing became of these discussions. The WVRA committee spent the following months seeking alternatives but by June 1965 decided to enter into negotiations with the K&ESR. A special general meeting of the WVRA was called for the following month to discuss the way forward. The choices facing the meeting were to cooperate with either Pickin's K&ESR Company or the K&ESR Preservation Society. Negotiations had taken place with both and the committees of the Preservation Society and the WVRA had discussed terms for a merged society while the company had offered the WVRA 'a wide amount of control' in the running of the railway.

Both proposals were put to the meeting. A vote to assist the re-opening of the K&ESR line was passed by 52-1 and a proposal to merge the WVRA and the Preservation Society was agreed by 41-7. However, this merger was opposed by two prominent K&ESR Society officials, who did not want to be burdened with any of the WVRA's

SECR-design 'Matchboard' Brake Third corridor carriage No S3554S at the Worth Valley Railway in 2015. The term 'Matchboard' comes from the vertical panelling strips on the lower part of the carriage sides. Withdrawn in 1961, it was bought in July 1962 by Roy Edwards for the proposed Westerham Valley Railway preservation scheme. When this failed the coach was sent to the Worth Valley Railway, being delivered by rail to Keighley in January 1965. It is now owned by the Vintage Carriages Trust and is currently restored to early BR carmine and cream livery. ***Author***

financial commitments, nor waste valuable time on a merger at a critical stage in their negotiations with BR. This delayed matters but further discussions resulted in a renewed decision to recommend amalgamation. In the meantime, the K&ESR Society had raised a loan of £15,000 and promises of £7,000 from members, which had enabled it to assure BR of its ability to proceed with the outright purchase of the line.

End of the line

The WVRA held its final annual general meeting in Bromley on 21 December 1965 at which it considered two proposals – to amalgamate the WVRA and the K&ESRPS and to transfer ownership of locomotive No 31263 to the 'H' class Trust. David Kitton told the meeting of the committee's final struggles to save the Westerham branch. Terence Boston had tried to persuade first Marples and then his successor Tom Fraser to hold an enquiry into the council's plans to use the railway for its road schemes. Both Ministers refused.

The committee had then considered alternative plans. A service from Chevening to Westerham was ruled out as the council wanted Westerham station for a new road and most of the remainder was earmarked for the South Orbital. Other closed lines were investigated but the new government had blocked sales of railway trackbeds; when they were allowed again BR would require immediate cash payment. The idea had been explored of buying a disused track bed where members would gradually rebuild the railway from regular subscriptions but no suitable site could be found.

That left one other option – to pool resources with another society with similar aims, which had led the WVRA to contact the K&ESR Preservation Society. Since then much had happened. Pickin, who had been negotiating with BR, had withdrawn his option to purchase. The K&ESRPS had opened negotiations and had received a draft contract for the line. At a meeting on 13 December they had agreed to sign the contract and had voted for amalgamation with the WVRA. All that remained was for the WVRA to approve the amalgamation. It was carried by an overwhelming majority.

* * *

So ended the scheme to preserve the Westerham line. On 1 January 1966 the WVRA and the K&ESRPS merged to become the Kent & East Sussex Railway Association, members of the two bodies transferring to the new one. (Membership of the WVRA counts towards the K&ESRA's long service awards, and at least one WVRA member achieved 50 years membership.) The committee of the new body comprised members of both its predecessors.

Its hopes were soon dashed, however, when the Ministry of Transport refused it a Light Railway Order. It claimed that the association had insufficient financial reserves to cover any unforeseen emergency such as the collapse of a river bridge and that a re-opened line would cause problems at level crossings between Robertsbridge and Bodiam, including that over the A21. These arguments sound all too familiar and the suspicion lingers that, once again, the line's plans to run commuter and freight services fell foul of the 'playing trains' rule. It was only when these plans were dropped and the K&ESR concentrated on the isolated Tenterden to Bodiam section of the line that it met with success.

A little of the actual Westerham line may have survived; when the station site at Westerham was being demolished in 1978, the developers Rush & Tompkins allowed K&ESR members to remove some of the platform railings for re-use.

The branch track was lifted by March 1967. Westerham station building was demolished in 1966 but Brasted survived until the spring of 1977 when it was cleared to make way for the M25.

Following the collapse of the Westerham preservation scheme, preserved 'H' class No 31263 was transferred to the 'H' class Trust which stored it on a temporary basis at Robertsbridge. An appeal was launched for funds to restore it to working order. *Author's collection*

STEAM INTO THE FUTURE WITH No. 263

Only a memory now, but a familiar sight in Southern England for nearly sixty years, one of the famous 'H' Class tank locomotives hard at work.

Now read how one of the class survived the breakers, and how you can help it to—
STEAM AGAIN

7

THE ROAD TO HELL[116]

Rumours that the Westerham branch was to be sacrificed to enable the building of the proposed South Orbital Road began to circulate even before closure of the line was approved. At the 1961 TUCC hearing, Kent County Council admitted that using part of line for the South Orbital Road would be considered if the line did close and, as we have seen, negotiations between BR and the council for the sale of the line were under way even before permission had been given for closure.

When the Sevenoaks MP, John Rodgers, raised these rumours in September 1961, John Hay, the Parliamentary Secretary at the Ministry of Transport, replied:

'When we had our talk on 13th September about the closure of the Westerham–Dunton Green line you mentioned to me a current rumour that the Minister might have been influenced in reaching his decision by the possibility that certain proposed road improvements could be more economically carried out if the line were closed. I have made careful enquiries and I can assure you that any such suggestion is unfounded... The line of the road has not yet been fixed and the Minister has not yet authorised any detail survey.'

Shoreham in Kent. The earliest 1926 plan for a new road through the Darenth Valley would have had it cutting the village in half just beyond the bridge. *Commercial postcard – author's collection*

Nothing has come to light to show that the line was deliberately closed so that the road could be built on its trackbed or even that it was a factor that Marples considered when he approved closure. On the contrary, there was confusion and incompetence within the Ministry during the late 1950s and early 1960s over the whole question of the South Orbital Road. The same, however, did not apply to the county council. Henry Bowdler, Kent's county surveyor wanted a new road through the Westerham valley to relieve the A25 and he was determined to achieve it.

The three problems

B'what were initially seen as the three separate that – problems that were identified as far back as the 1920s. The first was a new Thames crossing in the Dartford area, with approach roads to feed traffic to and from it. The second was a Sevenoaks bypass to take traffic out of its town centre. The third was a new east–west road to relieve traffic on the road from Guildford and Reigate to Maidstone – now the A25.

Planning was in its infancy before World War 2 and no less than three tiers of government were involved – Urban and Rural District Councils (the Sevenoaks area had one of each), County Councils, and the Ministries of Health and of Transport. It did not help that planning – even of major roads – was essentially a local responsibility[117]. The Ministry of Health vetted and approved local plans but the Ministry of Transport, formed in 1919, could only suggest and propose. At times the various tiers supported conflicting ideas, which makes for a complicated story but it helps to explain why little happened for 50 years and, when it did, the result was less than satisfactory.

The Dartford Tunnel and the Darenth Valley

In 1924 the Ministry of Transport proposed a tunnel under the Thames between Dartford and Purfleet, linking Kent with Essex. The idea was to avoid the need for traffic to travel most of the way into London and back out again just to cross the river. Not only was this wasteful but it added to growing congestion in the London area.

However, there were obvious fears that the narrow roads south of the river – and particularly that through the Darenth villages of Eynsford, Shoreham and Otford (now the A225) – would become overloaded with tunnel traffic heading south.

The Sevenoaks Rural District Council (RDC) proposed an 80ft-wide road that would pass right through the village of Shoreham. Not surprisingly, protests forced a rethink; a revised plan, published in October 1926, put the road alongside the Swanley to Otford railway, bypassing Shoreham to the east and joining the north end of the planned Sevenoaks bypass at Twitton.

A week later, the Ministry of Transport came up with its own idea for a road through the area, bypassing both Shoreham and Eynsford to the west. However, the scheme still proved unacceptable to many local residents so Dr Gordon Ward of the Sevenoaks Housing and Town Planning Association suggested that the new road should be built about half a mile further west, up on the valley side. As it happened, this is precisely where, 50 years later, the M25 was eventually built.

A year later, the Ministry changed its mind. A new road along the Darenth valley was both 'unnecessary and undesirable'. Instead, tunnel traffic heading to or from the south would be best served by a new road linking the tunnel approach to the Orpington bypass, where traffic for Sevenoaks and beyond would join the London-Hastings road (A21).

However, there was no point in building any of these new roads until the tunnel was built so there was no progress at all.

Bypassing Sevenoaks

The idea of a bypass for Sevenoaks town centre was proposed in a 1927 report of the West Kent Joint Regional Planning Committees. It was to leave the London road north of Dunton Green and pass between Chipstead and Riverhead. From there it was to cross the western side of Montreal Park and continue south via Hubbards Hill, rejoining the existing road at the foot of Riverhill. The gradient was to be approximately 1 in 25, which compared to the 1 in 9 of Riverhill on the existing road.

East–west road

Road planners in the 1920s recognised the need to cater for east–west traffic through Surrey and West Kent. Parts of the road from Guildford to Maidstone were improved in the 1920s, but most of these improvements were in the open countryside. The road still passed through all the towns along its route, including Westerham, and congestion was becoming rife. A new road was planned in 1927 to run through the Vale of Holmesdale passing north of Bletchingley, Oxted and Limpsfield in Surrey and Westerham, Brasted and Sevenoaks in Kent. This may sound familiar to those who use today's M25 but the proposed width of 80ft between fences, with a 40ft building line, is nothing like the modern road.

The thirties

The worldwide depression, which started with the Wall Street Crash of 1929, had huge effects on the UK economy. The overriding economic priority was to avoid a budget deficit and severe cuts in public spending followed but house-building in the south flourished, thanks to low interest rates, as did the car industry in the Midlands. The number of cars on British roads doubled during the decade, with a dire effect on a road system that had changed little for years, especially around London.

In 1934 the Minister of Transport asked the Chief

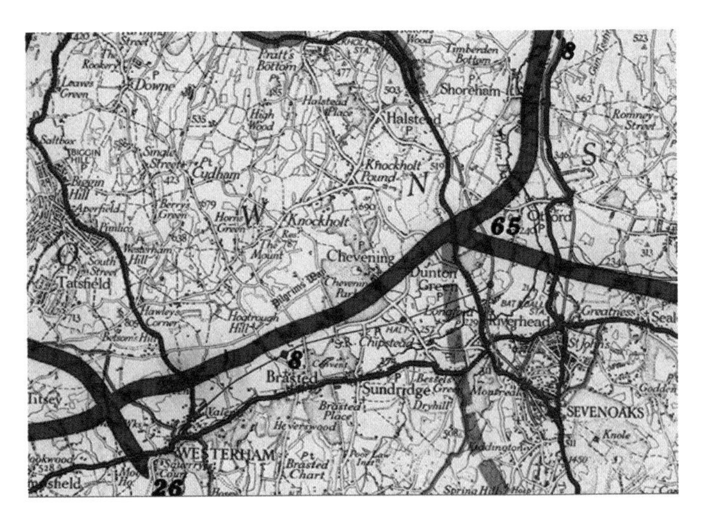

Figure 7.1: Bressey's 1937 proposals for the South Orbital Road between Westerham and Dunton Green and connecting roads. *Crown copyright*

Engineer for Roads, Sir Charles Bressey, to '. . . study and report on the need for improved communications by road . . . in the area of Greater London, and to prepare a Highway Development Plan for that area . . .' He was assisted by the architect Sir Edwin Lutyens. Among their proposals when they reported in 1937 was a South Orbital Road which was to start at a new bridge over the Thames at Egham and head south past Chertsey and Byfleet. After crossing the Leatherhead to Guildford road near Fetcham, it was to continue east past Kingswood, Merstham, Godstone, Oxted, and Westerham. Here the road would swing north-eastwards past Chevening, Eynsford and Lullingstone (where a new London airport was to be built), before joining the Dartford Tunnel approach at Swanley.

As a glance at a map will show, apart from a few short divergences, much of Bressey's route is followed by today's M25. The road was to be a 'parkway', up to 200ft (60m) wide, with restricted access and flyovers at major junctions but its purpose was more for pleasurable motoring than to take traffic away from London.

Bressey's map shows the problem of routing the road between Westerham and Dunton Green. The valley is narrow and is occupied by the A25 road with the towns and villages of Westerham, Brasted and Sundridge strung out along its length. South of the A25, the hills rise too steeply to leave room for a new road, while to the north the options were to route the new road along or beside the Westerham branch, further up on the downs beside the Pilgrims' Way, or somewhere between the two.

By the 1930s the Pilgrims' Way had assumed almost hallowed status, which left the planners with two choices. The new road could run immediately beside the Westerham branch or it could run parallel to but separate from the railway, leaving a narrow strip of land between the two. Bressey opted for the latter (see Figure 7.1.

The wandering bypass

Since it had first been proposed in 1927, there had been a stream of alterations to the planned route of the Sevenoaks bypass. By 1929, the scheme had been altered to skirt Montreal Park and the revised plan had the road crossing the Westerham branch immediately west of the existing railway bridge in Dunton Green.

In February 1936 Kent County Council revised the northern end of the bypass so that it avoided Dunton Green. In 1938, another change, which involved the bypass crossing the railway at Chevening, brought objections from Earl Stanhope at Chevening House and his neighbour Sir Edward Meyerstein at Morants Court. Money was allocated for the project but World War 2 broke out before work could start.

Work starts on the Tunnel

After protracted delays caused by the 1930s economic problems and arguments as to who was to pay the £3.2 million cost, work finally started on the Dartford Tunnel in 1937. To assist in the work, a short branch was laid in from the Southern Railway's North Kent line between Dartford and Stone Crossing, controlled by a new signal box[118]. Unfortunately, work had only reached the stage of boring a 12ft (3.7m) pilot tunnel when war broke out and the project was suspended. It resumed in 1956.

Post-war developments

Plans for new roads were filed away for the duration of the war but in 1943, with events starting to turn in the Allies' favour, the London County Council (LCC) asked its architect, John Forshaw, and the leading planning expert Professor Patrick Abercrombie to draw up a comprehensive County of London Plan for the post-war development of London with traffic as one of its four themes. A year later, recognising that London's traffic problems could not be solved within the LCC's boundaries, it was replaced by the Greater London Plan. This recommended a series of ring roads within and around London.

The A to C Rings, which ran within the LCC area, play no part in our story[119]. It is the eastern and southern sections of the D and E Rings which matter to us.

The D Ring was to bypass the built-up area of London – what we now know as Greater London. From Swanley, where it joined the Dartford Tunnel approach, it was to skirt Orpington, Selsdon and Sanderstead. After passing south of Croydon, it was to run between Epsom and Ewell before crossing the Thames by a new bridge at Walton.

The E Ring wasn't a ring at all, more a horseshoe on its side, open to the east. It started at a junction with the A12 Chelmsford bypass in Essex and passed round the north and west of London. From Staines its route was largely the same as Bressey's plan for the South Orbital Road but when it got to Sevenoaks, instead of following Bressey's route to Dartford, it continued east to join the A20 at Wrotham, following roughly the line of today's M26. The only link between the E Ring and the D Ring (and thus the Dartford Tunnel) was to be the A21.

The map that accompanied Abercrombie's plan showed that the E Ring was to run immediately beside the Westerham branch between Brasted and Chevening. It also showed the Sevenoaks bypass, but on its pre-war line, crossing the Westerham branch at Dunton Green. (See Figure 7.2)

It is hard to understand the purpose of the E Ring as the D Ring was to be London's bypass. The E Ring was to be an 'orbital parkway', described later as 'a tree-lined saunter through the home counties, designed and built as much for the pleasure of driving through the open country as for any practical purpose.'[120] There were to be ample lay-bys to allow for parking of cars for short periods, with easy access to local roads to allow for picnic parking.

The E Ring was too far out to relieve inner London traffic and had no part to play in meeting regional traffic needs; one wonders why Abercrombie included it. The answer must be that Surrey and Kent county councils were determined to relieve the A25 Guildford–Maidstone road, taking traffic out of the towns along its route, and presumably Abercrombie felt unable to ignore their demands. He needed their co-operation. However, if the D Ring had been built, it would have been difficult to justify the E Ring and it would probably not have been built.

This raises an important point. Kent was as bothered about its problems on the A25 as about bypassing London. It would do everything in its power to get the road built and its subsequent actions must be seen in that light.

Delays

In the event, post-war shortages of materials121 and funds limited what could be done but confusion and muddle made up for lack of progress. In 1945, Kent decided that the county did not need motorways, nor an express road on the line of the D ring. Instead, it wanted the E Ring to connect with the Dartford Tunnel by the A224 and the A21 to form an Outer London Ring. A 1947 review of Abercrombie's Plan supported this scheme, recommending that the D Ring be dropped and the Dartford Tunnel linked to the E Ring on both sides of the river.

The Outer London Ring now comprised the proposed tunnel approach between Dartford and the A224 at Chelsfield (to be a trunk road), the A224 Orpington bypass to Halstead (a general-purpose road), and the A21 from there to Polhill (status undetermined). The Sevenoaks bypass would then connect it to the E Ring (the South Orbital) to Westerham and the county boundary. As objectors pointed out, Abercrombie's D Ring motorway, 12 miles out from the centre of London, had been replaced by a mix of new and existing roads of varying width, character and distance from London. Any link to Croydon was not expected before 1972.

However, in 1957 the then Minister of Transport Harold Watkinson decided that the D Ring was to be built after all but, as a general-purpose road based largely on existing roads, with flyovers and limited access junctions only where they could be built without significant demolition. Instead, the E Ring was to be built as a motorway of almost entirely new construction.[122] However, by February 1960 the Ministry had excluded the South Orbital Road from its 10-year programme and there seemed to be little justification for including it, though it was recognised that something would have to be done 'fairly soon' about the tunnel approach.

Review of the South Orbital In early 1961 – as the future of the Westerham branch was being decided – renewed debate opened on the future of the South Orbital with serious differences of opinion within the Ministry of Transport as well as between the Ministry and Kent. The term 'South Orbital' was being applied indiscriminately to parts of different schemes and there was indecision as to which roads were to be motorways, trunk roads, or ordinary classified roads – something that mattered because it determined who could use the roads and who paid for their construction and maintenance.

To add confusion, no-one could agree how the A224 and A21 roads between Chelsfield and Sevenoaks should link the D and E Rings. Would they be ordinary roads connected at either end to motorways or would they have to become part of the motorway network, denying them to certain types of traffic? The Ministry thought that this would be impracticable, while short lengths of motorway sandwiched between all-purpose roads would be undesirable. In a fine spirit of fudge it proposed that the tunnel approach between Dartford and Chelsfield should be an all-purpose trunk road but built to motorway standards.

An Origin and Destination (O&D) Survey carried out in 1960 showed that most of the Dartford Tunnel traffic would, in fact, be heading towards or beyond Croydon. This led Kent to decide, after all, that the E Ring would be too far out to be of use for this traffic; a Chelsfield to Croydon link was critical and the council wanted the main London ring road to be built as a motorway on the line of the D Ring.

In a delightful piece of obfuscation, one civil servant recommended that:

'the Ministry accept the need for a "South Orbital" road and propose to get on with it as soon as funds permit in the presence of many other schemes up and down the country of very great importance. However, the Ministry wishes to be certain that this road is constructed on the right alignment in view of the great increase in traffic and general changes in traffic pattern since the existing line of the South Orbital was laid down. We therefore propose to carry out an investigation as quickly as possible into this.'

In reply, J. D. W. Jeffrey, an Assistant Chief Engineer for Trunk Roads, accepted the need for a link south of London but he was not satisfied that it would be met by the E Ring. Nor was he convinced that the plans to improve the A25 were of sufficient national importance to qualify as a trunk road project. Kent's hopes of getting its A25 relief road built (and paid for by government) were sliding away.

The position summarised

With work on the Dartford Tunnel under way, it is worrying that such basic questions were still undecided. Eventually, the issues were summarised in a Ministry report, dating from 1961 (see Appendix 18). The South Orbital was to form an outer ring for Greater London at about 16 miles radius from the centre, joined in the east through the Dartford Tunnel. The tunnel approach from Dartford to Chelsfield might be included in the 1965–66 Trunk Road programme.

As far as our story is concerned, the Ministry faced two serious problems. One was the pressure to build the tunnel approach earlier. Residents of the Darenth Valley were convinced that the bulk of the tunnel traffic would travel south on the overloaded A225 to Sevenoaks even though the O&D Survey had not supported their fears. It was recognised, though, that there might be some overloading of the A225 until new roads were completed around 1967[123]. The report concluded that the real need was for a link between Dartford and Chelsfield which would carry both Croydon and south-bound traffic flows. Kent was asked to survey the route.

The second problem was whether the planned route of the road was the right one. As far as the Ministry was concerned, the South Orbital now consisted of two distinct parts: (1)

the approach to the Dartford Tunnel, which was to be connected by the existing but improved A224/A21 roads to (2)

an arc about 16 miles out from London running from the A21 at Dunton Green to the River Thames at Egham, west of London.

However, the O&D Survey showed that there was a need for Route A to be extended at least to Croydon, since half the tunnel traffic would come from that direction. Little tunnel traffic would come from the rest of the South Orbital so a ring road closer to London would be more useful and was more likely to relieve local roads[124]. On the other hand, the need to improve the A25 had been recognised since at least 1937 and a new road was preferable to piecemeal improvement but that was a separate issue to any ring road function. The report decided that an A25 relief road was needed from the A20 at Wrotham as a means of keeping traffic between Kent and the south-west clear of London.

This led the report to pose a number of questions:

* Was an outer ring road for London needed?
* If so, should this be the proposed South Orbital, Abercrombie's D Ring, something different from either, or both?
* If the A25 replacement wasn't to be a ring road, could it merit trunk road status?
* What was the relative priority of the roads and their components?

Timeline

Putting this into the context of the timeline of the Westerham branch, we can see that when decisions were being made about the closure of the line, there was no certainty as to which part, if any, of the South Orbital might be built at all. On top of this, the Ministry did not want to tie the hands of consulting engineers by planning the Dartford-Chelsfield section of the new road in advance. Insisting that they use the railway trackbed between Brasted and Chevening would, equally, have tied their hands. We can safely assume that – as far as the Ministry was concerned – road plans played no part in decision-making about the railway's future.

However, for Kent's roads department, the Ministry's increasing lack of enthusiasm for the South Orbital meant that relief for the A25 was at risk and this was compounded when the council found itself having to support the building of at least part of the D Ring.

Delegation to the Minister

The review of the South Orbital was most likely written for Marples, the Minister of Transport, in readiness for a meeting between him and a delegation of Kent MPs, councillors, and council officials in June 1961. At the meeting the delegation stressed that the tunnel approach between Dartford and Chelsfield should be opened as soon as possible to avoid traffic using the A225 through the Darenth valley. Bowdler, the Kent county surveyor, added that, if the O&D Survey was correct, the new link could not stop at Chelsfield as there were no adequate roads from there through to Croydon. He now wanted the D Ring built. Marples accepted the point but said that any new road inevitably increased the need for improvements elsewhere but it was not possible to do everything at once. However, he offered to have the alignment of the road beyond Chelsfield looked at again as the O&D Survey did suggest that the road should continue towards Croydon.

With a public inquiry looming into the plans for the tunnel approach, the Ministry decided to investigate alternatives put forward by objectors, led by Eric Lubbock, the new MP for Orpington[125], before deciding which scheme to support. In a memo dated July 1962 it said that, by considering different ideas before the inquiry, it could not be accused of ignoring the opposition.

Uncertainties grow

A complicating factor was that in 1962 the government decided to accept the recommendations of the Royal Commission on Local Government in Greater London and create a new Greater London Council, which would take in much of north-west Kent[126]. The much-disputed D Ring between Chelsfield and Croydon would no longer be Kent's concern. As far as the South Orbital Road was concerned, the county was now able to focus solely on the route that would relieve the A25. But even if such a route was chosen, it was unclear whether the railway line should be used. The Ministry's annual report Roads in England and Wales rejected the idea of using disused railways for road building. The 1963 edition said that 'there is no prospect of any large-scale use of abandoned railways for road purposes.' It pointed out that:

'Even where an abandoned railway line is available on an important traffic route which requires a new road, the permanent way is usually far too narrow for straightforward conversion, and any overhead bridges usually give inadequate headroom. The majority of lines already abandoned, or likely to be so, are single tracked with a formation width of about 14 feet . . . a dual carriageway all-purpose trunk road requires an overall width of 87 feet, and a motorway with three lanes in each

Figure 7.2: Road plans in 1944 – Abercrombie's D and E Rings in West Kent. The only link between the D Ring and the E Ring was to have been the existing A21 road.

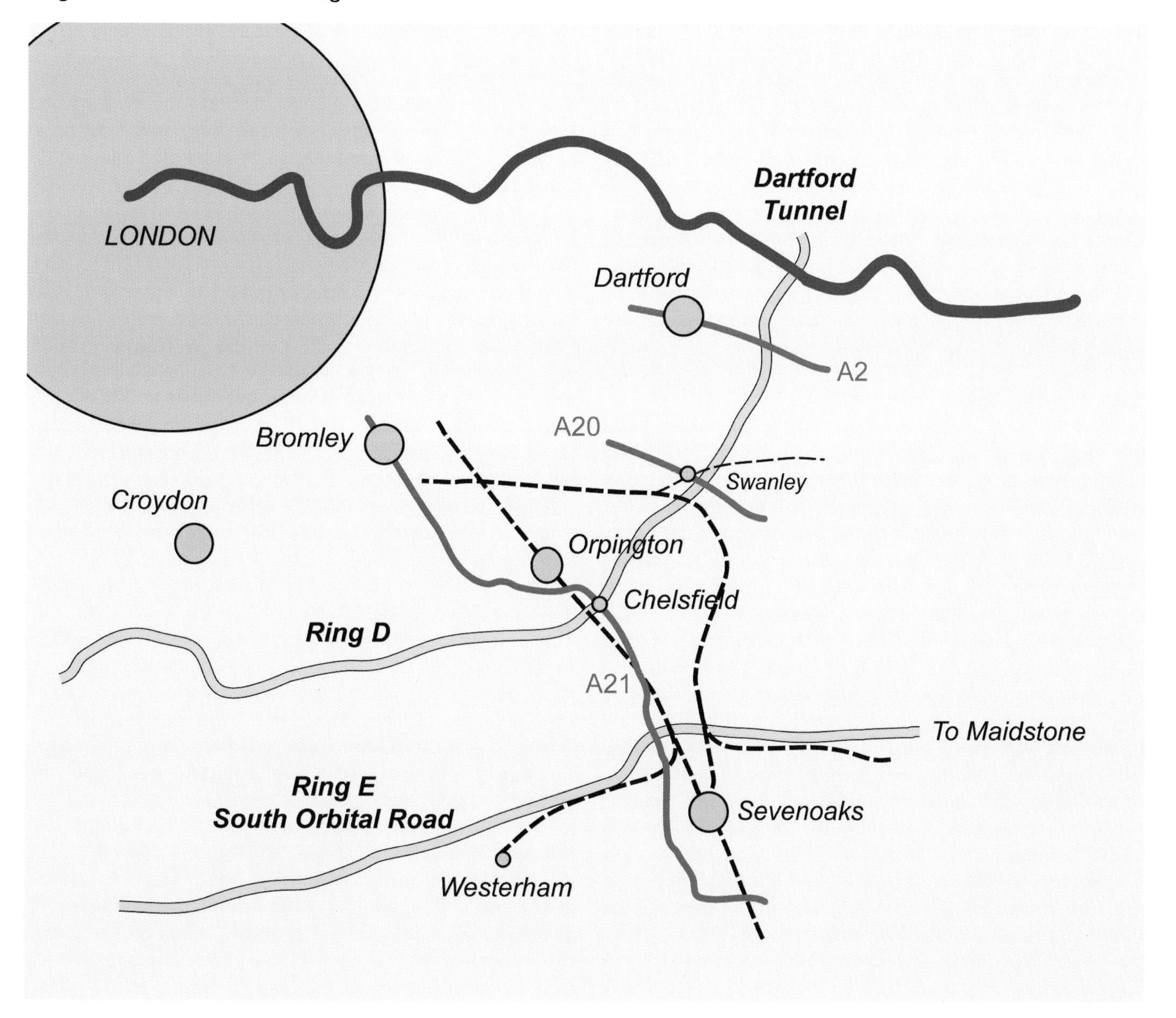

direction requires 129 feet. Thus, the new high capacity roads generally needed on important traffic routes could not be built along railway lines without the purchase of additional land, extensive engineering works where the railway ran on embankment or in cutting, and the reconstruction of all tunnels and bridges.'[127]

Reading the evidence

What can we gather from this situation? At the time the Westerham branch closed, no-one could decide whether the D Ring or the E Ring should form London's ring road. Any road built to relieve the A25 might not be a trunk road, never mind a motorway. There was no sign that the Ministry accepted the need for it or had any great enthusiasm for it.

The impetus for the South Orbital came from Surrey and Kent County Councils. We have already seen that Kent's roads department was negotiating with the Southern Region's estates department to buy the Westerham line in the spring of 1961, well before Marples had agreed to close it. The evidence from the early 1960s reveals a huge contradiction between the Ministry's vacillating over the South Orbital Road and Kent's determination to buy the railway line. Kent clearly feared that the South Orbital might never be built or, at best, it might have been reduced to a county-funded project. Did it think that by buying the Westerham trackbed it could make the road more affordable? If it was built as an ordinary road it might have been no more than a single carriageway, so the limited width of the railway trackbed may not have been an issue.

Change of plans

In October 1964 Labour won the general election and announced a 40 per cent increase in spending on road building[128] and in December 1965, Barbara Castle took over as Minister of Transport[129]. Within months, she decided that the South Orbital was to go ahead based on the E Ring, though the decision was not welcomed in parts of the Ministry. Its London Highways Division viewed the situation with apprehension, not from opposition to the South Orbital (it accepted the need to relieve the congested A25 east of Leatherhead), but from fear that the whole South Orbital would be built before work began on the D Ring. It wanted the South Orbital to be built between Maidstone and Leatherhead and the A246 improved from there to Guildford. Construction of the D Ring, for which the demand was much greater, should then precede the South Orbital north-west of Leatherhead.

After some delay, a compromise was reached which did not preclude the D Ring but which allowed the Minister to announce the building of the full length of the South Orbital. By the end of 1966 Kent and Surrey County Councils were told to complete preparatory design work for a motorway standard road from the A30 at Staines, in the west, to Dartford in the east, with a spur to the M20 at Wrotham.

However, while the section from the Sevenoaks bypass to Staines was to be a motorway, the section north from the Sevenoaks bypass to Chelsfield was to be no more than an improvement of the existing A21 up Polhill. This created the peculiar situation in which motorway was to run from Staines to Wrotham, while Dartford traffic would have to turn off the motorway at the Sevenoaks bypass and join a local road. A plan, probably dating from about 1970 (see Figure 7.3), shows an intersection at Chevening between the South Orbital (running east-west) and the A21 which is of broadly similar design to that at South Mimms. The A21 flies over the east-west road, with a roundabout above both. This also gave access to a proposed service area in the south-east corner of the layout which would have occupied part of the former railway trackbed east of Chevening.

M25 opening

The first section of the South Orbital – by then named the M25 – opened between Godstone and Reigate in February 1976. Dartford (J2) to Swanley (J3) followed in April 1977. The section from Sundridge Road (the A25) to Godstone, which took in the trackbed of much of the Westerham line, opened in November 1979 while the northwards link at J5 followed in July 1980. The M26 from Sevenoaks to Wrotham finally opened in September 1980 but it was over five years before the Swanley to Dunton Green section of the M25 opened in February 1986, replacing the use of the parallel A21 up Polhill. A planned interchange at Westerham was never built and traffic for the town has to leave the M25 at either Godstone or Sevenoaks and use the very A25 that the motorway was intended to relieve.

The D Ring in the south of London – which became Ringway 3 under the London Ringways plan of the late 1960s – was never built.

The Sevenoaks bypass

Much of the story of the Sevenoaks bypass has already been told in Chapter 6 as it was so intimately involved in the collapse of the preservation scheme. Work started on the bypass in 1964. Sir Charles Pym, Brasted resident, former chairman of Kent County Council, and campaigner for the branch line had the ironic duty of cutting the ribbon to signify the start of work.

The road opened in 1966 but only after encountering colossal problems that led to the tabloids branding it as 'the road that couldn't be built'. On the section overlooking Sevenoaks Weald, between Hubbard's Hill and Riverhill, the work triggered landslides. Engineers discovered that five major mud slides were pouring into a vast underground lake, faults that dated to the end of the last Ice Age. The road-line had to be abandoned, along with a number of bridges that had already been built.

It turned out that only nominal site investigations had been carried out before work started. A subsequent investigation identified shear surfaces associated with ancient landslides that could occur in clay soils in south east England on slopes of as little as three degrees and showed that movement could be triggered by construction work. The importance of pre-existing shears and was already known and the shallow shear surfaces could easily have been found by careful trial pitting, but the initial investigation consisted only of boreholes at intervals along the road centreline[130]. The road had to be redesigned at a cost of £1¼ million. Just two per cent of that sum would have built a bridge over the railway at Chevening. It was incompetence and waste on a huge scale.

Further waste occurred when the M25/M26 was built on a different alignment to that proposed when the bypass was built and Chevening Road bridge had to be rebuilt for a second time to carry it over the motorway as well as the bypass.

Looking back

As we have seen, there is nothing to support the idea that Marples agreed the closure of the Westerham branch so that the South Orbital could be built on its course. The Sevenoaks bypass and Kent's desire for an A25 relief road played a part in the collapse of the preservation scheme. However, by that stage the WVRA had enough problems of its own that made its success unlikely, and that was without the determination of senior civil servants and managers in BR that the scheme should not succeed. The infilling of the cutting at Chevening simply administered the coup de grace.

Once Kent had bought the railway, it was inevitable that the M25 would be built on its course when work finally began in 1977, but the irony was that it contributed little to the land-take needed for the road. As many people had warned, the route along the Gault Clay followed by the railway was far from ideal for road building. When it was decided to widen the motorway in 2013 the instability of the Gault Clay made it impossible to add lanes to this section. Instead, in an arrangement that many feel is unsafe, the hard shoulders were converted to running lanes.

Three drainage lagoons had to be installed at Brasted and Chevening to cope with the excess water that the WVRA surveyors warned of. The water that overflows from them regularly adds to local flooding. The junction arrangement at Chevening between the M25, M26 and A21 is widely condemned as a nightmare of bad road engineering.

Of the two roads involved, the Sevenoaks bypass cost £5.6 million and the M25 from junction 5 to Westerham £13.5 million. It was claimed that the taxpayer saved £120,000 by using the railway for road building – less than 1 per cent of the total bill, little more than petty cash. Vastly more was wasted by mistakes on the schemes, including the abortive Westerham interchange.

Words such as 'scandal' and 'incompetence' are far too mild to describe the situation.

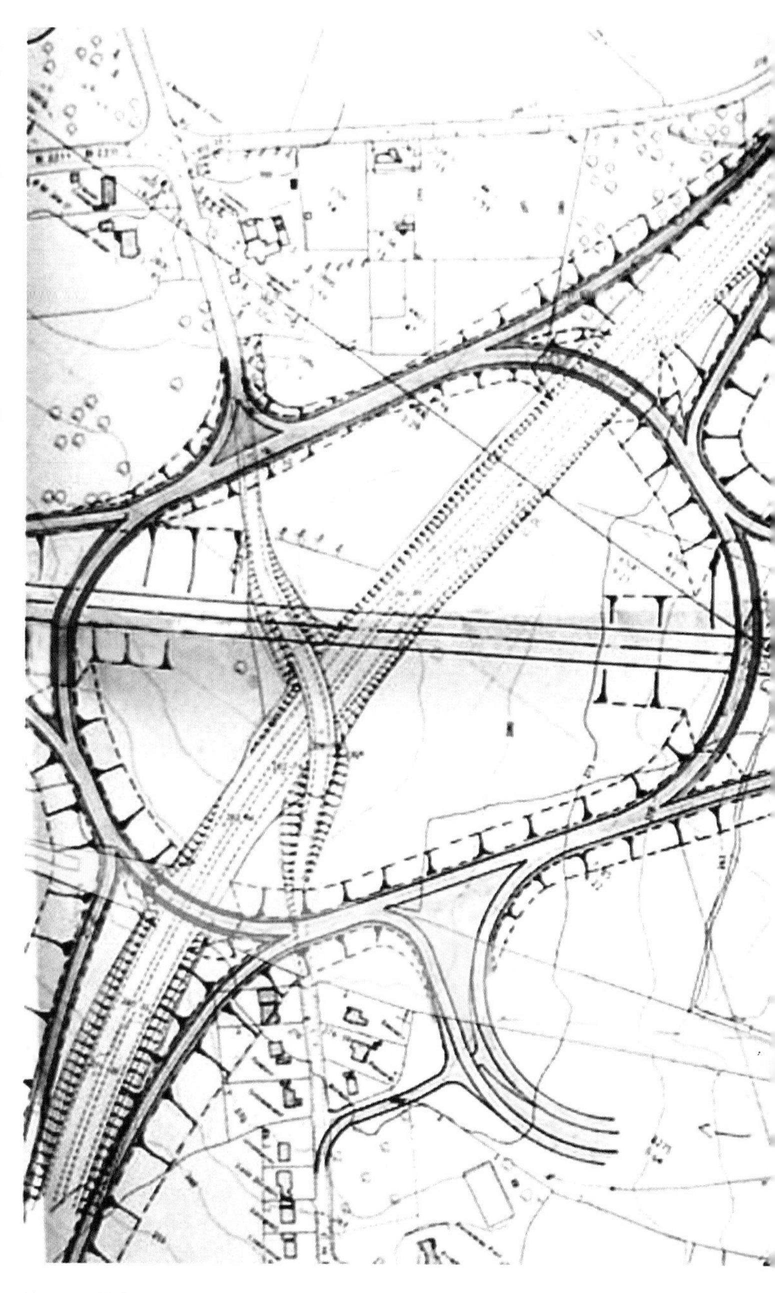

Figure 7.3: The proposed roundabout intersection between the South Orbital Road and the Sevenoaks bypass (A21) at Chevening (early 1970s). It also gave access to the planned Chevening Service Area. The A21 runs from bottom-left to top-right. The railway formation (shown shaded) lies beneath the bottom segment of the roundabout and its exit to the service area. The roundabout would have replaced the bridge carrying Chevening Road over the bypass.

Epilogue
In Retrospect

What was it that doomed the preservation of the Westerham line? In truth, a host of factors came together that stood in the way of its success. One thing, without a doubt, was BR's total antipathy to the idea of railway preservation, the reasons for which are not easy to pin down. There is little doubt that the proliferation of preservation schemes as more and more closures were announced was seen by both BR and the Ministry of Transport as more than just a nuisance. They had real concerns, not least because the ability of enthusiasts to run railways successfully had still to be proved, but instead of working with the enthusiasts it was easier to block schemes.

Like some other schemes of that time[131], the Westerham scheme was ambitious, aiming to provide a full public service where BR had failed; that cannot have appealed to BR managers. However, unlike some of the others which quickly fell by the wayside, the Westerham scheme appeared more likely to succeed. Its target was a manageable length of line, close to London, with a junction offering easy interchange with BR at Dunton Green. It threatened to embarrass BR if it did succeed and some of its proponents did little to disguise their delight at such a prospect. It is little wonder that BR wanted nothing more to do with the line. The opportunity to sell to the county council offered a way of getting rid of an embarrassment once and for all.

But why was the Kent county surveyor, Henry Bowdler, so keen to buy the line's formation? The answer is that Bowdler was a dedicated but frustrated road builder. In December 1965 he told the national conference of the Institution of Highway Engineers that 'this country has dragged its feet to such an extent that we now find ourselves at least a generation behind with our road-building programme and slipping farther back each year'.[132] Three years later he warned that the opening of the Channel Tunnel and the likelihood of Britain joining the Common Market would put intolerable traffic loads on the road system west of Maidstone and entering the London area. His primary concern was to get those routes in the fringe area of London improved to satisfactory standard[133] – including relief for the A25, which could divert traffic away from London.

He had little faith in the senior echelons of the Ministry of Transport, which appeared not to understand that Kent's roads needed improvements to handle the HGV traffic to its ports[134]. Did Bowdler think that, by buying a potential route for a road that he regarded as vital, it might help to push the Ministry in the right direction?

Why was BR so keen to sell the line to the council for road-building? To some it was, of course, a way of avoiding a potentially embarrassing enthusiast takeover but there were other motives too. A few BR managers misguidedly thought that new roads could make it easier to reach main line railheads but maybe they thought that the planned new road was intended simply as a solution to local traffic problems. Did they have any idea of what it would turn out to be? I doubt that Bowdler made that clear to them.

There were also those in BR who believed that, as managers of a nationalised industry, their decisions had to consider the wider national interest. That may have been the case in the early years of state ownership but it was no longer so in 1962. BR managers were supposed to act in the best interests of BR and BR alone. Marples himself was quite clear on this.[135]

* * *

However, this does raise the question about the role of Graham Tunbridge and his Southern Region estates department in this whole affair. There were undoubtedly close links between Tunbridge and Bowdler and their departments and, in the light of Tunbridge's subsequent conviction for corruption (see Cast of Characters on page **xi**), we have to wonder about his motives.

Unlike some councils (the Isle of Wight County Council, for example), Kent had no policy of buying disused railway land; selling the Westerham line to the council was a one-off transaction that did not justify a special relationship between Tunbridge and Bowdler[136]. Did Tunbridge hope that, by doing a favour for Bowdler, it might be repaid at some later date in a way that would have been of interest to Tunbridge's corrupt paymaster, Poulson? The Channel Tunnel was something in which all three men would have had a shared interest, and improved roads to the BR-owned Channel ports might have opened up opportunities of interest to Poulson.

There is no suggestion that Bowdler was corrupt but, at the very least, the dealings between him and Tunbridge over Westerham crossed the boundaries of propriety. Tunbridge's job was to sell redundant railway lines for the best possible price once it had been agreed that they should close – not to set up cosy deals in advance. Between them, Tunbridge and Bowdler certainly created an impression that something fishy was going on and they left the Ministry of Transport open to the charge that the Westerham closure was engineered to allow the trackbed to be used for road building. Maybe Bowdler would have said that the ends justified the means.

* * *

But while external forces conspired against the Westerham scheme, we cannot absolve the WVRA from all blame for its collapse. Its inability to raise the price demanded by BR was a fatal flaw. It had assumed from the beginning that BR would grant it a lease and it was in difficulties as soon as BR demanded an outright sale. Schemes such as the Keighley & Worth Valley and the Kent & East Sussex lines were eventually offered mortgages by BR in the late 1960s and early 1970s, because it helped BR to dispose of lines that no-one else really wanted. The Westerham scheme came too early, it faced too much official opposition, and there was another willing buyer.

Once the WVRA had to seek capital, it ran into exactly the same problems as its predecessor in the 1870s – it could not raise hard cash. BR had only to ask where the

A drainage lagoon built on the railway formation at the point at which it emerges from under the M25 west of Chevening. This is the view looking west with the motorway in the background. ***Author***

money was coming from for negotiations to stall. Even when Beeching agreed to accept the offered £30,000, he probably realised that the WVRA had little chance of raising even this amount. Any scheme involving a single major backer was always bound to come with overwhelming drawbacks. In other places, local authorities helped preservation schemes by buying the land from BR and leasing it to a railway society, but that was never the case in Kent.

It did not help that months were wasted in negotiating a price for the line, the blame for which lies equally on BR and the WVRA. Why did BR initially quoted a price of £60-70,000 to the Association, of which £41,500 was for the track, when it sold to the council for only £40,000 all in? Did it really have no idea of the value of its redundant assets? Did it ask the preservationists for too high a price to deter them or did it ask too little of the council?

Had the WVRA been able to complete a deal with BR early in 1962, the scheme might have succeeded but that was not to be. Even if the council had not been determined to buy the line, Gray's fixation with the commuter service to the exclusion of all else blocked its success. Dealing with the issue of the replacement buses and BR's subsidy for them complicated negotiations and dragged them on for far too long. Nor, despite being an economist, did Gray properly understand the scheme's finances, which undermined confidence in him and not just on the part of officialdom. Some enthusiasts may have welcomed the idea of running a 'proper railway' with a purpose but others realised that the need to subsidise a weekday service for a handful of relatively well-heeled commuters would be a constant drain on the steam preservation side of things and its volunteer supporters. It must also be said that Gray's approach did not help matters, either.

Funding the purchase by selling off surplus land would have doomed it. Today, when the appetite of preserved railways for land for sidings, sheds and workshops is plain to see, how would the Westerham line have survived with a couple of sidings at Brasted and maybe a couple more at Dunton Green?

* * *

BR's opposition to the Westerham scheme was overt; the Ministry of Transport's was less obvious but more insidious. Its stonewalling was the final straw that put paid to the scheme. Were civil servants opposed to commercial private railways because they did not want private operators being able to show that local railways could be run profitably at a time when their political masters wanted BR to slim its network? The Ministry hid behind other excuses to block the scheme – safety, speed limits, and bridges. For nearly two years, it refused to say whether it might allow the WVRA to run a commuter service. When it looked as though it might have to decide about the bus subsidies, it bowled a googly by suggesting that maybe LT, and not BR, should be paying for the replacement buses.

When it comes to the patronising attitude shown towards railway enthusiasts by many of the 1960s civil servants and particularly the colonels of the Railway Inspectorate, words fail. Both McMullen and Robertson lived long enough to see the growing success of railway preservation but not, sadly, to witness its most incredible achievements. Fortunately, the next generation of inspecting officers was of a different calibre and the heritage railway sector has much to thank them for in their unstinting support, advice and occasional admonishment.

* * *

Westerham's public transport link to Sevenoaks has continued to decline. Buses now operate only hourly during the day and to be in London before 9am means catching the 07.08 bus from Westerham. The last bus back is at 19.48, connecting with the 19.10 from London. London Buses provides a far better service from Westerham to Hayes and Bromley, running half-hourly from early morning till after midnight but most of Westerham's London commuters drive at least part of the way.

And on a wider scale, the motor vehicle rules Westerham's valley today.

Chapter notes

Introduction

1. Having put a massive, if unsuccessful, effort into saving Westerham and an equally supreme effort into the successful Kent & East Sussex re-opening, David went on to try to save Real Cider.

Cast of Characters

2. This was an organisation structure that had been pioneered on the Eastern Region – see Fiennes, chapter 6. Bolland was appointed early to the Line Traffic Manager position on the Southern's South Eastern Division; similar positions on the Central and South Western Divisions were not created until the following year.
3. *The Times*, 15 January 1974, page 4, 'John Poulson tells of gifts to rail man': report of Poulson's trial.
4. Knight, Stephen, *The Brotherhood*, chapter 15, Granada Publishing, London, 1984.

Chapter 1. Closure Looms

5. Anyone seeking a detailed account of the decline of BR's finances in the 1950s should read Gourvish's *British Railways 1948-73: A Business History*.
6. To clarify the structure of the nationalised transport industry in the 1950s, the overriding body was the British Transport Commission, appointed by the Minister of

Transport. The BTC delegated day-to-day operations to a number of subsidiary Executives, one for each form of transport. These included the Railways Executive (operating under the title of British Railways or BR) and the London Transport Executive (LT). BR divided up its activities into geographical Regions, corresponding largely to the former companies, each headed by a Chief Regional Officer. The Westerham line was part of the Southern Region. The Railway Executive was abolished in 1953 and BR was then run directly by the BTC; each Region gained an Area Board and the Chief Regional Officers became General Managers. This lasted until 1963, when the BTC was abolished and the railways came under the British Railways Board (BRB).

For brevity and to avoid a plethora of confusing initials I have used the term BR when referring to the railways in general unless there is some specific need to differentiate between parts of the organisation.

7. The Act that had nationalised the railways and inland transport.
8. Because it fell within the London Passenger Transport Area, the Westerham line came under the London area TUCC.
9. CTCC report on the Lewes to East Grinstead line closure, February 1958.
10. Had the line continued in use after 1961, BR would almost certainly have restored the off-peak service. Curiously, the line's weekend services almost certainly lost money but there was never any serious consideration of withdrawing them entirely.
11. The use of this term has caused some confusion because 'one-engine-in-steam' working has a specific meaning in terms of railway signalling. The Westerham branch was never signalled on the 'one-engine-in-steam' basis.
12. The road bridge at Chevening was rebuilt around this time and it may be this expense that led to the instruction to avoid any more substantial works on the line.
13. Despite this bar on any expenditure, in September 1955 the CCE produced a plan for substantial track alterations at Westerham. The existing crossover near the water tank between the platform line and the run round loop (known as No I Siding) was to be removed. Instead, the line through the site of the engine shed was to be extended and connected to a new double slip at the entrance to the goods yard. There was also to be a new connection between the run-round loop and the goods shed siding near the buffer stops. At a time when freight traffic was almost non-existent, it is hard to see how this could have been justified.
14. BR first closed the Bluebell line in 1955, only to discover that the line's original Act of Parliament required a minimum service of four trains a day over the line. BR had to re-open the line until it obtained another Act of Parliament in 1958 to repeal the minimum service requirement.
15. The National Archives (TNA) CAB 129/83 Minister of Transport to Cabinet, includes BTC memorandum *Review of Financial Situation*
16. The report correctly said that freight had declined. Photographs taken in 1947 show a healthy number of wagons in Westerham yard but later pictures show only the odd wagon at Westerham or Brasted – but at least freight was operated cheaply by using the branch engine on its way to and from Westerham at each end of the day. In 1960, as a result of a tally clerks' strike at the Surrey Docks, the City Timber Company experimented by sending timber from the docks to Brasted by rail. 100 timber standards were to be sent by rail but the experiment does not seem to have continued.
17. TNA CAB 129/83 BTC memorandum *Review of Financial Situation*
18. Harold Watkinson, Minister of Transport & Civil Aviation, House of Commons, 23 July 1958. (Hansard HC Debates vol 592 col 422)
19. To be fair to BR, if the Modernisation Plan was indeed a failure, it was by no means BR's fault alone. See Further Reading.
20. Serpell was to claim that he was a regular user of the Westerham branch (see Gould page 115). In fact, he lived at The Red House in Tonbridge until 1966, when he moved to Lamberhurst.
21. Hansard HC Debates 10 March 1960 vol 619 col 642 on

Chapter 2. The Fight Begins

22. In fact, this was a red herring. It was not clear, even as late as March 1962, whether Tonbridge steam depot would close before 1964, the planned target date for Stage II Electrification of the Southern Region's Central Section. (See National Archives file reference AN 151/63)
23. Producing financial data in the pre-computer age was a laborious task, aided only by mechanical calculating machines, pencils and paper. There were no tools for carrying out the sophisticated analyses that we take for granted today. That said, though, in an organisation of the size of BR in the 1950s and 60s, the lack of financial management tools and practices was a fundamental weakness.
24. In his autobiography, the veteran railway manager Gerry Fiennes castigated Bolland's approach. (Fiennes, G. F., *I Tried to Run a Railway*, Ian Allan, 1967)
25. In a few extreme cases, such as that of the Wells-next-the-Sea line described by Loft in his book *Last Trains*, BR ended up worse off after closing a line because the costs of closing it were higher than the savings.
26. In 1961 the difference in price between a weekly season ticket to London from Westerham (37s) and Dunton Green (31s 9d) was 5s 3d, equating to just over

1s a day. On a mileage basis the daily difference was slightly higher at 1s 3d.

27. Sir Philip Warter was chairman of the Associated British Picture Corporation (ABC) cinema group, and held various other directorships. He was appointed a member of the British Transport Commission in 1958 and in 1961 Beeching appointed him as deputy chairman, a position that he held until October 1963.
28. In 1961 a weekly season cost 34s from Sevenoaks compared to 37s from Westerham.
29. If this seems muddled, the Ministry of Transport's attitude to the provision of replacement services was even more confused. See Hansard House of Commons Debates 17 July 1958 vol 591 col 1457 and 23 July 1958 vol 592 cols 421-2 (available on-line).
30. The team also visited Sevenoaks (Tubs Hill) and were unimpressed by what they saw. Despite their criticisms that the station needed urgent rebuilding, it was to be 1977 before the old wooden station buildings were replaced by a new glass station building on the down side of the line and what they described as 'dangerous' outer platforms demolished.
31. Both methods of costing have their drawbacks. On a full cost basis, the resulting fleet would be nearly twice the size it needed to be but on a marginal basis, there would be no spares.
32. In contrast, the figures for replacement buses only ever included the costs of the two buses actually operating the service. No spares were allowed for them or for the parcels lorry.
33. Later more detailed costs allowed for the third car – even to the extent of including the cost of platform extensions (presumably at Chevening) to accommodate the longer train.
34. The explanation is that someone thought that even the peak service was intended to be hourly.
35. In fact, the branch train was used for a midday Tonbridge–Maidstone West trip (with a different crew) but the branch was never credited with the share of the costs involved.
36. Curiously, none of BR's figures for steam working mention the costs of converting set 610.
37. BR had claimed that it would save £11,600 by closing the line – so half of that could have been saved by electrification alone.
38. This was still less than the earnings of the off-peak trains before they were withdrawn in 1955.
39. The Bexhill West line finally closed in June 1964.
40. The fact is that BR had little idea whether its other modernisation projects were 'worthwhile' or not. See Gourvish page 301 onwards.
41. BR was later to do a U-turn on this and once again blame losses for the closure.
42. Gibbins relies on it repeatedly in his book *The Railway Closure Controversy*.
43. In the early 1960s it suffered a number of small battery fires and was withdrawn from service. It survives in preservation on the Royal Deeside Railway which has re-opened a mile or so of the Ballater branch, which closed in 1966.
44. This was a distant signal which would only ever show a yellow light.
45. See Henshaw, pages 88-89.
46. Approval to close the Allhallows branch followed in December 1960. This was the complete opposite of the Westerham case: the TUCC rejected closure in March 1960 but the CTCC refused to accept the decision and passed the case back to the TUCC, which finally approved it.

Chapter 3. Closure in the Balance

47. Far from bringing them to a head, the issues he raised were not to be properly answered until Barbara Castle tackled the dichotomy between commercial and social railways seven years later.
48. TNA PREM 11/3577 note of meeting on 12 December 1960
49. This suggests that Marples saw no role for the inter-city railway as a part of the network. Presumably his new motorways were to take over that transport function. The contemporary critical review of the Euston main line electrification should be seen in that light.
50. This was a problem that the CTCC itself had come to recognise. By coincidence, the need for technical support to be able to challenge BR effectively was discussed at the same CTCC meeting at which the Westerham line case was decided.
51. The report revealed that the estimate of bus fare income was based on an expectation that only 136 passengers would use the buses.
52. This did not stop BR and the Ministry of Transport quoting the losses made by steam as justification for closure.
53. An early ACV vehicle was briefly tried out on the Allhallows branch in 1953.
54. The result of their improved suspension design and use of disc brakes which, unlike clasp brakes, do not clean the wheel tread.
55. They were closed because, ostensibly, they continued to lose money despite the cheaper costs of operation that resulted from the use of railbuses. With our new understanding of the Westerham closure, we have to wonder if these lines were being run as efficiently as possible or whether they were simply swept away in Beeching's fervour to get rid of all local lines.
56. A director of Lep Transport, a major international freight forwarding business, and a prominent member of various transport industry bodies.
57. He was later to become the first president of the Great Eastern Railway Society and was one of the founders and president of the East Anglian Railway Museum.

58. He might have added that, in the case of Brasted station, interest was being charged on a building that was not only old but unused and derelict.
59. That is curious. Hancock worked for the Eastern Region; knowing that the subject of railbuses was bound to come up, it seems odd that he hadn't briefed himself on the way in which his own region operated them. It seems to be just another occasion when BR assumed that everyone would accept its claims unquestioningly and when the lack of knowledge on the part of BR managers was exposed.
60. Given that, as later studies were to show, most BR lines lost money in the late 1950s, presumably this meant that closure of most of the network should have followed.
61. This was nonsense. The steam service would have needed a third driver but there was little point in BR working out the costs involved. With diesel or electric working the duties could have been just as easily married in with other work – if not more so.
62. Like many of Shervington's answers, this made no sense. The new signalling system gave six signal sections between Sevenoaks and Tonbridge. Four trains could occupy these sections at the same time but they would all be approaching signals at danger and would be crawling from signal to signal. To run at speed under clear signals there could only be two trains between Sevenoaks and Tonbridge.
63. It had and, since the work had only been carried out in 1958, it should have lasted for 30 years, bringing down the annual cost of renewals to around £1,000 a year.
64. It was now Jones's turn to get his facts wrong. The weekly fares to London in 1961 were 34s from Sevenoaks, 35s from Brasted and 37s from Westerham so, regardless of any other losses, BR would have lost over £1,000 a year in fares even if all branch passengers used the bus. If passengers did as BR suggested and drove to Dunton Green, their weekly ticket would have cost even less – just 31s 9d – increasing the loss. On the other hand, if passengers drove to more distant railheads, making shorter rail journeys, the losses would have become substantial. If just 70 Westerham passengers drove to Bromley, from where the weekly fare was only 20s 3d, BR would have lost £3,000 in fares from them alone. We know that by the summer of 1962, only 48 of the original 140 branch season ticket holders were still taking advantage of the bus concession – 92 had made other arrangements.
65. It is not clear whether the note-taker became confused here. The whole purpose of a sinking fund is to set aside money to replace capital equipment as it becomes obsolete, to fund major maintenance or renewal of a capital asset, or to repay capital.
66. The correct rate at the time was 6 per cent.
67. The background to this discussion is that the South Eastern Railway created shares with which to buy the Westerham Valley Railway Company in 1881. Those shares were later exchanged for Southern Railway shares and, when the railways were nationalised in 1948, railway shareholders were given government-issued British Transport Stock in exchange for their shares. This stock carried a guaranteed interest of 3%, payable by the BTC. (It was a way of financing nationalisation without having to find actual cash to buy out railway shareholders.) It was about the Westerham line's share of these interest charges that this whole debate arose.
Parkin was right but a commercial company would have written off assets that were, in effect, useless but on the railways the original capital debt remained and carried interest charges until part of it was finally and belatedly written off by the 1962 Transport Act. The interest charges on the written-off part of the debt were then picked up by the Treasury. Until then, ignoring the capital debt of closed lines meant that the rest of the network simply picked an ever-growing burden of interest charges. Walsh was right. The interest charges didn't go away and weren't saved by closing a line – they just increased the costs of operating the remaining lines.
68. It is an accepted commercial principle that assets which do not make money have no value and should be written off.
69. If BR thought that 12 months was a long time for a closure case to take, it was to be in for a shock when the Beeching closures began to work their long-winded way through the system, many closures taking two years or longer.
70. This is precisely what BR did when the Isle of Wight line was electrified in 1966-7. The use of old Tube stock was first proposed for the Island in 1961. Maybe they could have been used to Westerham too!
71. Which poses the question: why BR did not do the same in such a difficult case? In any case, Bernard Walsh only got the better of BR because his expertise was way above that of the railway managers he was up against.
72. The 'Chalkpits' case was a contemporary planning case in which a minister had controversially decided to overturn the advice given by his Inspector.
73. The full text of Marples' reply to the debate can be found in Appendix 14.

Chapter 4. Postscript to Closure

74. Hansard HC Debates 27 June 1962 vol 661 col 1175
75. This was not helped by the election in October 1964, which inevitably delayed unpopular closure decisions, and the change of government which resulted.
76. Gourvish, page 436-438
77. This is despite the considerable financial benefits that the concession offered and shows how unappealing the replacement buses were when, just 12 months on, only a third of the former rail passengers were willing to take advantage of them.

78. Gourvish, page 280
79. Hansard HC Debates 24 April 1956 vol 551 col 1646

Chapter 5. The Vexed Questions

80. The DREs were, in effect, the Ministry's engineers and administrators in the field. Their responsibilities ranged from co-ordinating a number of county surveyors and their work on designing new roads to deciding mundane questions such as whether a set of traffic lights or a pedestrian crossing should be allowed on a main road. They had an interest in getting roads built which their policy and planning colleagues did not always share. At times they could be fairly close to the county surveyors.
81. However, the Southern's commercial officer was worried that the idea of holding onto the trackbed undermined BR's claims that substantial development in Westerham was unlikely, naïvely adding that they should not stand in the way since road improvements could improve access to the main line.
82. The Ministry of Transport had the power to refuse an LRO and its Railway Inspectorate also had to be assured of the fitness of the new owners and their ability to run the line safely.
83. The term 'playing trains' was one that found much favour with a number of people in BR, the Ministry of Transport, and the Railway Inspectorate.
84. Less ambitiously, it now runs the Chasewater Railway in the Midlands.
85. It was not until the following October that the merged body was retitled the Westerham Valley Railway Association (WVRA).
86. This was an error. It was about 48 acres.
87. The planning officer told Hawkins that he was happy with local light industry on the Westerham station site but less so with housing. No development of any kind would be allowed at Brasted but if the sidings were removed at Dunton Green, the site could be used for car parking. If the road schemes went ahead, the council would need most of Westerham station site plus the track bed between Chevening and Brasted.
88. In any case, as Chapter 7 shows, back in 1962 the Ministry of Transport could not even decide whether the South Orbital should be a trunk road (the definition of a road of national importance) or not. Clearly, BR managers took their cue from the Kent roads department and the Southern's own estates department that the scheme was of vital importance.
89. This was a serious question. When the Bluebell reopened its fares were restricted to the same level as BR's fares – 3d a mile second class and 4½d first class – under the Independent Undertakings (Railway Passenger Charges Scheme Application) Order 1959, which set its return fare at 2s 6d. This restriction was abolished by the Transport Act 1962.
90. BR subsequently decided that there would be no inherent difficulty in retaining the connection, subject to certain safeguards. The existing points would be clipped and padlocked and worked by a ground frame.
91. It was, of course, entirely wrong for Cobb to imply that BR had a sale lined up for £60,000.
92. On 29 October 1961, the last day of the Bluebell's 1961 season, the railway had extended into Horsted Keynes station itself.
93. In the event, the proposed Westerham bypass was never built in this form. Instead, the narrow Beggar's Lane was upgraded to take the traffic completely away from the town, a much more sensible solution.
94. Fortunately, in this case, while BR insisted on an outright sale of the line to the Keighley & Worth Valley Railway, the North Eastern Region granted the preservation company a mortgage.
95. An editorial in the *Sevenoaks Chronicle*, perhaps inspired by Gray, wondered whether BR was anxious to avoid an experiment which might prove that the line could be run at a profit. Having failed to make it pay themselves, they didn't want anyone else to succeed.
96. Raising a bank loan would have been difficult if not impossible. In July 1961 the government had introduced severe restrictions on bank lending and bank rate was raised to 7 per cent.
97. Though this is the sum that BR had expected to pay an agency if staff had been withdrawn from Westerham station. (See Appendix 8.)
98. The Talyllyn Railway was only 25 miles from the Festiniog and both were doing tolerably well.
99. Some Association members claimed that Gray had hopes of being elected onto the local and county councils and subsequently becoming a parliamentary candidate.
100. Shirley, an Australian, had been seconded from Unilever to bring badly needed financial skills to the railways. He is remembered as a volatile, abrasive and controversial character with a passion for tackling wasteful spending. See Gourvish, page 338.

Chapter 6. The Men From the Ministry

101. Minute (35) G. Davis to Pearson 30th July 1962 TNA MT 110/62
102. Months later, Col Robertson of the Railway Inspectorate was to comment that 'We, as an Inspectorate, are not much worried about the bridges . . .' It was all a fuss about nothing.
103. By 1989, Allan's Dart Valley company announced that the line was uneconomic and decided to find another operator or close it. Volunteers formed their own charitable trust company – the South Devon Railway Trust – to take the railway over and run it. The trust later bought the freehold for £1.15 million, raising the money through a share issue, loans, donations and revenue.

In the meantime, the Dart Valley company bought the

Paignton to Kingswear branch when it closed in 1972. The price was £250,000, partly recouped from the sale of the Royal Dart Hotel at Kingswear and other surplus land. This approach had parallels to the proposed Westerham scheme. Unlike the Buckfastleigh line, the Kingswear line has always been run as a commercial concern with no volunteer involvement.
104. The limited headroom under the line's bridges may also have required a speed limit.
105. See Gould page 122
106. Shortly after this, LT checked the use of the 5.58 bus from Westerham to Sevenoaks. There were no more than four passengers; they were asked if they had previously used the train – none had.
107. McMullen's naivety is astounding. Leaving aside the advantage that hindsight gives us in knowing how these 'little railways' have developed since 1963, his idea that local authorities could run railways within some loose safety framework was laughable. It must be remembered that, in the 1960s, many local authorities, rural and urban district councils in particular, were small and running a railway would have stretched their resources and skills to the limit.
108. TNA MT 57/149
109. Despite this, similar questionnaires were sent to a number of subsequent applicants for Light Railway Orders.
110. Only BR, as the land owner, could have opposed the CPO.
111. The council's only acceptable terms were for a lease limited to five years (less one day) at a premium of £14,000, or whatever the excess cost of the bridge amounted to, and a rent of £3,000 per annum, without any option to renew or right to compensation.
112. Quite why the council bought the track has never been explained. Maybe it genuinely intended to lease the line to the WVRA or maybe the urgency of the sale meant that BR did not have time to arrange contractors to lift the track and it had to sell it with the land.
113. A similar questionnaire was sent to the Hayling Light Railway Society, for the same purpose and with the same effect. This intention was confirmed in a BR document about the demolition of several disused Southern Region branch lines, in which developments since the Westerham line was closed were described: 'The negotiations were complicated by Ministry of Transport reluctance to the operation of a service by a body with such little standing, and they attempted to thwart the Society by requesting them to complete a long and detailed questionnaire.'
114. It seems to have dawned on someone that justifying the sale on the basis of the savings to the council risked creating grounds for legal action against BR.
115. Pickin had some unconventional ideas for running the line. One was that he would own the railway but anyone would be allowed to operate trains on it. However, when he wanted to run a train of his own, everyone else would be required to clear the line for him.

Chapter 7. The Road to Hell

116. Chris Rea's two-part song *The Road To Hell* is said to inspired by the frustrations of M25 motorway traffic.
117. It was only in 1936 that the Trunk Roads Act transferred responsibility for 30 major roads from county councils to the Ministry of Transport. The only one in Kent was the London–Folkestone–Dover road – the A20 plus short lengths of what were then the A259 and the A2.
118. *Railway Magazine* 1938 Issue 1 (Vol 82 p487) 'A New Thames Tunnel Branch – What the Railways are Doing'
119. The C Ring, for example, comprised today's North and South Circular Roads.
120. Marshall, Chris, *Ringway 4*. http://www.cbrd.co.uk/histories/ringways/ringway4/
121. Steel was rationed between 1951 and 1953.
122. This decision was prompted by specific problems with the D Ring in north-west London but a minute signed by the Minister (in TNA file MT 95/317) makes it clear that the changes applied to the whole D Ring and the orbitals.
123. In fact it was 1977 before the M25 opened south of Dartford and then only as far as Swanley. Relief for the A225 did not come until 1986. What the O&D Survey did not make clear was how the A225 traffic figures might vary depending on the toll to be charged for the tunnel. The survey figures assumed a toll of 4 shillings per car but traffic on the A225 was expected to vary from 27,000 vehicles if no tolls were charged down to 5,000 vehicles with a 7 shilling toll. In the event, the initial toll was only 2s 6d per car.
124. The expected increase in passengers handled at Heathrow Airport (forecast at 12 million a year by 1970 and 15 million by 1975) suggested that there would also be considerable road traffic between the airport and the southern/south-eastern suburbs which would be well-served by the D ring. (In fact, Heathrow handled only 5 million passengers a year in 1969 but this increased to 27 million by the end of the 1970s.)
125. The Liberal Eric Lubbock seized the seat from the Conservatives in a spectacular by-election victory on 14 March 1962.
126. The Local Government Act was passed in 1963 and the new Greater London Council came into being in 1965. The areas of Bexley, Chislehurst and Sidcup, Crayford, Erith, Beckenham, Bromley, Orpington and Penge were transferred to it from Kent.
127. *Roads in England and Wales*: report by the Minister of Transport for the year ended 31 March 1963: HMSO, London July 1963
128. In August 1963 a report was drafted for Marples

recommending 10 new motorway projects, including the South Orbital (TNA MT/121/298). It is likely that this formed the basis for Labour's plans.

129. By this time the Westerham preservation scheme had been killed off by the construction of the Sevenoaks bypass.

130. The borehole reports are available on the British Geological Society website.

Epilogue. In Retrospect

131. In 1959, for example, the nascent Bluebell scheme, which sought to reopen the complete Lewes to East Grinstead line, was joined by another that planned to re-open much of the 180-mile Midland & Great Northern Joint Railway system in Lincolnshire and Norfolk. Schemes to re-open the Keighley & Worth Valley Railway and the Kent & East Sussex Railway had emerged by 1961.

132. *Commercial Motor*, 17 December 1965, news item, 'Britain Lagging in Roadbuilding'.

133. Bowdler, H., 'Highway Implications of the Channel Tunnel', *Journal of the Institution of Highway Engineers*, 1968, Vol 15, No 6, p5-11.

134. Baldwin, Sir Peter et al: *The Motorway Achievement – Building the Network in Southern and Eastern England*, Phillimore 2007, page 86

135. See, for example, the matter of BR and the North British Locomotive Company revealed in TNA ref: CAB 129/102/20

136. It was only in 1966 that it became national policy to give local authorities first refusal on surplus railway land – Ministry of Housing & Local Government Circular No. 57/66, dated 17 October 1966.

A Trip Down the Line from Westerham to Dunton Green – Then and Now

Westerham Station

The view from the buffer stops at Westerham, which were positioned just a few feet from London Road. Just to the right was a gate leading from the road onto the loading dock. ***Bluebell Railway Museum – John J Smith***

Going . . . This was once a railway station. Amazingly, the advertising hoarding survived after everything else had gone. *Tony Harden*

Gone . . . Taken from the far side of the road but otherwise the viewpoint is the same – truly! *Author*

A collection of classic vehicles parked on the forecourt at Westerham on the last day of service, illustrating only too well the increasing problem that the branch was facing. *Ian Nolan*

Seen from slightly further back but the station forecourt provides a clue. *Tony Harden*

The branch train in the platform at Westerham on Sunday 13 September 1959. *Bluebell Railway Museum – Alan Postlethwaite*

From a slightly wider view, Westerham station slumbers in August 1962, the grass is growing as it awaits the arrival of those who hoped to preserve it. *Ian Nolan*

The same view in the early 1970s when the station building had been demolished but the platform remained. The roof of a Green Line RF coach is visible in the centre of the photograph. The Westerham section of route 706 was reduced to peak hours only in 1969, then cut to one up in the morning and one back in the evening in 1973 before being withdrawn completely in 1975. It wasn't only trains that were being cut! *Tony Harden*

Only the office block in the background, which occupies the site of the old Crown Hotel, identifies this as the same location. The goods shed would have been under the rear part of the building on the left. The crane base may have been moved from its original location. *Author*

This house, on the south-western corner of the station site at Westerham is often mistaken for the station master's house, owing to its current name of "Station House". In fact, the railway bought two houses, nos. 1 and 2 Oak Villas in Madan Road, for senior staff. The building illustrated was outside the railway boundary and was used by Hortons, a local merchants, as an office. *Author*

The Crown Hotel featured in the background of many photographs of Westerham station. It was built after the railway arrived (if the Oxted extension had been built it would have crossed the road on a bridge here and continued through the site of the Crown) and didn't long outlast it. Railway officers occasionally used the Crown as a handy location for 'out of the office' meetings. *Author*

Looking along the line of the platform towards the signal box. Its alignment was roughly through the right-most of the two trees. The signal box was at the rear of this building. The road in the foreground, which gives access to the industrial estate is called The Flyers Way, to commemorate the branch train (see inset). The inset also shows the stump of the tree that graced so many photographs of the Westerham station building. *Author*

The Aqualisa building occupies the Dunton Green end of Westerham goods yard. The site of the engine shed, water crane and water tower are under the rear of this building (under the brown-clad extension seen in the inset). The signal box was a little to the left of the picture. *Author*

Looking east, the line of the track as it left Westerham and passed behind the houses on Madan Road. Some of these houses have now extended their gardens over the trackbed, as seen in the distance. *Author*

Westerham to Brasted

'H' class No 31239 is just half a mile into its journey as it leaves Westerham on the 5.28pm to Dunton Green on Sunday 17 April 1955. *Bluebell Railway Museum – Colin Hogg*

The same scene but looking back (west) towards Westerham! The farm track joins the old railway formation just a few yards ahead and the course of the railway can be seen in the middle right of the photograph, heading towards the site of Beggar's Lane bridge. *Author*

The site of the bridge over Beggars Lane. This was once little more than a farm track but after the railway closed it became the A233 Westerham eastern bypass , in connection with the never-built M25 Westerham interchange. The course of the railway runs through the line of scrub to the right of the picture. The new road is not on the line of the old lane so the railway bridge was roughly where the car is parked. The new approach to Charman's Farm, seen on the extreme right, appears to have cut into the railway embankment. The land to build the railway here was bought from the Warde family of Squerryes Court, lords of the manor of Westerham, who have now re- acquired parts that the county council did not require. *Author*

The line of trees and scrub across the middle of the picture marks the line of the trackbed as it rounds the curve away from Beggars Lane bridge and heads towards Brasted. At the left-hand end of the trees the M25 takes over the trackbed. *Author*

The bridge over Hogtrough Hill at Brasted with the station approach on the right. Despite demoting Brasted station to an unstaffed halt as an economy measure in 1955, BR then spent money on changing the signs so that no-one was in any doubt that it was now a mere halt. *Bluebell Railway Museum – Alan Postlethwaite*

The road has been re-aligned so that the bridge no longer crosses it at a skew. *Author*

Brasted station

Brasted station on 13th September 1959. The station had been unstaffed for four years by the time this picture was taken. There are a number of wagons in the yard, probably far more than were justified by local needs. Quiet goods yards were often used to store withdrawn wagons before they went for scrap. *Bluebell Railway Museum – Alan Postlethwaite*

Brasted station in about 1968, after the WVRA moved out and the track had been lifted. The aborted repainting of the building is obvious. The coal yard was still in use – indeed the fence has been moved to this end of the station building to enlarge it – and continued to be for some while until work began on constructing the M25 in 1977, albeit served by road. The station building stood empty and unused. *Tony Harden*

The station building stood in the area now occupied by the bushes on the far side of the works exit off the motorway. Taken on 28 October 2006, the 45 anniversary of the line's closure. *Author*

Brasted goods yard. The line of upright sleepers in the centre of the photograph shows the site of the coal staithes that were built after the line closed. *Author*

A feature of Brasted goods yard from the 1930s was this former LBSCR van body, photographed on 13th September 1959. It was supported on bricks and was used by the coal merchant as a store. Unusually for discarded van bodies, it retained its underframe and W-irons. It survived the closure of the line and was still in place in 1965 but sadly it wasn't preserved. *Bluebell Railway Museum – Alan Postlethwaite*

The platform side of the van in May 1960. *Author's collection*

When BR converted Brasted to an unstaffed halt, it went to the effort and expense of replacing the enamel station sign. This was removed after closure, revealing the marks of a much earlier sign beneath. *Richard Ferris*

On 11th March 1961 the permanent way hut at Brasted looked as though it had seen better times. *Bluebell Railway Museum – Alan Postlethwaite*

Even in the last months of the line's life, and despite the station having been unstaffed for over five years, its name was still picked out in flints on the bank opposite the platform. In its early days, Brasted had its own signal box, which was situated at the far end of the station just beyond the visible telephone pole. Curiously, even though the box was demolished in the 1920s, the board crossing that was provided to reach it survived until the end. *Bluebell Railway Museum – Alan Postlethwaite*

Brasted to Chevening

Looking west from Brasted Hill Road bridge round the curve towards Brasted station. *Bluebell Railway Museum – Alan Postlethwaite*

Taken from an almost identical viewpoint on 4th December 2015. The left-hand cutting side appears to be the original. This demonstrates that even here, where the railway formation was wide due to the instability of the ground, what a small contribution the railway land made to the motorway's requirements. *Author*

Signs of the previous year's track renewals are evident as 'H' class No 31520 emerges from under Brasted Hill Road bridge and propels its train for Dunton Green away from Brasted. This is the view along the notoriously wet Combe Bank cutting on 13th September 1959. *Bluebell Railway Museum – Alan Postlethwaite*

Today from the same viewpoint. *Author*

The view west from Combe Bank bridge where the line passed through Combe Bank Wood. Note that the motorway is on a raised embankment within the cutting, presumably in response to the very poor ground conditions as a result of the underlying gault clay. *Author*

Looking east from Combe Bank bridge. The line of the railway was on the left-hand side of the motorway at this point; the road was shifted south to ease the curve that will take it off the railway formation and towards Junction 5. The next bridge, Chevening Road bridge, is just beyond the gantry. From here the railway continued roughly straight ahead. *Author*

The view west from Chevening Road bridge. Whereas the motorway curves at this point, the railway was virtually straight, cutting across the line of the road from the far right – the photograph was taken from directly above the lined of the track. *Author*

Looking east from Chevening Road bridge where the motorway leaves the railway formation. The line of the railway passed through the right-hand support of the gantry and continued straight ahead. There is a brief isolated section of trackbed in the field beyond. *Author*

The remains of accommodation bridge No 1421 between the point where the motorway leaves the railway formation and Chevening Halt. This is a coping stone on one of the bridge abutments. The bridge appears to have been filled in. *Author*

'H' class No 31518 departs from Chevening Halt with the 11.50 train from Dunton Green to Westerham on the last day of service on the branch. The slip road linking the northbound A21 to westbound M25 now occupies the immediate foreground. *Ian Nolan*

A short isolated section of railway formation remains between the M25/A21 intersec tion at Chevening and the point at which the line is subsumed beneath the motorway. This view, taken from roughly where the engine is in the previous photograph, is looking west. The M25 can be seen merging in from the right. Inset: the Southern Railway concrete fence posts seen in Ian Nolan's 'then' picture still survive. *Author*

The point just west of Chevening at which the railway formation disappears beneath the A21 Sevenoaks bypass and its slip roads. *Author*

Looking west across the A21 from the site of Chevening Halt. The course of the railway continues straight across at this point before disappearing under the M25 about half a mile further on. The motorway itself is just to the right but it, and the slip road between the northbound A21 and the westbound M25, are hidden in the trees. *Author*

Chevening Halt

Chevening Halt, looking east towards Dunton Green. *Author's collection*

The filled-in site of Chevening Halt, looking east towards Dunton Green during construction of the Sevenoaks bypass 1965-66. One of the original bridge parapets survives, complete with smoke stains. *Tony Harden*

Looking south across the road bridge at Chevening Halt during road building works. The cutting containing the halt has been completely infilled, as has that on the Dunton Green (east) side, but the western bridge parapet remains. My memory tells me that the platform was simply buried and is still down there. *Tony Harden*

Believe it or not, this is roughly the same view over the site of Chevening Halt, looking across the cutting in which it was situated, now sandwiched between the road bridge and the A21. The road level has been raised to bridge the A21. The southern edge of the railway cutting is marked by the line of leylandii trees. This photograph was taken in 2006. A repeat visit in 2015 revealed an almost impenetrable jungle here. *Author*

Chevening Halt in May 1960, seen from the top of the steps leading down to the platform. The Sevenoaks Bypass and its link roads to the M25 now cross the former railway line at the far end of the platform. *Author's collection*

Chevening to Dunton Green

The trackbed emerges at the end of Chevening cutting. The line here was built on land compulsorily purchased from the Morants Court Estate. The owner, William Tonge, objected to the railway as it would spoil his view. In fact, he had plans to divide up his estate into plots for house building and the railway would interfere with that scheme. 140 years later that is exactly what has happened. *Author*

Looking east from Chevening bridge towards Dunton Green. The cutting has been infilled, probably as a handy place to dispose of surplus material from the M25 construction. The trackbed continues between the trees in the middle distance. Much of the land between here and the London Road bridge at Dunton Green, including the trackbed, has been bought by a property development company and has been divided into building plots in the hope that Green Belt restrictions will one day be lifted. *Author*

The line between Chevening and Dunton Green was virtually straight throughout. This view, looking back west towards Chevening, was taken from the point at which the Darent Valley Path crosses the trackbed. *Author*

The section of trackbed between London Road bridge and the Darent Valley Path is overgrown and part way between the two a culvert that carried a stream beneath the line has been removed. The paved base of the culvert can be seen here. *Author*

On the outskirts of Dunton Green an accommodation crossing gate lies abandoned in the undergrowth. The landowner, William Tonge, wanted the railway company to have to build bridges to link up his severed land. He got crossings instead. *Author*

On the outskirts of Dunton Green a small housing development has been built on the trackbed. Beyond it is the London Road bridge, which has now been converted into a pedestrian subway (see inset). Until the Sevenoaks bypass was built, this bridge carried the A21 road. The buildings on the left are on the site of the East Surrey Omnibus Co (later London Transport) Dunton Green bus garage. There was a pedestrian footbridge adjacent to the road bridge but it has since been removed. *Author*

On the last day of the Westerham branch, class D1 4-4-0 No 31739 rounds the curve from Dunton Green station and descends at 1 in 73 towards the bridge under London Road. *Bluebell Railway Museum – Colin Hogg*

A panorama of the branch, marked by the line of trees and bushes, as it curves round from the main line (to the left). The houses at the left are on the site of Dunton Green goods yard; those in the right background are in Lennard Road. *Author*

Dunton Green station

The subway that runs from the station forecourt and under the branch tracks. It was built by agreement with the landowner, Samuel Wreford, and opened in late 1882. It enabled two level crossings, one across the Westerham line just west of Dunton Green station and the other across the main line on the London side of the station, to be closed. It provides a short-cut to the village. *Author*

Dunton Green forecourt in 2006. The main station building was on the right. The substation equipment occupies the site of the cross-passage linking the London and Westerham platforms. The Westerham platform was to the left. Inset: the substation equipment has since been replaced with a single unit. *Author*

Looking through the passageway at Dunton Green that linked the main London-bound platform to the branch platform. On 15 May 1961 'H' class locomotive No 31177 was waiting for its connecting passengers to arrive before setting off for Westerham. *Bluebell Railway Museum – Alan Postlethwaite*

The view from Dunton Green footbridge in 2006, looking south. The course of the Westerham branch is marked by the trees as it curves away to the right. The new flats in the background are on the site of the goods yard. Just in front of them is the covered exit from the subway. The main station building was to the left, the cross-passage to the Westerham branch passed through the substation hut, and the Westerham platform is marked by the buddleia on the right. *Author*

End of the line. This is roughly where the run-round loop points, the headshunt and the connection to the main line were. The land at Dunton Green was excluded from the sale of the branch to Kent County Council and it appears that it is still owned by Network Rail. *Author*

The north end of the platforms at Dunton Green. They have been extended since 1961 and now cover the site of the connection between the branch and the main line. The crossover from up to down line was in the immediate foreground. The hut on the right appears to stand on the foundations of the signal box. The trees and scrub on the lineside have grown from nothing in the past 50 years. *Author*

Dunton Green twilight. Southeastern Class 375 No 375618 calls at Dunton Green with a London-bound train. The footbridge was originally at Grove Park. *Author*

Index